MY AMERICAN

REVOLUTION

MY AMERICAN

REVOLUTION

ROBERT SULLIVAN

FARRAR, STRAUS AND GIROUX

NEW YORK

Farrar, Straus and Giroux
18 West 18th Street, New York 10011

Copyright © 2012 by Robert Sullivan
All rights reserved
Distributed in Canada by D&M Publishers, Inc.
Printed in the United States of America
First edition, 2012

Grateful acknowledgment is made for permission to reprint two quotations from
Hudson River Almanac, text courtesy of the New York State
Department of Environmental Conservation. All rights reserved.

The image of the signal on page 232 is from The Pictorial Field-book of the Revolution:
or, Illustrations, by Pen and Pencil, of the History, Biography, Scenery, Relics,
and Traditions of the War for Independence, by Benson John Lossing
(New York: Harper & Brothers, 1859).
The image of the map on page 234 is reprinted by permission of the
National Oceanic and Atmospheric Administration.

Library of Congress Cataloging-in-Publication Data
Sullivan, Robert, 1963–
    My American Revolution / Robert Sullivan. — 1st ed.
        p.   cm.
    Includes bibliographical references.
    ISBN 978-0-374-21745-7 (alk. paper)
    1. New York (N.Y.)—History—Revolution, 1775–1783.   2. New York
(State)—History—Revolution, 1775–1783.   3. New Jersey—History—Revolution,
1775–1783.   I. Title.
    E230.5.N4S85 2012
    974.7'03—dc23

                                                                    2011047037

Designed by Abby Kagan

www.fsgbooks.com

1   3   5   7   9   10   8   6   4   2

For Suzanne

As to the history of the revolution, my ideas may be peculiar, perhaps singular. What do we mean by the revolution? The war? That was no part of the revolution; it was only an effect and consequence of it. The revolution was in the minds of the people.

—JOHN ADAMS, in a letter to Thomas Jefferson, 1815

We are a landscape of all we know.

—ISAMU NOGUCHI, c. 1980

It is hoped that the reader will relate with the people of the time and will enjoy reminiscing while he reads.

—LAURA P. TERHUNE, *Episodes in the History of Griggstown*, 1976

CONTENTS

꿩

PART ONE

✥

THE PANORAMA
OF THE REVOLUTION

WHAT IF RIVERS COULD TALK? What if ancient creeks, crossed hundreds of years ago by tired feet, could bubble up in verse? What would make the skies speak again of battles that had happened as they watched, centuries ago? And do the hills around us remember all that they have seen? Whenever I ponder these questions, or questions like them, or whenever I just want to get out of my apartment for a while and poke around, I buy a ticket to the top of the Empire State Building—especially in the spring, when the city is just turning green. On a bright, clear day, when the sun shines on the still-green hills of Brooklyn, on the plains of Queens, and on the saltwater marshes of the Bronx and Staten Island and beyond, I ride to the top of the Empire State Building and, invariably, find myself looking out across the blaring, ship-dotted panorama that is New York Harbor to see the American Revolution.

I see it across wide rivers and small streams glistening in the warm-weather sun that shines on New York, New Jersey, and the coves of Long Island Sound that eventually become Connecticut. I see it beyond Dutch-named kills, and even past old paved-over creeks in the middle of Manhattan, vertiginously sited below me, though still in many ways a hill-carved island. I see it up toward the Bronx, in the gentle public housing–dotted hills, where both the British and the Americans would have waded across the creek called Mosholu, a word translated variously as "smooth stones or gravel" and "clear water" from the language of the Lenni-Lenape tribes native to the city. The Mosholu was known to troops on both sides of the eighteenth-century nation-establishing battle as Tibbetts Brook. Tibbetts Brook is still there today, less flowing than dumping into the Harlem River, and the stream that will not go away may spend a portion of its course from north to south inside a sewer built with a high-arched brick ceiling, an underground architectural feature that quietly quotes the classical world.

I have sometimes thought, in fact, that from the top of the Empire State Building the harbor is like the shield of Achilles, displaying the ocean-bound strait called the Narrows, off Staten Island, where, in 1776, the British sailed in with forty thousand troops, a forest of masts deckling the edge of Staten Island. Indeed, from the observation platform, the harbor is like a great poem or painting, extolling the East River, which Washington used to escape after being routed by the British out near the big old Brooklyn cemetery visible to the southeast. The harbor sings the story of the shore—near hills in the Bronx and Westchester, where, in subsequent clashes with the British, the Americans did not lose. The harbor sings, too, the story of the Hudson River near the George Washington Bridge, where the Americans did. For a few quarters, the coin-operated, high-powered binoculars sing the race of the newborn American army as it fled through New Jersey, across the marshes that today are demarked by an incinerator's towers, by power plants, by disused factories and big-box stores and the slow, sparkling pulse of the New Jersey Turnpike.

In this wide prospect, the vista is a great palimpsest of the Revolution, a painted-over canvas of ancient routes walked smooth or transformed into traffic-jammed highways, of colonial villages grown like weeds into great cities, such as Newark, Elizabeth, and New York. If I could zoom in on the backstreets of the old towns on the banks of the Passaic and Hackensack Rivers, I'd see the road markers, on utility poles and street signs, still demarking that 1776 escape: "The Retreat to Victory." And there is no need for a spyglass or zoom lens to see the New Jersey hills where the Continental troops held dances early one spring, and where, in 1777 and then again in 1779–1780, during the coldest winters known to New York and colonial Americans alike, men built huts and fires and waited out a deathly freeze. It was to these hills that these long-gone troops marched, starting from the Delaware River, which Washington had most famously crossed. As for the crossing itself, it happened at the outer edge of the circle one can see on a clear day from the Empire State Building, a day's march past a rise that I need binoculars to just make out from the observation deck.* I know this hill from my own attempts to attack the Revolutionary landscape, as well as from ancient maps, where it is denoted as Remarkable Hill.

Because this is where it happened: the Revolutionary War, the new-born American military's struggle for independence, the nation's birth. Let Longfellow go on about Paul Revere's ride to Boston and there-abouts; let Emerson memorialize the shots that rang out at Lexington

---

*The term "Empire State" is sometimes attributed to George Washington. After the Revolution, and before he was elected president and sworn in on Wall Street, Washington wrote the following in a letter to New York City's Common Council, which had just sent him a ceremonial city key: "I pray that heaven may bestow its choicest blessings on your city—That the devastations of war in which you found it, may soon be without a trace. That a well regulated and beneficial Commerce may enrich your Citizens.—And that your state (at present the Seat of the Empire) may set such examples of wisdom and liberality, as shall have a tendency to strengthen and give permanency to the Union at home—and credit and respectability to it abroad." "Seat of the Empire" was a phrase in circulation at the time, heard in the debate in Europe over whether the seat would move from London to the now-independent colonies, with New York its about-to-be capital. It is also argued that New York's nickname arose in the time of canals, in the mid-1800s, when New York, owing to the Erie Canal, was promoted again as the seat of a westward-reaching, waterway-connected realm. But even canals lead back to Washington, who was a canal booster, before, during, and after his presidency. He saw the Potomac, manipulated with canals and connected to the Ohio River, as the key to unlocking the continent, as well as a key to increasing the value of his own western lands. "Hearing little else for two days from the persuasive tongue of the great man," a visitor to Mount Vernon wrote, "I confess[,] completely infected me with canal mania." (According to the *Encyclopedia of New York City*, George Washington was also the first person to use the epithet "New Yorker.") Al Smith was the former governor of New York who ran for president in 1928 and lost in a landslide to Herbert Hoover; as the first Catholic facing a Republican in the last minutes of pre–Great Depression prosperity, he was defeated, a reporter said, by the three Ps: Prohibition, prejudice, and prosperity. Smith became instead the first president of the Empire State Building, in 1934, and on taking the position he wrote to 1,257 principals of public and parochial schools. "Part of the geographical education of every child within 50 miles of New York [should be] at least one geography lesson from the top of the Empire State Building," he wrote. "Under the guidance of his instructor he will see States, Cities, Rivers, Islands and Mountains laid out in one grand map." The building's publicists added: "The city, in an instant, becomes an open book."

and Concord. It is within the view of the Empire State Building that the Revolutionary War was fought, and where the first president sat in a chair beneath a ceiling decorated with the moon and the stars and the sun.

Go ahead and take a look at a map of America. Find those first thirteen colonies, the original ones that declared their independence from the British crown on July 4, 1776, the colonies with names you memorized when you were a kid. Remember that Vermont was not yet a state, that Maine was still part of Massachusetts. Recall that there was a line down the left side of the about-to-be-a-nation that more or less followed the peaks of the Appalachian Mountains—an old mountain chain, incidentally, that once would have been among the tallest in long-ago geologic time, before being worn down by that winner of all wars: time. Certainly battles were fought in Canada; and we well know that the British finally surrendered on a peninsula of land in the area of Yorktown, Virginia, at the mouth of Chesapeake Bay.

But look closer to see where George Washington and his army spent their time, where exactly the majority of battles were lost and, less often, won. The action in the Revolution, it turns out, was centered in the area of Connecticut, New York, and Philadelphia, in a patch of territory that, as one contemporary historian has noted, takes about twenty minutes to fly over in a commercial jet—enough time for, say, pretzels and a Diet Coke. The resulting demarcation, if you draw it as a rectangle, blow it up, put it on TV, and stand a meteorologist before it, looks a lot like a local weather map, specifically those you see on news programs in and around New York. Indeed, if the landscape of the Revolution were a forecast, the weatherman would direct the viewer at home to the points of the compass and say: *We've got the Hudson River valley dropping down from the north, and Connecticut and the Long Island Sound dipping in from the northeast, with a big blast of New Jersey, coming in like a storm from Chicago!*

The land on this weather map is the very first Middle America. The Middle America we think of as middle today is not New York and not L.A. and sits at the center of the nation. Likewise, the Middle America that was middle in 1776 was not Williamsburg, Virginia, and not Boston, Massachusetts; it was a place in between. It was also middle in a number of other ways: a mix of cultural affiliations, of income levels, of jobs. There were speculators and fishermen in the cities, and farmers out in the New Jersey countryside, all fighting one another before the war with Britain even began—fighting with absentee landlords in England and Manhattan, fighting for rights having to do with religion and money. As opposed to New England, which was squeezed for arable land and in economic decline (farmers packing up, markets moving elsewhere); as opposed to Virginia, which was mostly in debt, the Middle Colonies were the land of economic opportunity—Pennsylvania was called "the best poor man's country in the world"—and the Middle Colonies' newly arrived immigrants crafted a definition of liberty that was characterized mostly by its expansiveness, by its disparate indefinability.

Boston has its Liberty Trail, and Virginia has Mount Vernon, where George Washington farmed and fished, ran a mill, and manufactured various kinds of alcohol. But the British were fought—and, to a large extent, avoided—in the Middle Colonies. Dozens of battles, all of them less well known than the Battle of Bunker Hill, took place in the area of New York; Connecticut and New Jersey were home to hundreds of skirmishes. And New York City itself was the place where Washington officially began the Revolution, as well as the place where it ended, on Evacuation Day, a day celebrated for a century and a half with parades and flags throughout New York City, though no longer. And then, when the war was over and a new government formed and a president inaugurated, that first president took up residence in a house on a plot of land that is today unmarked and frequented by skateboarders. If the Revolution itself were still being described on that local TV newscast, we'd have British troops coming in from Sandy Hook at the mouth of New York Harbor and moving up past Staten Island, with colonial regiments blowing down from New England, via the Hudson River valley and the Connecticut coast. For five years, we'd see the skirmishes between New Jersey loyalists and various New Jersey rebel militias, battles that, if they were denoted by a TV news icon, might be indicated by a persistent dark cloud.

And yet, this Revolutionary landscape is today not so much neglected as forgotten, or rushed by, its founding details mostly lost to constant inspection, trammeled by the machinations of business and real estate. Massachusetts lauds its Minutemen as patriots; in comparison, New Jersey and New York seem insecure, or less certain, despite some encouragement over the years. "I cannot but remember the place that New Jersey holds in our early history," Abraham Lincoln once said. He recalled being enthralled, as a child, by the story of the Revolution in New Jersey, which, by the time he reached adulthood, was a less-told tale. "In the early Revolutionary struggle, few of the States among the old Thirteen had more of the battle-fields of the country within their limits than old New-Jersey," Lincoln said.

If Washington is the Father of Our Country, in other words, then this is the country he was first father of—this is the country that he begat, the forgotten first land.

FATHER

Father of Our Country was, after all, more like a job than people today, I think, tend to realize. It was an actual position, in many ways, from which, in a matter of months or even weeks, one guy was fired, another hired, a George for a George, "George" being a name derived from the Greek, meaning "earth worker," or "farmer." King George III was the one fired, obviously, and George Washington was the next in line, a shooting star that showed up on cue. Father of Our Country turns out to be a thing about Washington that America did not fabricate later on, as opposed to the story about him cutting down a cherry tree and not lying about it, or the notion of his teeth being wooden, when they were not wooden, in point of fact, but made of gold and ivory and lead, as well as being made of teeth taken from horses, donkeys, and his slaves.

The father position was associated with the writings of a British political philosopher, Henry St. John (pronounced *sinjin*), better known as Viscount Bolingbroke. Bolingbroke was himself the opposite of what we as Americans have come to think of George Washington as being. Whereas Washington was reluctant to write and speak, trained in the arts of surveying, farming, and animal husbandry, always finding a smart young officer for secretarial purposes, Bolingbroke was urbane and literary, at the center of a circle that included Jonathan Swift and Alexander Pope. It is written that Oliver Goldsmith once saw Bolingbroke run naked through a park drunk, and the *Encyclopaedia Britannica* remembers him as "a poor manager of men who tended to lose his nerve in a crisis."

Bolingbroke saw the British government as a broken and corrupt machine, its power newly vested, under the leadership of his rival, Sir Robert Walpole, in the financial contrivances of the city, in the machinery of debt and credit. Power, he believed, ought to be vested in the landed gentry, whose (to him) benevolent ruling power was derived from their long-lived-on land. His treatise, entitled *The Idea of a Patriot King*, defined that king as the unique individual who could rise above personal ambition, and whose character, motivated by selflessness and public spirit, would transform society with a disinterested patriotism. Though not well read in England, Bolingbroke was esteemed in the colonies, by John Adams in Boston, and by Thomas Jefferson, James Madison, and George Washington in Virginia.

It's a long story, of course, and let us not forget that many versions of the Washington story exist. Suffice it to say, though, that when George III took the throne, the American colonists first crossed their fingers for a patriot king, and then, when the English George failed them, they looked to a military hero on the horizon, a George who had been brought up in the tradition of disinterested patriotism, who had spent years enthusiastically practicing the called-for public reluctance. It is astounding to a reader today to see how suddenly the transition occurred, to see the term "country" used in Virginia in the 1760s referring specifically to Virginia, transformed into another "country"—"the Cause of our Common Country." And very soon, we hear Washington himself speak of "the great American body."

Oh, how the colonies wanted the king to be their king. Oh, how the place that was about to become America blamed Parliament for their troubles, Washington himself referring to the invading British armed forces as "the ministerial troops." This is *after* the Boston skirmishing, just before the war officially commences in New York. At last, though, in January 1776, the king, speaking in Parliament, accused the Americans of revolting "for the purpose of establishing an independent empire." The colonies were mortified; the colonists disowned King George immediately, renouncing him in newspapers as "an unnatural father."

"Your name darkens the moral sky and stinks in the nostrils of the world," said a writer referring to himself as "Soldier" in a broadside. The king was called a monster in human form, likened to Cain.

As I say, it is a long story, and you might read any number of

historical accounts of the breakup of the king and his American colonies, the point being that the replacement father began in his post not
after the war or after the Constitution or after the first White House or
after an obelisk was chosen to represent him in the place that, as it ended
up, he himself chose to call Washington, D.C., on account of his plans
for the country and his own personal real estate development goals.
The replacement father began his fatherhood almost immediately. He
took his new position right here, in the middle of the Middle Colonies,
within view of an Empire State Building that was not yet built.*

In New Jersey, at the start of long, never-certain war, a Hessian commander was startled to hear a New Jersey couple sing: "God save great
Washington! God damn the King!" Even before the first major battle of

---

*By the time Thomas Paine called the king "The Royal Brute," in his pamphlet *Com-
mon Sense*, it was almost a relief for Americans. Paine crowned the law itself the new
king and drew an image of a shattered crown being spread across the land, like seed,
or manure. I don't want to delve too far into an exploration of Paine's subtext here,
but I would like to note that in an essay on Paine called "Familial Politics: Thomas
Paine and the Killing of the King, 1776," written in the early 1970s, a time when
people were enthusiastic about both the American Revolution—due to the upcoming
two hundredth anniversary of the Declaration of Independence—and subliminal
explorations—it being the 1970s—the historian Winthrop Jordan saw a link between
Paine's personal life and what Jordan calls Paine's "patricidal accomplishments."
Paine's father was a poor Quaker, his mother the Anglican daughter of an attorney,
eleven years her husband's elder; they were not happily married, and Paine's references to his father are affectionate, to his mother nonexistent. "The lower status of his
father may well have angered Paine, and his affectionate remarks may have masked a
hostility he could not admit," Jordan wrote. "His own inability to get along with
women may have been owing to an inability to identify with his masculine parent.
Armed with these facts it is possible to stretch Paine out on the couch and have at
him." Jordan, who in 1968 won the National Book Award for *White over Black:
American Attitudes Toward the Negro, 1550–1812*, was one of a long line of scholars
and thinkers: his father a history professor, his mother the great-great-granddaughter
of the Quaker abolitionists and women's rights advocates James and Lucretia Coffin
Mott ("In a true marriage relation, the independence of the husband and the wife is
equal, their dependence mutual, and their obligations reciprocal," Lucretia Mott
wrote in 1879). An obituary published at the time of Jordan's death, in 2007, said:
"Disinclined at first to follow in his father's field, Winthrop Jordan earned a bache-
lor's degree from Harvard in 1953; his major—a gentle act of rebellion—was not history but social relations." Jordan himself wrote in an essay: "I took no history courses
in college. Partly this was owing to being a history professor's son."

the Revolution, a town in Massachusetts incorporated and took the name Washington, becoming the first geographical place named in his honor. A few weeks later, in what is today known as the Washington Heights section of Manhattan, Mount Washington was named in honor of the new father; soon afterward, the name Washington showed up as the name of a district in North Carolina, a town and a mountain in New Hampshire, counties in Maryland and Virginia. It is thought that the first time the appellation was applied formally—the first time Washington was referred to in print as the "Father of Our Country"—was in the 1779 edition of the *Lancaster Almanack*, which, like most colonial almanacs, concentrated mostly on cycles of the moon and growing seasons, less on politics and philosophy. If political at all, almanacs were more likely to deflate kings, to attack pomposity. Here is an example:

> *Fly not too high my Genius, know thy Wings*
> *Weak-feather'd are, to soar to th'highest things;*
> *Undress'd and Unadorn'd is the Quill;*
> *To please the Critik, deficient is thy skill.*
> *Let not thy fancy aim at things sublime,*
> *High flights do often times become a crime.*

The journals of soldiers and officers read to me like accidental eclogues, pastoral dialogues written in the moments between contemplating battlefields and death. Here is an excerpt from the journal of an officer, set on the bank of the Passaic River, in the city we now call Paterson, where he sat with George Washington, ate lunch, filled his canteen at a spring beside an old oak tree, "composed some excellent grog," and described the falls:

The Pasaic appears to be about 30 or 40 yards broad—but the water does not cover at the falls near this extent. There a smooth and gentle sheet tumbles down into a deep aperture or cleft of the rock, which crosses the channel, while, at the same time, several lesser portions seem to steal thro' different openings, rudely encountering each other in their descent, till they arrive at the bottom where they all mix together. This conflict and the dashing of the water against the asperities and contrasted sides of the rock produces a fine spray that issuing from the cleft appears at a distance like a thin body of smoke. Near the bottom of the falls it exhibits a beautiful rainbow in miniature. Here the water composes itself as in a large basin of solid stone and then spreads into a pretty broad channel, continuing its course uninterrupted to New-York bay.

I went out to the Passaic Falls recently, on the edge of Paterson, New Jersey, a beat-up city. It was on a day when the river was high, when the falls were raging, and the smoke that General McHenry described was thick. I brought a friend from Boston who couldn't believe how secret and beautiful it seemed.*

A PLAN OF ATTACK

Like my father before me, I was born in this country, and even now continue to bang around in the vast but forgotten battlefield, a no-longer-so-hallowed ground. I walk and work and ride buses and bikes and subways and occasionally flag down a cab in the very precincts that Washington and his mapmakers surveyed and marked, fortified

---

*The Great Falls of the Passaic River were once quite widely known, even famous. When Alexander Hamilton saw them, he promptly planned an industrial base around them, to create an independence founded on manufacturing. During the Paterson silk strikes in 1913, the International Workers of the World gathered near the falls to demand (in vain) an eight-hour workday; they gathered, as well, on the nearby hill in Haledon. In the 1940s and '50s, William Carlos Williams used the falls for inspiration in his Greek epic–like poem *Paterson*. "From the beginning I decided there would be four books following the course of the river whose life seemed more and more to resemble my own life as I more and more thought of it: the river above the Falls, the catastrophe of the Falls itself, the river below the Falls, and the entrance at the end to the great sea," wrote Williams. Robert Smithson, an artist known for what is today called land art, or earth art, also grew up around the falls. "I guess the Paterson area is where I had a lot of contact with quarries and I think that is somewhat embedded in my psyche," he said. Once, I was a newspaper reporter in Paterson and would eat lunch at the falls, imagining Allen Ginsberg being arrested nearby— arrested, in fact, by the very mayor, Frank X. Graves, Jr., whose office I stopped into every day. Ginsberg was mentored by Williams, who wrote the introduction to the younger poet's *Howl* and included Ginsberg's letters in the final book of *Paterson*. Williams was also a doctor. He delivered Robert Smithson.

and ditched and armed with cannons and pikes—the place he studied all through the war with maps, on foot, and with a spyglass, hoping, first, to defend the city (a lost cause, he decided fairly early on, due largely to the city being an indefensible archipelago); and, second, to recapture it, which he never really did. Of course, for the better part of my life, I thought haphazardly about the land over which Washington would have strategized endlessly; I walked like a mindless incumbent in the streets of the First Inauguration, an unwitting spectator to the giant natural coliseum in which the American rebels fought their war, in which they instigated a new nation. But during my time here, I have slowly come to see the past in the place, to attack it more strategically, as far as history goes.

A couple of years ago, I began to work like a scout, going out on reconnaissance missions into a landscape that might not appear ancient, camouflaged as it is by cities and strip malls, by toxic waste sites and high-end commercial properties. Sometimes I went alone, sometimes recruiting family or friends, sometimes escorted by the like-minded— for example, a guy I know who is hoping his elementary school–aged sons might grow up with a sense of the history around them that seems secret. (The day I met this guy, in an office overlooking New York Harbor, he asked me, out of the blue, "Can you imagine what it looked like in 1776, when the British fleet sailed in?") Like American military strategists during the Revolutionary War, I considered the tactics of the French cartographers, who were highly trained, mapping battles after they were won or lost, entrusted with secrets of great importance, and (most reassuring from my own vantage point) often mapping as they went along.

I might take a subway up to Washington Heights and simply look down a hill that the Americans defended from a British approach. I might ride a ferry with stockbrokers headed from Wall Street to the suburbs of New Jersey, in order to imagine the course of a whaleboat as it raided a Tory stronghold along the Upper New York Bay. Once, I walked the three-day route of the army, screwing up my back in an epic fashion. Another day, at the site of the Battle of White Plains, on the anniversary of the battle's commencement, I stood in an empty playground in a hilltop residential neighborhood and spotted another man, dark glasses, avoiding eye contact, seeming a little tense. "Battle of White Plains?" I asked him.

"Yeah," he said, relaxing. It felt as if he were making a confession. "I just read about it in a book."

Eventually, I formulated a plan of attack on the view from the Empire State Building—a way into the Revolutionary past. This would not be a cut-and-dried chronological assault on the war. After all, the past in the landscape does not come to us on a schedule or in a straight line, but in something more like a circle, or as a rush of water with eddies and pools. It was often that I was reminded of the line by the New England seer: "Time is but the stream I go a-fishing in." In my case, while fishing for the Revolution, I have tended to pull out the history of New York, stories of New Jersey, and in my creel I see big fish representing the history of New York Harbor, as well as small fish that remind me of the story of myself.

As I look back now, I see stages to my years of walks and ponderings and small site-inspired epiphanies, as well as to my more martial and complicated actions in small groups, and I would summarize them as being part of three campaigns. In the first, I ventured out of New York to the edge of the panoramic view, to find a place through which to break back into the city and its layers of history. I chose the Delaware at the point where the Americans famously crossed back, as well as a place to which they continue to return. As historians (and the history programs that run over and over again on television channels) have instructed us, this is, if not the Revolutionary War's crucial turning point, then a turning point crucial to the construction of America as an idea. In the actual chronology of the war, the Delaware Crossing occurs long after the Boston Massacre and seven years from the Treaty of Paris that formally ended the war. In the chronology of modern America, it occurs every year as one of the oldest reenactments, dating to 1876. It is a place that writers and artists alike have chosen to dwell upon—though perhaps especially artists, who seem most compelled to revisit the Delaware Crossing, often as the clock ticks through centennials and bicentennials, when history is emphatically reconsidered.*

---

*The plaques and tablets that mark old boulders and rocks, for instance, are generally attached in the years connected to anniversaries. In 1926, plaques went up on banks in anticipation of the 150th anniversary of the Declaration of Independence, just before

The second front in my first campaign involved mountains, which, like rivers, can serve as a kind of threshold, in a war as well as in life. Thus, after crossing the Delaware, I followed the troops on into their winter refuge, the little-noted Watchung Mountains, which were America's Revolutionary War capital. That there are any mountains in and around New York City is, like the presence of battlefields and the unrecovered bodies of Washington's soldiers, a surprise to New Yorkers and all who claim to know New York. Eventually, the Watchungs would become as important to my authorial strategy as they were to Washington's winning (or, more precisely, his not-losing) of the war.

And when I crossed the Watchungs, I descended back into the city, where I began my next major campaign, which was, like the war itself, dependent on the seasons, the wind and weather, the snow and the sky. For this is how I have come to see the Revolution, as well as the inauguration of the new nation—in terms of the calendar, the times and dates of the Revolution mixed up in the relentless stream of seasons, like an almanac. Summer fog in the harbor reminds me of the American forces making their way across the currents of the East River in August, a historic retreat. The chill of fall reminds me of the war's end, when Washington, in anticipation of British ships sailing north, and of the British troops' evacuation, marched slowly down the Hudson Valley, at last returned to New York City, an earthquake marking his first night back. And in the winter, when the wind blows down the river, and salt is thrown on our sidewalks and slush spreads across the city streets, I watch the puddles freeze and icicles fall, and recall the time, in 1780, when the island city became landlocked, frostbitten forces from both sides skirmishing on frozen waterways, guns on sleighs in

---

the stock market crashed. The 1939 New York World's Fair was dedicated to George Washington, on the 150th anniversary of his inauguration, and plaques and monuments sprouted again in the 1970s. In Chinatown, there is a monument to Confucius, donated in 1976 by the Chinese Consolidated Benevolent Association of New York City on behalf of the Chinese community, in commemoration of the Bicentennial of the Revolution, which includes a quote from a Confucian text describing what is called "The Great Harmony": "When the Great Principle prevails the world is a commonwealth in which rulers are selected according to their wisdom and ability. Mutual confidence is promoted and good neighborliness cultivated. Hence, men do not regard as parents only their own parents nor do they treat as children their own children."

snow. In the end, the city is a kaleidoscope of times present and times past, a kaleidoscope turned by the winds and the tides.

In my final campaign—perhaps the longest to coordinate, though ultimately less time-consuming to execute and recount—I returned to the mountains, to stake out a point, a moment in time. Perhaps I have spent too much time considering poets and historians, but I think of art as an on-again, off-again partner with the Revolutionary War; statues and markers, paintings, and even poems change the war's story slowly, like winds or streams, various artistic depictions defining various Americas. To me, historical markers function like the great landscape paintings, invoking faded actions like colors from a palette, to inspire a reconsidered vision of the land at hand. After a while, I decided to create a marker of my own, as I shall describe. It was invisible, in a sense, as well as cumulative, weaving together the Revolution's wide-ranging and quiet reverberations. Not to give it away, but I signaled.

A CHALLENGE

Sometimes, on my excursions, I was in the rank and file, another person under command—as when, a few years ago, I got a call from a friend, a naturalist named Mike, who wanted to take me to a small hill, a drumlin. "There's a place you have to see," he said.

On a spring morning, we headed up to the Bronx, to Pelham Bay Park, situated at the mouth of the Hutchinson River. To get there we drove up along the East River, eventually crossing the Harlem and Bronx Rivers, then on to Pelham Bay. We parked at Glover's Rock, a big rock with a plaque dated 1960 that stakes out the site as the place where General John Glover, from Massachusetts, held back the British, as the plaque says, "long enough to save Washington's troops from destruction." The plaque is, according to local historians, probably wrong about the specific site, but the general idea (rebels held back British troops) is considered accurate.

We hiked farther into the park, Mike stopping suddenly at one point along the side of the road to pick up a small bird, a yellow warbler, just dead, likely hit by a car. He gently touched its chest, indenting the yellow down, then carefully placed it back in the grass.

At Split Rock Golf Course, we crossed a parking lot. As golf carts battled parking cars, we walked up onto a hole, to stand before an old oak—at least two hundred years old, as far as anyone can tell. Its canopy was sixty feet wide, its remaining limbs long and tired. At this moment, the golf-course worker running the concession stand spotted two non-golfers with backpacks and hiking boots, and opened fire. "Hey, hey, you can't walk here!" he shouted.

Mike talked to the guy and the guy stood down, though Mike did not mention our interest of the history of the place, nor did he mention the Revolution.

"Hey," the concession-stand guy offered, "did you know you are standing on the site of the Battle of Pelham Bay?" A couple of golfers were waiting back at the concession stand, but the guy was on a roll. "And this tree," he continued, as if letting us in on a special offer, "was there back then."

Mike and I walked into the woods on the trail that on colonial maps was marked Split Rock Road. We inspected a salt marsh that had managed to survive improvements and degradations, a little hidden fortress of diverse estuarine ecology; except for the view of Co-op City behind it, the place would likely have been recognizable to eighteenth-century visitors. The ecology of the walk showed off New York's middleness: the flora and fauna of the park itself, in the most northern portion of New York City, is more New England than places on the southern tip of Staten Island, where plant species are related to those in South Jersey and the Maryland shore.

We reentered the golf course near the fourth hole, where a party was about to tee off. We waited, the ball at last rising up out of the long trench made by a long parallel hill. We crawled up the hill between several fairways, and I became concerned about the approaching golfers, who, I feared, did not see us. Sure enough, a ball was lofted toward us, though it fell safely to our west, near the rough, which looked treacherous from a golf perspective. On top of the hill, we touched an old stone wall. From General Glover's report: "We kept our post under cover of the stone wall before mentioned till they came within fifty yards of us, rose up and gave them the whole charge of the battalion."

"This is the place," Mike said.

From the course description: "A shot-maker's course, it is a challenge that forces you to use every club in your bag."

FAMOUS

On many occasions—as I continued my forays into the view from the Empire State Building and the landscape of the Revolution—I was on my own, making brief journeys, not wearing any costume but setting out in a way that was, believe it or not, transformational, if only for me. I surveyed the waters of New York Harbor, seeing signs that George Washington himself saw, and I watched for groups and individuals who seemed somehow revolutionary. I sat down, too, with the notes of the founding fathers of New York City history—the first historians, who have themselves become footnotes in a semi-neglected history.

One summer day, I was in a wistful mood, having driven to Pennsylvania for the funeral of an uncle, my father's brother. He was a veteran, like my father, and as I helped my father out of the car, a phrase was ringing in my head: *old generals.* My uncle lived not far from where Washington and the American army had crossed the Delaware. A few months after the funeral, I decided to visit my parents and see the winter encampment of Washington's troops, out in Morristown, New Jersey, where they were living at the time. I went to Penn Station, passing, on my way, the corner where my father and his brother once ran a liquor store, and took a train out through the industrial swamps of Jersey—bright-white herons playing in gray waters impounded by railroad tracks. Past receding garbage dumps, the Passaic River, running dark through Newark, was traveling from its source in the hills near Morristown, having cascaded through Paterson's Great Falls.

It was at a time when Morristown was in the news, though not for the Revolution. The mayor had proposed deputizing police as immigration officers, the better to deport illegal aliens, many of whom lived in crowded basements. "They don't have anything to fear," the mayor was quoted as saying. "Unless they have something to fear."

In the Morristown train station's waiting area, a poem by schoolchildren was written in Spanish and English, printed on posterboard—"Famoso A Tu Manera," or "Famous in Your Way":

> *Famoso quiero ser de manera que recordado sea, por quien yo soy y
> por lo que hago. . . .*

*Famoso quiero por ayudar a la gente que necesita mas ayuda de la
que necesito.* . . .
Famoso soy como un lapiz para su artista. . . .

The translation, hanging alongside:

*I want to be famous in the way that I will be remembered for who
I am and what I do.* . . .
*I want to be famous by helping people that need more help than
I need.* . . .
I am famous as a pencil is to its artist. . . .

Outside the station, day laborers were sitting on the curb, as shiny cars
sat patiently in the commuter parking lot, their drivers off for daytime
forays into New York City. I walked across the Morristown Green, and,
before preternaturally lifelike statues of Hamilton and Lafayette giving
Washington the news about French participation in the Revolution,
statues constructed very recently, I stood for a moment, a third man.

I started up a long hill that I had never really thought about before,
though as a kid I had tested for my driver's license in an old armory at
the top. I passed an office building that I had painted one summer as
a high school student, the paint peeling badly now. I proceeded up to
Fort Nonsense, during which time I gained my very first strategic insight into the hills that Washington had relied on during the war, the
Watchung Mountains—i.e., the hill was a slog. In about half a mile, I
met two women walking. They were speaking Spanish, pushing strollers
with infants in them, and accompanied by an elementary school–aged
girl. Eventually, they turned up a driveway into a garage sale. I followed; I like garage sales. This one was unusual—an odd mix of typical
garage-sale odds and ends along with unopened boxes of contact lens
cleaner, hair conditioner, office supplies in bulk, and feminine-care
products. It was a yard sale–*cum*–discount drugstore closeout sale.

I bought an old book on George Washington, a volume of the
American Heritage Book of the Presidents and Famous Americans
series, as well as a relatively recent paperback entitled *Everything You*

Need to Know About Latino History, which included an entry on Bernardo de Gálvez, the Spanish governor of Louisiana who sold munitions to the American rebels during the Revolutionary War and gave them permission to travel through Spanish Louisiana, as well as permission to use the port at New Orleans, all crucial to the rebel effort: "Many of Gálvez's men were actually Mexican *criollos,* and most of the money to help the early American revolutionaries came from Mexico."

The Morristown resident managing the sale was in her forties and was chatting idly with an older woman. In halting English, the two women with strollers inquired about children's clothes. The woman running the sale smiled and brought out two black plastic garbage bags from behind the display tables. As the women with strollers sorted through the garbage bags, the older woman began talking to the elementary school–aged child. She was speaking very loudly, saying over and over, "Is that your brother?"

"Yes," the little girl said, politely.

"Hello! Hello!" the woman said to the baby. She woke the baby. "Oh, you're a big one," the woman said. The baby was crying now, screaming, startled by the woman who was now leaning down in his face. "You're a big one, all right. Are you going to play football when you grow up?" The woman looked back at the child's mother, as she continued to shout at the crying child. "You're going to play football, right? Not soccer?"

The women with the strollers smiled again, a little anxiously, I thought.

"Football!" the older woman repeated. The mother moved to comfort the crying baby.

REHABILITATE

The walls of the hill spouted little fresh-looking streams as I climbed for about an hour up the road toward the Continental Army's encampment at Morristown. At last I found a vantage point, and tried to figure out if I could look back to New York City from Morristown—I could not. I was just beginning to understand where Morristown was in the Revolutionary landscape; for my entire life, the meaning of these hills had eluded me, though I thought I recalled hearing something about signals from somebody. George Washington chose Morristown as his winter headquarters not just once, but twice; to scholars, Morristown is known as the Revolutionary Capital of America, though not really to anyone else. "It is not clear—and probably never will be—exactly why Washington chose to spend the winter at Morristown," a historian wrote not too long ago.

On the other hand, after you set out to hike, and even camp, around New York and New Jersey with the Revolution in mind, and look back toward the Empire State Building, you gain some insight into the Founding Country, at the very least.

On the way down the hill, I came back into Morristown via another old road, past a site that I would eventually come to understand was where the first batch of Revolutionary War wounded were treated, an early hospital. Across from the site, coincidentally, was the building where my father was staying while undergoing some rehabilitation of his own. He was having trouble walking, and when I arrived he was exercising his leg.

Time is at its most visceral when you visit your father in a hospital setting. As the son, you feel young and old simultaneously. I cannot say I know yet how you feel as the father when your son visits you, but I do know that my own father appeared irritated with me when I walked in, for what reason I can only speculate. When I told him that I had just walked from Washington's 1776 winter headquarters in Morristown out to the hilltop site where the troops spent that winter—a couple of miles—he perked up. "Washington was apparently a ladies' man," my father said.

"Martha stayed with him in Morristown—I know that," I said. I was referring to the fact that Mrs. Washington spent the duration of the Continental Army's winters in Morristown, living with her husband.

"You know," my father then said, pausing in his exercise, "there was something about George Washington and these hills." My father thought for a second. "He used them to signal to New York City," he said. "So if the British were coming he'd know. Something about fires and the hills"—he paused to lift his leg—"and he had lookouts, I think."

My father got better and eventually returned home, but I kept thinking about those hills, especially after I spent some time at the place where Washington once rehabilitated himself and his army, the spot, a few days' march to the south, where he crossed the Delaware.

PART TWO

ACROSS THE RIVER AND OVER THE MOUNTAINS

THE RIVER

སཝ) cཚ

IN THE PANTHEON of founding landscapes—the Battle of Bunker Hill, the winter at Valley Forge, the battlefields of Lexington and Concord—the first among rivers is the Delaware. Washington crossed it from a place that is today a village in Pennsylvania called Washington Crossing. Washington Crossing is home to Washington Crossing Historic Park, directly across the river from the New Jersey version, in Titusville, called Washington Crossing State Park. The two parks face each other on opposite sides of the thousand-foot stretch of river, a before-and-after of the United States where, since 1952, a reenactment of Washington's 1776 crossing has taken place annually, river permitting.

I had heard about the reenactment since I was a kid—it shows up in New York's newspapers and on the local TV news—but had never witnessed it, or even visited the site, until a couple of years ago, when on a blustery fall morning I commandeered a car and drove through Brooklyn, where I live, and then across the Verrazano-Narrows Bridge and through Staten Island. Following, roughly, the path of the British in 1776, I came down the New Jersey Turnpike to Trenton, the capital of New Jersey. In Trenton, I crossed the Delaware on a narrow, old bridge. The river was wide and running fast; vigilant seagulls sat on little islands of broken tree limbs, the islands beaten by the white current. I passed through quiet little towns and was eventually greeted by a giant limestone statue depicting Washington's crossing of the Delaware—stone men in a stone boat—donated by the people of Bedford, Indiana, the town that supplied the limestone for the Lincoln Memorial, the Pentagon, and the Empire State Building. I parked at the visitor center and walked directly to the Pennsylvania-side riverbank. The river seemed wider and deeper than at Trenton. In the sun, the face of the Delaware resembled the back of a sturgeon, a rippling armor. On the high bank I found a marker, words carved into an old rock by the Bucks County Historical Society, in 1895:

NEAR THIS SPOT

WASHINGTON

CROSSED THE DELAWARE

ON CHRISTMAS NIGHT 1776

Inside the visitor center, I paid admission and was directed to a room where a videotape was presenting the story of the crossing. I sat down to watch it, alone. "Our vision of Washington's crossing, like the Delaware, is timeless, forever etched in our national consciousness," the narrator said. The video detailed the story with graphics and scenes of reenactments: Washington's army, beaten and ragged when they arrived at the Delaware and crossed into Pennsylvania, taking all the boats from the Jersey side with them. I thought about the claim for timelessness, and it occurred to me that an essential fact to consider about the Revolutionary War is that as soon as it began, it looked as if, from a military point of view, it was perhaps over, the Continental Army driven out of New York City, about to be crushed. It took generations for the Delaware Crossing to become significant in the popular remembrance of the war, to be considered timeless, but it eventually became a good place to sell the war as a comeback, a conflict championed by a new nation that was down for the count but got up again at the last minute.

The visitor center is constructed in modern hindsight, timelessness a given. As I recall, arrows moved through maps in the video as though the routes were preordained. An actor pretending to be a Hessian mercenary made fun of the American soldiers, saying in a thick faux-German accent: "Zee Americans are nosing but a bunch of varmers." The narrator talked about the river as if it were a colleague working closely with Washington: "The river gave him time."

The narrator next told the story of Charles Willson Peale, the painter, who, according to his diary, did not recognize his own brother as he crossed the Delaware in the dark, bonfire-lit Christmas night. The person playing the part of George Washington sat at a table, alternately writing and pausing to look as if he were pondering what to write. When the narrator said that Washington had agonized over the conditions of his troops, the actor playing Washington shuddered, took a deep breath, and slammed his fist on the table.

There followed scenes of actors getting into boats—it was getting me revved up for seeing the reenactment of the crossing, a few weeks away. And then the video came to an end. "Enjoy the now serene setting," it said. "Take the time now to explore an important place in American history."

I wandered into the auditorium, where there was a full-scale copy of *Washington Crossing the Delaware*, originally painted by Emanuel Leutze in 1851. In the lobby I bought some replica colonial currency and a ballpoint pen, a tiny Leutze-inspired boat sliding back and forth in its viscous interior. I really wanted to find out about the reenactment, and when I asked for a contact, the receptionist wrote down a name, Casey Jones; but when I returned, a few days later, the park was closed, the doors of the visitor center locked. Due to a recession, Pennsylvania had made some budget cuts. For the first time in the half-century history of the reenactment, the crossing was in jeopardy.

A PAINTING

The history of the reenactment of the crossing of the Delaware begins with a painting, *Washington Crossing the Delaware*, the egg to the chicken of the contemporary idea of the American Revolution.

Born in Germany, Emanuel Leutze took up drawing in the United States, while at the sickbed of his father, who had campaigned against the monarchy in Germany, then fled to Philadelphia, in 1825. After establishing himself as an artist in America, Leutze returned to Europe, where, after the failed German revolution in 1848, he painted the Delaware Crossing. He was inspired by a poem, "Vor der Fahrt," or "Before the Journey," by Ferdinand Freiligrath, a German writer who would later edit Marx and Engels's newspaper *Neue Rheinische Zeitung*, which called itself *Organ der Demokratie* (*Voice of Democracy*). The poem, published in 1846, is about a group of men who proclaim a love of freedom and, in the company of the ghosts of past freedom-loving heroes, sail off to find some. While working on the painting, Leutze had old uniforms and props sent to him from the United States; he used the Rhine as a stand-in for the Delaware. When he was done, the German painters whose politics were akin to Leutze's—i.e., those politically disposed to German nationalism—understood that the painting had, in fact, a lot to do with Germany. In a poem that a group of artists wrote about the painting, they described the Delaware as a river that "flows afar in western lands between America and here."

After Leutze completed the huge painting—it is twelve feet tall and twenty-one feet long—his studio caught fire. He cut the canvas from the frame, but it had been damaged in the smoke; as a result, George Washington appeared enveloped in a fog. Leutze then painted a copy, or perhaps two. The damaged version of the first painting toured, to great acclaim, and was eventually hung in the Bremen Art Museum, where British bombers destroyed it on September 5, 1942. The copy was sent to the United States, where people adored it. During Leutze's time in America, the public had fallen in love with history painting. "A field for historical art had opened in the New World," said Henry Tuckerman, the author of *A Defense of Enthusiasm*, "and as Leutze left home because he found no adequate scope and inspiration, he returned when both were ample."

The painting arrived in New York in 1851. "This exciting picture, which is now all the talk, meets with great success," one newspaper said. Within a month, twenty thousand people were reported to have seen it. Editorialists hoped the painting would have healing effects on the nation, at a time when southern states were debating secession. "The sight of such a splendid work of art will do more for the union of this country than a thousand speeches," said *The New York Times*. Henry James remembered staying up past his bedtime to see the painting as a child, the gallery lit with gaslight, the giant ornamental frame topped with an ornately carved wooden eagle. "I live again in the thrill of that evening," he said.

Washington Crossing the Delaware was bought and sold several times and eventually donated to the Metropolitan Museum of Art, in New York, in 1897. In the 1950s it went to Texas for a short time, and in 1952 it hung in a Methodist church in Washington Crossing,

Pennsylvania, where people apparently enjoyed being married in front of it. Mostly it has hung at the Met, where it is now refurbished and stuck, too fragile to roll up, too big to leave the American wing. In 1931, Met officials attempted to take it down for a while—a mistake. Immediately, public and patriotic organizations erupted. The two hundredth anniversary of the birth of Washington was coming up, in 1932, and people were planning on celebrating, in part by seeing this particular work of art. The museum announced that only paintings considered masterpieces were permanently displayed, and that the Leutze was neither a masterpiece nor historically accurate, a communication that did not go over well with the public, who fired off letters to the editors. "Shall we scrap our patriotic canvases in all the capitals and replace them with cubistic Hoovers Crossing the Potomac?" a letter to *The New York Times* asked.

The museum relented, realizing perhaps that it was facing a losing battle. "In spite of obvious defects, it has great interest for many people in the country who were accustomed to seeing copies of this picture in their school books," said William Sloane Coffin, the Met's director. In his statement, Coffin sounds beat up, as if it were not easy dealing with the outcry about a painting that is more than just a work of art. In a matter of weeks, New York's governor, Franklin D. Roosevelt, was threatening to take *Washington Crossing the Delaware* away from the museum. Attendant to the clamor, Coffin made every attempt to stay calm about the dispute. "There has been considerable discussion in the public press regarding the painting," he said.

Amid the painting controversy, the Great Depression was deepening, and Coffin, aside from being director of the Met, presided over several public and private low-income housing projects. People were not paying their rent and, according to biographers, turned to him for greater amounts of charity. His wife was telling him he was doing too much already, and, meanwhile, he had begun to sell off his own property to meet overdue bills. Coffin had the painting reinstalled in February 1932, in time for the bicentennial celebration of George Washington's birthday. Not much later, Coffin walked into his home, uncharacteristically ignored his family, lay down in his bed, and died of a heart attack. "Mercifully," his wife said later, "he has gone as he would have wished, in full stride, with flags flying. I remember realizing that, and feeling confusedly grateful for him, that those constant problems, of which he never complained, had fallen from his shoulders."

His son, William Sloane Coffin, Jr., a clergyman and civil rights activist, speaking to his own biographer, remembered his mother on that day this way: "I can still see her face—lots of tears but very much holding it together and just telling us that Dad had died and everything was going to be all right."

CORRELATED

When I next returned to Washington Crossing, late in the fall, the prospects for the nearly canceled reenactment had improved. "Save Our Crossing" said the banner that greeted me when I drove into town. The local visitor bureau had set up a new association, Friends of the Crossing. There was a rally, a petition, a fund-raiser—and a local home builder won an auction and thus would be permitted to sit in the boat with the reenactor playing George Washington, assuming anyone crossed. There was an acting site administrator, Doug Miller, who, like me, had never seen a reenacted crossing. When I arrived at the shut-up visitor center to meet him, I peered through the windows, expecting him to walk out of the shadows, until I realized his office was in one of two large metal containers behind me. They resembled payloads on tractor-trailers. "We call this Dumpster Number One, and that's Dumpster Number Two," Miller said when he appeared.

I went to lunch with Miller in downtown Washington Crossing, in a little strip of shops on General Washington Memorial Boulevard—at the original Dominick's, established in 1974, after the family arrived in the United States from Carini, Sicily, later to set up six other Dominick's in Pennsylvania and New Jersey. Miller asked for two pepperonis and a root beer. I looked at the menu, decorated by the Leutze painting, and repeated Miller's order. We talked about the recent history of root beer in the area and chatted briefly with a local fireman, Paul Sullivan, who said he had charted the history of river levels at the times of the reenactments and discovered that the river is still in charge of the crossing. "High river volumes pretty much match when they didn't cross," Sullivan said.

As we sat and talked, Miller went through some of the most recent scholarship on the crossing, which indicates it was carried out against a Hessian force that was *not* hungover from a New Year's Eve party, as tradition suggests, but was, despite its military professionalism, over-worked and stretched thin—mercenaries lacking needed resources. Miller laid out the scene for me, as he imagined it, on Christmas Eve 1776, when Washington, low on finances, with his troops' enlistments about to expire, had planned for several Delaware crossings. Only Washington's group made it, thanks, presumably, to the regiment known as the Marbleheaders, the Massachusetts soldiers often in charge of amphibious operations during the Revolution.

"So what we're talking about, then, is that they have to march about eight miles down this road," Miller was saying—he pointed down General Washington Memorial Boulevard. "They get over across the river, and there's a bonfire. Yes, they use the bonfire to warm up, but it's also a direction point for the boats, to guide them—it's dark, it's snowing. The Marbleheaders are rowing people across for something like nine hours straight. They all get to the other side. They start marching. They march for nine miles. They fight the Hessians. Then what are they going to do?"

The firemen were leaving and Miller waved goodbye, then took a slug of his root beer.

"So what are they going to do?" Miller went on—it was as if we were talking about people who still lived in the area, people you might meet while grocery shopping. "They have to come back here, and they have to take the captured Hessians with them. So then they have to march back and across again, and then, when they get back here, where are they going to stay? There's only about half a dozen little houses in the area, so they have to start marching again—so that's about two days of marching without any rest. Incredible!"

VETERAN

We walked back to Dumpster Number One, or maybe Two—they were identical. Outside the Dumpster, Miller talked about the growth in the public's interest in reenactments. "Did you know there are guys doing battles from Vietnam now?" he said. Inside, Miller introduced me to

Jennifer April. She was sitting at a desk, working the phone and going though piles of form. She had been fired by the state and then rehired. "She's a veteran," Miller said. "She has been through this."

Miller was standing in the Dumpster, relaxed, his hands in his jacket pockets, looking relieved, frankly, that he was working with April. April looked swamped with paperwork. When the crossing was over, whether anyone crossed or not, her time with the state would run out—in this way she was akin to a soldier in the Continental Army, her enlistment clock ticking. She had already sent out guidelines to reenactors. "While wrapping one's feet in rags produces a desirable visual effect, it is dangerous given the weather, terrain, movement on the boats, etc.," the letter said. "Please wear shoes under the rags. Additionally, wrapping one's shoes in rags is an acceptable method of hiding modern shoes from view."

I showed up a few weeks later, for the dress rehearsal. It was freezing, pouring down cold rain, though a couple hundred spectators had come; the reenactors were dressed for eighteenth-century winter rain. At around noon, the boat captains and their crews packed into a back room of the visitor center, temporarily opened. A surprise was to be unveiled. The local congressman, Patrick Murphy, the first Gulf War veteran to serve in Congress and a Democrat who had barely won a traditionally Republican seat, had managed to match the reenactors with funding from Lockheed Martin, the global defense contractor, maker of jet fighters, engines, and missile systems, with a plant just a few miles away. Miller stood before the reenactors to make the announcement. It was a dramatic moment, though Miller kept it low-key.

"Hi, I'm Doug, and I'm the new guy here," he said. He told the reenactors about the four hundred thousand dollars from Lockheed. The reenactors broke into a cheer. An executive from Lockheed raised his hand and smiled, looking strangely out of place as a neatly dressed businessman surrounded by men dressed as Revolutionary War soldiers, some with bandages, some with bloody bandages—or bandages that looked bloody, anyway. Again the reenactors cheered.

"*Huzzah!*"

When I spoke to Miller a few days before Christmas, the river was running high, charged by rain, and he was playing down expectations. "Washington and his guys did it in this kind of weather," he said, "but I'm far more cautious about the safety of everyone. Safety is paramount."

Though Miller himself is a reenactor—trained as a colonial blacksmith and also able to handle eighteenth-century field artillery—he stressed that he would not be dressing as a Revolutionary soldier during the crossing.

"I am not a reenactor on this day," he said. "I am a site director. When they are asking for the director, they don't want to see a guy in a funny costume. They want a site director."

"I'm psyched, and scared," he added. "If anything goes wrong, it's on me."

CONTROVERSIAL

I studied the Delaware, of course—stared at it, photographed it, video-taped it, and watched its quiltlike surface race by, the wind accompanying it, the nearly leafless trees waving it on beneath the fast-moving autumn clouds—but I also studied the Leutze painting, as have many Americans. The Leutze painting is like a river itself, changing with the political currents of the day, reflecting cultural skirmishes and political combat.

In 1913, the Cleveland *Plain Dealer* ran a parody of Rosalie Jones, a well-known New York suffragist, depicting her as George Washington, spoofing Jones's march on Washington, D.C., for women's suffrage—a two-week walk from New York City to the capital of a nation whose Constitution did not allow women to vote until 1920. In 1918, in the midst of World War I and a tide of anti-immigrant sentiment, Leutze's painting was attacked as being inaccurate, by Bernard Cigrand, a dentist who is sometimes called the Father of Flag Day. Cigrand pointed to Leutze correspondence that indicated that German soldiers were used as models, that Leutze had been mistakenly referred to as an American native, that the river in the painting was not the Delaware.* "The entire

---

*In 1949, in honor of Washington's 217th birthday, a television program called *You Are an Artist* was broadcast live from the site of the crossing, its purpose being to illustrate landscape painting techniques. A press release announcing the NBC program, hosted by Jon Gnagy, said: "One of the main points Gnagy will make is the significance of the 'crossing' in molding history since the Revolution, pointing out that the crossing symbolizes the crossing of the colonies from defeat to vic-

atmosphere is of German character," Cigrand complained. He disparaged the painting, calling it un-American. "The spirit of Washington,
in making democracy safe for the world, will yet cross the Rhine," he
wrote. When the *Newark Sunday Call* critiqued the painting, in 1931, it
wrote that Washington probably had stood up in his boat, though in a
boat that was different from the one in the painting; in the illustration
that the *Call* ran as a corrective, Washington does not look terribly
confident, and the soldiers in the back of the barge are huddled together, like hobos around a fire. In the 1950s the painting was prominent again, due in part to the 175th anniversary of the Revolution, in
1951; the predominant analysis of Washington at that time extolled
his sterling character, which, of course, the Leutze painting exuded:
Washington became the Delaware-crossing father of an expanding
Cold War economy that looked back on the twenties as a decadent,
sickly time. "It's possible to pinpoint the time when the picture,
painted in 1851, and long admired, began to decline in popularity,"
wrote an editorialist in the *Kennebec Journal* (Augusta, Maine), in
January 1956. "It started in the great debunking era of the 1920s, when
jaded writers began to pick apart American history in a frenetic effort
to reveal that all heroes had clay feet."* In 1974, Robert Colescott painted

---

tory." Gnagy was the art director for Philadelphia's War Service Committee during
World War II, supervising camouflage design. According to the art materials company
that continues to sell his instructional drawing kits, he was, with his trademark Vandyke
and plaid flannel shirt, America's pioneering television artist. "Jon was the first act on
the first commercial television show ever, broadcast May 14, 1946," the company
notes. "It was seen by about 200 viewers living within 80 miles of NBC's tower atop
the Empire State Building." On the show, Gnagy drew an oak tree. Later, Andy War-
hol cited him as an influence, maybe ironically, maybe not; Gnagy cited Cézanne. The
director of education at the Museum of Modern Art adopted a resolution stating that
"television programs of the Jon Gnagy type are destructive to the creative and mental growth of children and perpetuate outmoded and authoritarian concepts of education." Gnagy responded: "I'm in sympathy with the esoteric viewpoint but I can't
do esoteric work and remain on the air."
*The word "debunk" was coined in 1926 by W. E. Woodward, a southern writer who
defined it as "taking the bunk out of ideas and opinions" and first applied the term to
George Washington, in a biography that made Washington out to be selfish and
greedy as well as not too smart and willing to beat a man at any deal, charges that
raised the ire of patriotic societies and churches that then attempted to debunk

George Washington Carver Crossing the Delaware: Page from an American History Textbook, featuring African American oarsmen rowing, as well as fishing, drinking from a jug, and banjo playing.

In the twenty-first century, painters of the crossing have attempted to be meticulously accurate, if not literal, as if they had a point to prove about the importance of exactness, a disdain for analogy. For her book about the crossing, *When Washington Crossed the Delaware: A Wintertime Story for Young Patriots*, Lynne Cheney, the wife of former vice president Dick Cheney, worked with Peter Fiore, an illustrator who lives near the site of the crossing and regularly paints landscapes in the area. According to a biographical sketch of the artist in *Orange* magazine, published in the Hudson River valley's Orange County, Fiore grew up in New Jersey but lived in the Bronx, and worked at his father's liquor store when, the article stated, "it was tougher than it even is now." In the *Orange* piece, Fiore recalls his oldest memory of his grandmother, from when he was about two: "The light from the

---

Woodward. Woodward later argued he was only saying Washington was the equivalent of a 1920s-style CEO, "the typical captain of industry attitude," possibly a left-handed compliment, given that the stock market crash was blamed on those captains in Woodward's time. Attempting to steer a course between bunk and debunk, watching various Washingtons rise and fall over the centuries, I often think of the Washington drawn by the historian Paul Longmore, who, in 1988, wrote *The Invention of George Washington*. Longmore's Washington is smarter than the mythic Washington, who stands below Jefferson, Hamilton, and Adams in terms of estimated intellectual firepower. As a person of his time, Longmore's Washington is almost an anachronism: the fatherless Washington (Augustine Washington died when George was eleven) was inculcated with an ideology that was out of date, a romantic republicanism that enabled him to help found the nation but hurt him in governing, since he perceived partisan divisions as disloyalty. "He understood what was expected of him," Longmore wrote. Longmore's portrait of Washington as an ambitious man who steps forward with reluctance makes Washington's accomplishments seem more monumental to me. Longmore, who died in 2010, had been a leader himself, in the disability rights movement. After a childhood battle with polio, he required a ventilator to breathe. To type *The Invention of George Washington*, he put a pen in his mouth and tapped at the keyboard. Shortly before his death, Longmore gave a speech in honor of Ed Roberts, the first student with severe disabilities to attend the University of California at Berkeley. Standing beside his wheelchair, Longmore made the point that the disability rights movement could not be credited to one person. "Great leaders do not create great movements," he said. "Great movements give rise to great leaders."

chandelier hits her hair and turns it a white silver and it hits the table and makes the surface look like it can float."

CORNY

A version of *Washington Crossing the Delaware* that was revolutionary in terms of the art world in which it was produced was Larry Rivers's *Washington Crossing the Delaware*. If the Leutze painting spoke to the ideals of democracy and whatever else Leutze was speaking to from where he stood as a German (and sometime American) interested in German nationalism, then a painting that might be described as celebrating a personal nationalism in the time of a relatively unified modern American painting scene in New York is Larry Rivers's *Washington Crossing the Delaware*. "The idea of Larry Rivers was born with *Washington Crossing the Delaware*," Rivers wrote in his autobiography.

Larry Rivers himself was born Yitzroch Grossberg in the Bronx, to Polish immigrants. He spoke Yiddish until he was six and considered himself, as he put it, "a fake American—sort of American by mistake." He grew up across the street from the Bronx Zoo, in the area that the Continental Army passed through in 1776 shortly before the Battle of White Plains and two months before the crossing of the Delaware—a time in the Revolution when the Americans had a little momentum going, even if they were about to be clobbered and chased out of New York. Grossberg played piano, to accompany his father on violin, then switched to saxophone and proceeded to study at Juilliard. While performing as teenager, Grossberg was introduced by a comedian as Larry Rivers and His Mudcats. He kept the name. On a vacation in Maine, he met the painter Jane Freilicher, the wife of the jazz pianist Jack Freilicher, and later a member of the Jane Street Gallery, often said to be New York's first artists' cooperative. As Rivers described her at the time, she sounds like the Abigail Adams of 1950s New York City painting—smart, low-key, and, as Rivers once recalled, "in touch with something that seemed marvelous." One way she was in touch with something was through painting, which she encouraged Rivers to take up.

Living in the twenty-first century, I sometimes find it difficult to imagine how revolutionary Rivers was when he painted his *Washington Crossing the Delaware*, but as an exercise in historical reenactment I like to try. It's my version of putting on period clothing. Rivers's painting was done when Jackson Pollock and Willem de Kooning were pioneering abstract expressionism. When the critic Clement Greenberg was insisting that abstract expressionism was the only way to paint, Rivers was painting in an older European style, inspired by past masters like Pierre Bonnard. As George Washington first made his name in a bold and risky frontier skirmish in the French and Indian War, Rivers first made his name with paintings of Bertha Burger, his ex-mother-in-law, nude. Like Freilicher, Rivers was showing at the Tibor de Nagy Gallery. But to support himself and his two sons, he took odd jobs, including promoting a pen at Hearn's, a Union Square department store, by representing himself to customers as a fictional person that the store called Jack Harris, Famous Artist. While America during the time of the Revolution embraced public figures who spoke in the codes of heroic humility, who modeled themselves after the Greek Stoics, Rivers began to paint, with rags and charcoal, what he described as autobiographical paintings, "a visual gossip column." "My life interests me," Rivers told an art critic.

It was in the summer of 1953 that Rivers painted his *Crossing*. It was a few months after President Harry Truman had announced the development of the hydrogen bomb. Samuel Beckett had recently premiered *Waiting for Godot*. Sir Edmund Hillary and Tenzing Norgay had reached the summit of Mount Everest, and, in Washington Crossing, Pennsylvania, a couple of men in a boat had crossed the Delaware, commencing the modern Washington's Crossing reenactment. The Cold War, which, I would argue, was a kind of abstract war, was escalating, and it was for Rivers a time when, as the artist described it, he had suffered "some personal defeats."* He had just finished reading *War and Peace*. In interviews around that time, he reported wanting

---

*On the day of the crossing of the Delaware, close to what would one day become Dominick's Pizza in Washington Crossing, Pennsylvania, Washington wrote to a friend and congressman: "It is in vain to ruminate upon, or even reflect upon the Authors or Causes of our present Misfortunes. We should rather exert ourselves to look forward with Hopes, that some lucky chance may yet turn up in our Favor."

to paint something that was *not* abstract expressionism; at a time when figurative painting was considered trite, he wanted, he said in 1960, "to take something corny and bring it back to life." In the context of painting in New York in 1953, Leutze's *Washington Crossing* was corny. Rivers set about painting his *Crossing* on Long Island, in a shack owned by Fairfield Porter, a writer and painter who was a descendant on his mother's side of Peleg Wadsworth, a Revolutionary War general. In painting his *Crossing*, Rivers was, as many writers would note, declaring war on the downtown art scene.

Sure enough, when the painting was done, it was attacked by the abstract expressionists, many of whom, like Rivers's friend the poet Frank O'Hara, hung out at the Cedar Tavern, on University Place in Greenwich Village. The Cedar Tavern was an artists' bar, as opposed to the White Horse Tavern, a writers' hangout. Gandy Brodie, a painter, called Rivers a "phony." *Washington Crossing* was bought by the Museum of Modern Art. O'Hara, who worked at the museum, called the painting "corny" but then changed course and wrote a poem extolling it, "On Seeing Larry Rivers' *Washington Crossing the Delaware* at the Museum of Modern Art," which included these words: "we see the calm cold river is supporting / our forces, the beautiful history . . ."

In 1958, a fire swept though the Museum of Modern Art. Thirty-one people were hurt, three visitors and twenty-eight firemen. When the fire crews made it inside, Barry Geller, an electrician from Brooklyn, was found dead, lying facedown in six inches of water. Employees broke a fifth-floor window to drop onto an adjoining roof; the director, René d'Harnoncourt, exited the building weeping. The mayor's wife comforted firemen lying injured on the sidewalk across the street. Nelson Rockefeller, the museum's chairman, said that by using small nozzles, the firemen had saved 4 million dollars' worth of art. The fire commissioner marveled as the mostly female employees, soaked in water as the blaze continued, ferried paintings into the courtyards and adjoining office buildings. One of Monet's *Water Lilies* canvases was destroyed, hacked by firemen; on another, the oils blistered in the heat. The paintings in two exhibitions—one of paintings by Georges Seurat, another of paintings by Juan Gris—survived. *Washington Crossing the Delaware* was initially considered beyond saving.

STONES

Recently, Larry Rivers's *Washington Crossing the Delaware* was shown in a museum for the first time in years. Simultaneously, Leutze's *Crossing* was temporarily taken down—the Metropolitan Museum was using Civil War–era photos of the painting to re-create the large eagle-topped frame that Henry James would have seen as a boy. The shifting of artwork felt, to me, planetary, as if stars that had appeared forever in an autumn sky suddenly disappeared and were replaced. I decided to see the Rivers painting with someone who knew the artist, a witness.

I rose from the subway in midtown Manhattan, gazed out on a sea of yellow cabs, as well as the large black sport utility vehicles circling the block, empty, awaiting orders from shoppers on high-priced Fifth Avenue sorties. On the way to the Met, I stopped at the Tibor de Nagy Gallery, where a show called *Painters and Poets* commemorated the sixtieth anniversary of the gallery, an encourager of the New York school of poets, which included O'Hara, as well as of collaborations between painters and poets—Fairfield Porter and James Schuyler, for instance. At the gallery, seeing pamphlets and news clippings alongside the paintings, I felt as if a revolutionary art scene were being reenacted for me: a film by Rudy Burkhardt that spoofed a madness for money and 1950s corporate culture; what were called poem-paintings by John Ashbery and painting-poems by Larry Rivers; a painting by Jane Freilicher and a treatise on politics and literature in a 1954 journal called *SEMI-COLON*, which opened with a one-sentence manifesto written, it seemed, in sight of a battle that is still ongoing today:

> Now that the existence of the highbrow has become a political issue in the United States, and in fact the most bitter one of the last presidential election, with eggs from one side and apologies from the other, the formation of a sentence that exceeds in complexity the capacity of the typewriter to impart in spurts of its mechanical brain the rhythms by which the fingers of reporters, experts and magazine fictioneers excogitate the zeitgeist involves the possibility of lese-majesty, particularly if the thought it begins with encompasses the energy to pick itself up at the end of a pause and move on; this situation revealing once and for all that the synthesis of literature and politics, not to be achieved in our time by subjecting the first to the force-rhetoric of the

second, nor, contrarywise, through spraying the vast events and hero-demons of this century with the PRiticism of English department mysticism and journalistic mythocracy, simply is, because, since what happens in literature is politics for politicians, and what happens in the world is drama or dream for poets, literature and politics were inseparable from the start for anyone whose mind has not been blasted by !!! nor so short-winded it can only sprint from . to .

French surrealist writing was in the air like gunpowder.

I felt—or imagined I felt, anyway—the enthusiasm of young artists encouraging each other, in addition to writing letters to each other, hanging out with each other, sleeping with each other, probably borrowing money from each other, as well as warring. I remembered being in midtown, as a kid out of college, reading O'Hara's *Lunch Poems*, walking around, thinking poetic thoughts, writing bad poetry, drinking at the Cedar Tavern with friends who were painters, imagining that we, too, would paint and write or write and paint, never imagining, though, that we would later realize the bar had moved a few doors down since the days those artists were drinking. Robert Smithson once said: "I think [the Cedar] was a meeting place for people who were sort of struggling to figure out who they were and where they were going." On a back wall at Tibor de Nagy were some prints called *Stones*, in which Rivers and O'Hara, who had been lovers and then were not, wrote and drew together on lithography stones, the act of printing itself uniting word and image, *lapis philosophorum*. "They call us the Farters of Our Country," the writing from *Stones* began.

ASSOCIATED

Approaching the Museum of Modern Art's façade, I thought of the fire trucks in 1958, and, in the lobby, met David Joel, who, after graduating from art school in 1986, had been hired as an assistant by Rivers and worked with Rivers until Rivers's death in 2002. Joel was forty-seven, my age at the time. Now, in addition to working with the Rivers estate, he paints murals, often dealing with history as a theme. We went inside and ascended the stairs. When we arrived at the painting, we were both quiet for a moment: Washington's still-trembling nose (O'Hara's description) stood like a split second frozen in the rag-drawn blur of war-preparing movement around him, a painted Polaroid of general fear, of self-centered poise in the field of abstract confusion.

At last, Joel began speaking about Rivers and Frank O'Hara.

"Larry and Frank were very interested in going down in history, or as Frank would say"—Joel grinned, then made his voice go deep and deadpan, with a distinct Bronx accent, so that a few people in the gallery looked over—"Go down *on* history." He laughed, looking around the gallery. "I'm holding back, because I don't want to freak anybody out," he said.

Joel recalled Rivers obsessing over research, studying magnified aspects of images, and then painting, almost in an inspirational flash. He remembered that when Rivers was told people were wearing ties to an event, Rivers might wear two. "He was a very literal man," Joel said.

Joel remembered some stories about the painting of *Washington Crossing* that he had heard from Rivers. "He said, 'Look, for me it was easy,'" Joel recalled. "'I lived at a time where there was a really specific art movement, and they were a prime target.'"

A museum visitor walked by, looked at us talking, looked at the painting, held up his camera, aimed the camera, shot.

"Larry said, 'I'm going to make the most controversial painting of our time.' He didn't say, 'I'm going to make the *greatest* painting of all time.'"

A woman with a stroller, the baby asleep, walked by, headed toward a Willem de Kooning painting, as if *Washington Crossing the Delaware* didn't exist.

"Larry knew that by painting historic material, you could tie yourself to history." Joel used his voice to re-create Larry's again. "'It's gonna come around, man!'" he said.

From listening to David Joel, I got the idea that when he made *Washington Crossing*, Larry Rivers felt he had come to a point where he had nothing to lose; this was a last-ditch effort that ended up not being the last ditch, not unlike the modern understanding of the 1776 crossing itself. "He had a reputation prior to this time and he changed his style—he changed everything," Joel said. Then Joel stepped toward the painting, inspected it more closely. "And I don't have to tell you that you've got a guy who's now called Larry Rivers, goes on to paint a painting about a river crossing, and that the picture Rivers paints is an attack, and the result of the painting almost mirrors revolution, and in this way makes a bridge to pop art. Pretty incredible."

Joel pointed out the repair of the burned painting—a slightly off-colored patch, a battle scar.

Before we left the painting, Joel showed me a letter that Larry Rivers had written to Frank O'Hara just before the painting was begun, a piece of documentary history. "I can't wait to start the most controversial painting of our time," the letter said. The next sentence is over-typed with Xs, a change in course. The letter resumes: "(I just changed my mind.) I was thinking Washington Crossing the Delaware, but maybe something Alittle [sic] more obscure like him crossing the Potomac or Washington At His Toilette I'm not sure."

"You know what upset him about this painting?" Joel asked at one point. "He said, 'For the rest of my life, I'm only going to be associated with *Washington Crossing the Delaware.*'"

IMPRESARIO

The history of the modern crossing of the Delaware—the contemporary version of the reenactment that has been attempted every year since Christmas 1952 and which appeared to be canceled the year I was finally planning on attending but then was uncanceled so that, river permitting, it would take place again—may have as its antecedent a crossing that happened in 1876, when a newspaper described a proposal for a reenactment of the crossing, with what was called a Centennial Army. "They should come over and occupy the old camps, extending down from Newtown to Brownsburge, and then cross over in Durham Boats," the *Newtown* [Pennsylvania] *Enterprise* wrote at the time.

The old marker, still at the site, was erected in 1895, and in 1929 a tower was built on the nearby hill, by tradition a viewpoint for Washington's troops. Beginning in 1939, the park was under the command of Ann Hawkes Hutton, the chairman of the Washington Crossing Park Commission. Hutton fought for years to make the crossing the centerpiece of memorializing the Revolution, to wrest control from Bunker Hill and Lexington and Concord, remembrances of which were more popular than the crossing at the time. (At one point, she seemed to have hijacked the Leutze painting, refusing to return it to the Metropolitan Museum, which had loaned it to her Pennsylvania park.) She lectured at high schools and to civic groups and eventually wrote a book, *George Washington Crossed Here*, which she sent to General Douglas MacArthur, who was then in charge of the American occupation of Japan. "Thank you so much for sending me your inspiring book," the general wrote from his headquarters in Tokyo, in 1951. Hutton's book was praised in newspapers around the country, as well as on the *Kukla, Fran and Ollie* show, a mention on TV that was in turn noted by *Automotive News*, probably because Hutton's husband managed a Chevrolet dealership and had sent the book to his customers. "Have you looked over the talent at your dealership recently?" *Automotive News* asked in February 1950.

"Few people are aware," Hutton wrote, "that along the Delaware that bleak December in 1776, a crisis was taking place." By 1956, Hutton had built up the remembrance of the crossing to such an extent that she could confidently say, "It has become almost another Mayflower business."

Hutton was the post–World War II version of a Liberty Boy, the kind of civic-minded, business-oriented booster who in colonial times laid the groundwork for Founding Fathers such as Washington, or in the case of the crossing, for St. John Terrell, who, in 1952, with a rowboat, a flag, a wig, and what looks like makeup, began the current yearly reenactment, looking like a poor man's version of the Leutze painting. Toward the end of his career, when Terrell would retire from the crossing while under attack, people would speculate that he had crossed merely as a promotion for the local theaters he managed, but he disputed that, calling the charge a myth.

"While I'm on the myth destroying," he said. "Even entrepreneurs have the Achilles heel occasionally." The crossing, he argued, started after he gave a lecture in which he offhandedly said someone ought to give it a try.

St. John Terrell was born George Clinton Eccles in Chicago, his father a lumber trader who left young George's mother when George was a child. He was raised by his maternal grandparents, who gave him his maternal grandfather's name, St. John (pronounced *sinjin*). As a young boy, he was the voice of Jack Armstrong in *Jack Armstrong, All-American*

Boy, a radio series sponsored by Wheaties. When he moved to New York as a teenager, he worked in his mother's fragrance business while attending Columbia University. In 1939, the year the world's fair opened in New York, in celebration of the 150th anniversary of the inauguration of George Washington, Terrell opened the Bucks Country Playhouse, in a colonial gristmill in New Hope, Pennsylvania. One of his partners was Moss Hart, who, like his partner, George S. Kaufman, wrote on a Bucks County farm near New Hope. In 1941, Hart and Kaufman premiered a play in the new theater, *George Washington Slept Here.*

The theater closed for a time during World War II, and Terrell, a pilot, was injured in a crash; he subsequently managed USO troupes in the South Pacific, where he tried, unsuccessfully, to convince the army to let him use a tent when there was no theater in Manila. After the war and a failed experiment with a "Smellodrama," an invention that released odors as it projected films, he patented a type of tent that allowed him to open his first "music circus," in 1949, in Lambertville, New Jersey, on a hill overlooking the Delaware River. Some of the people reported to have paid $2.75 a ticket to attend included Oscar Hammerstein, Noël Coward, Frank Loesser, Walter Kerr, Paul Whiteman, Eddie Cantor, Mary Martin, Sid Caesar, and Irving Berlin. Shirley MacLaine was a member of the 1950 season's cast, as were Audrey Meadows and Elaine Stritch. They performed shows like *Anything Goes, The New Moon,* and *Blossom Time.* The actors in the circus were mostly unknowns, and it was considered an adventure to see them, as it involved a drive up an old dirt road in the country to the top of a hill. Today, the grounds of the former Lambertville Music Circus are covered with a number of large houses with views of the Delaware, the street names a commemoration: Big Top Drive, Broadway Court, and Terrell Road.

The circus was a huge hit, and for twenty-one years Terrell ran summer shows—everything from drama to burlesque to rock-and-roll band competitions. *Time* called him "a Belasco of Straw Hat." He lived near the circus in an eighteen-room house built in 1739. On his résumé he listed his interests as astronomy, light plane flying, tennis, skiing, trap shooting, and Revolutionary autograph collecting. He hung signatures of soldiers who had crossed the Delaware on a wall in his house. He also hung photos of himself chatting with Presidents Kennedy and Johnson, and with a man identified as Count Phillip Lafayette, a descendant of the Marquis de Lafayette, as well as with Lord Cornwallis, the British general's descendant who in 1976 was in the insurance business in London. Terrell drove a 1940 Rolls-Royce, wore jeans and a cowboy hat. "Half the time he's the impresario, the rest of the time he's human," a friend said.

Terrell claimed that the very first modern crossing came about as a result of an off-the-cuff remark he made during a lecture he was giving on the history of the area. It was 1952, the winter before Larry Rivers would paint his *Washington Crossing the Delaware*, and Terrell may have been dressed as Washington. ("I frequently lecture in costume," he said later. "I don't pretend to be George Washington, I just wear his uniform.") In mentioning the site of Washington's crossing, he said offhandedly that he was going to memorialize the site by taking a boat out on Christmas Day. "One newspaperwoman in the audience," he remembered, "wrote her story and the headline read, 'Terrell Plans to Cross the Delaware.' That caused a couple of other newspapers to ask me if it was true. One thing led to another. Then the Washington Crossing Foundation called me and wanted to know what my intentions were."

Terrell recalled being diplomatic with the foundation. "I assured them I was going to do it in the proper patriotic spirit and not ridicule the crossing," he recalled.

FUNNY

In attempting to describe the very first recrossings, it is necessary to look at contemporary accounts of those crossings, to listen to the recollections of the reenactors at that time. In doing so, it seems clear that Terrell's first recrossings were significantly smaller than today's, less organized, less concerned with safety—more high-wire affairs. Terrell originally took about half a dozen people in one small boat. The boat was some sort of rowboat, more faithful (albeit semi-accidentally) to the Leutze painting, which, though it had been frequently debunked, had not yet been completely debunked; nor has it, I would argue, been completely debunked today—people *believe* in the painting. Terrell called criticism of the Leutze "nitpicking" and purposefully stood in the bow, as if standing up for the dead German history painter.

The boat would cross with great difficulty, sometimes blowing downstream out of sight of observers, who lined the banks. On more than one occasion the boat appears to have hit something, possibly a dock, and we know from news reports that in 1960 the boat was smashed by the tow truck transporting it. If the winds were bad, the number of crew members shrank accordingly. In 1962, for example, when the crossing was cold, according to the *New Hope Gazette*, "the ice on the banks forced [Terrell] to cross below the bridge—and the wind cut down his companions to three instead of the usual six." One year the boat went far downstream and had to be towed back. At that time, the reenactors included Lowell Birrell, who was portraying Colonel Knox, and Elmer Case and George Bailey, who were portraying other people—I can't determine whom. After the crossing, the crew and many spectators would repair to Terrell's house in Stockton, New Jersey, down the road. Terrell would remain dressed as Washington, and his wife at the time, Elrita Terrell, would also wear colonial-era clothing. An actress who attended the early crossings described these post-crossing gatherings as festive, and they remind me of the dances that you read of taking place in the very early spring in New Jersey that Martha Washington would help organize, when her husband would dance with the wife of General Nathanael Greene, and the troops would drink, carouse. "The crossings were always hysterically funny events," the actress said. "Something always seemed to go wrong."

Early on, Jack Kelly, the brother of Grace Kelly and a celebrated Olympic rower, became a member of the crew. In the late sixties, there are murky reports of high school students having "attacked the boats," according to a newspaper account, at which point the police were called in. In the seventies, with the bicentennial of the Declaration of Independence looming, historical accuracy loomed, too. So-called Durham boats—or authentic replicas of them—arrived. Also by this time, on the day after Christmas, photos of Terrell recrossing would inevitably appear in newspapers across the country. He began to be referred to as a folk hero. Charles Kuralt filmed the boats and the crossing point for his program *On the Road*, on CBS TV. In a memoir, Kuralt recalled seeing the boats first in a setting that was not as wintry as the Leutze painting. "I wish to hell it would start to snow," he remembers his producer saying. At that point, Kuralt recalled, he and the crew raised their eyes heavenward. "We looked up at the sky," he wrote. "A cloud passed over the sun. It started to snow." The snow covered the boats. The camera rolled.

SO DAMN CLOSE

At some point, the crossing became a great battle for Terrell. He cast himself as the noble warrior fighting against authenticity, against over-seriousness and too-solemn times, a fight he began to take very seriously. He had faced criticism early on; in 1957, E. J. Lever, a newly appointed member of the Washington Crossing Park Commission, sent a letter to the press disavowing any association with Terrell's crossing, calling it a "cheap, tawdry publicity stunt." He ridiculed Terrell's fire-breathing. "[The crossing] is a piece of ballyhoo and, as such, is hardly historically correct or authentic." A paper noted that Terrell pledged to go on with the reenactment. Terrell was quoted as saying his theaters operated only in the summer and that he breathed fire only occasionally. A cartoonist parodied the Leutze painting, replacing Leutze's Washington with Terrell's Washington. The flag in the cartoon read: "*Unfair!*" Mrs. Ann Hawkes Hutton, the commission's still influential former chair, was asked to weigh in on Terrell's crossing. "I think he has been doing a dignified job," she said.

As time passed, even fans began to question the reenactment, which inevitably changed as it repeated, even if it stayed essentially the same. The crossing began to be judged against itself. "How different from this year's reenactment of history which now attracts thousands of viewers in Washington Crossing and thousands more who watch on all newscasts," a local columnist wrote, comparing a late Terrell crossing to an early one. "Now there are forty foot replicas of the Durham boats carrying more than 100 persons (the only New Hope name now is Bob Heath), and the Senators, politicoes of all sorts, big businessmen and even an oarsman, Jack Kelly (Grace's brother) of the Olympic fame. There are speeches, presentations, reenactments, ceremonies and a memorial service."

The reenactment had become a tradition. "George Washington—alias St. John Terrell—makes yet another successful crossing of the frigid Delaware at Washington Crossing," reported the *New Hope Gazette*. And the expectations that accompanied the tradition began to weigh on its founder. "Every year it got bigger," Terrell would say toward the end. "Seems like in America you always have to beat last year's record or you're a failure." Penny Larsen Vine, a local resident, writing in the *Gazette*, bemoaned that the crossing was too well run by 1975. "I am certain it is all extremely impressive, I'm certain there are no mishaps and all goes off without a hitch, that it is organized to the last minor detail—but I'm also certain that none of the spectators had as much fun as we did. I can't help wondering if Sinjin (old George) himself has as good a time."

With the onset of the Bicentennial celebration, Terrell's crossing came under a final fatal attack. There had been a sudden surge of Revolutionary War reenactments across the nation, things that nonactors began to do at state parks and historic sites; the pageantry became more populist. In New Jersey, Terrell was appointed to a state Bicentennial committee, and he used the position to push for Trenton to be the centerpiece of the reenacted Revolution instead of Boston, but by then he had begun to lose control of even the Delaware Crossing. At the 1975 crossing, news helicopters drowned out Terrell's speech, and reports indicate that an onlooker was nearly injured. A cannon had recently been added to the reenactment, and Terrell appears to have stepped out of the ceremony just before the cannon fired, concerned for a bystander standing too close to a gun. Then a helicopter flustered him during the crossing itself. By all accounts, the 1975 reenactment sounds like a miniature war zone. "I refused to look up at them," Terrell said of the copter. "He was so damn close. I think they were news. Here we were, hollering orders at the oarsmen who couldn't even hear us. For a moment there, we thought we had a foul-up. It could have ruined the whole thing. But we made it." Two men in kayaks, protesting the Vietnam War, were pulled out by the police, one with a red gag in his mouth and a sign: "No Free Speech." The anticipated crowd of thirty to fifty thousand never arrived.

A DOG'S BREAKFAST

Ann Hawkes Hutton was gone. A new man, Howard Rohlin, was put in charge of Washington Crossing State Park. Rohlin and Terrell immediately clashed—Rohlin with degrees in history, Terrell with a penchant for it. "Rohlin has been trying to change everything," Terrell complained. "He even wanted me to read a speech he wrote. I said I would read the same speech I've been reading for twenty-five years— the one Washington wrote." When plans were drawn up for the 1976 reenactment—the bicentennial recrossing—they included a larger re-enactment of what were called the Ten Crucial Days, involving the crossing as well as the Battles of Trenton and Princeton. Terrell was not asked to be a part of the Ten Crucial Days events in either Trenton or Princeton. Locally, this was big news. "Despite Mr. Terrell's 24 years of experience playing the role of General George Washington, the individuals in charge of the Ten Crucial Days celebration not only did not ask Mr. Terrell to participate," the *Trentonian* said, "they didn't even consult the veteran actor in making their arrangements."

I get the feeling that Terrell was grinding his teeth as he crossed in 1976, muttering to his friends. When it was over, he mostly talked about not being invited to participate in the Ten Crucial Days. "I was available," Terrell said. A big sticking point between Terrell and Rohlin had been the issue of horses. The Bicentennial was a time when the rules of reenactment were fluid, as opposed to today, when they have become codified. Terrell felt strongly that horses ought to be a part of the Ten Crucial Days reenactment. Rohlin disagreed. "They had a theory that there weren't going to be any horses in the battles—that they were going to make it a festival for the common man," Terrell explained later. "But they hadn't studied their history. The common man has to be admired in his commonality, but nobody thinks of himself as common. We don't vote for the common man. We vote for somebody over the common man. You have to have someone you can identify with—who is a hero—whom you can admire."

"A world without heroes is dull place," he added.

Predictably, Terrell disparaged the reenactments of the Battles of Princeton and Trenton. He had become a victim of his own democratization of the crossing, as its popularity resulted in the organized and quasi-governmental ritual it is today. "There was nothing dramatic in the battle reenactments, yet the battles were tremendously dramatic moments in history," he said. He was going out angry. "If I haven't made my point in twenty-five years, it's hopeless," he said. "We have some new types up now who want to change the thing, add new stuff. I put my foot down. I'll do it once more, I told them, and I'll do it my way. Next year, you can do what you want." The 1977 crossing was to be his last. "I haven't trained a successor, but there's no such thing as an indispensable man," he said.

As they crossed, one boat landed far downstream. When the crossing was over, the press approached the acting general, as per tradition. "I feel relieved," he said. "The responsibility has been lifted."

In 1978, Jack Kelly took over, a promotion from within Terrell's crew. Kelly ended up calling off the first post-Terrell crossing, due to ice; the reenactors likely walked across the bridge. But Kelly described the following year's crossing as "the best one ever."

Terrell, who had become more of a historical reenactment purist in his retirement, wrote a letter to the editor. "Historically, it was a 'dog's breakfast,'" he said of the '79 crossing, "with no regard for accuracy or verisimilitude."

In February 1979, Howard Rohlin had died of a heart attack in the Taylor House, a restored building at the crossing site. Terrell, meanwhile, had moved on to other history-related matters. He attempted to rehabilitate the legacy of Richard III, orchestrating a mass at St. Patrick's Cathedral and then arranging meals prepared and served in medieval style—and eaten in period costume. Terrell died in 1989, from complications related to Alzheimer's disease.

A few days after the 1976 crossing, during the time when he was excluded from the Ten Crucial Days reenactment, Terrell showed up in the papers on a horse of his own, in what seems to me like a consolation reenactment of some kind. On the other hand, perhaps he had gone rogue. He was photographed wearing his Washington outfit on horseback, a formal (but, to my eye, resigned) look on his face, his nose raised, an old soldier pressing on. It was a completely staged photograph in which he was handing a map to the pilot of a C-141, a Durham boat–like military transport plane, at McGuire Air Force Base. This is a base named for Thomas B. McGuire, Jr., the second-highest-scoring ace in World War II, killed in combat in the Pacific. McGuire Air Force Base is sometimes called the most historic air force base in the United States, due partly to the fact that it has not been sold off and developed as a shopping mall, or condo-ized, as have many other bases over the years. One reason it has not been developed has to do with radioactive contamination. In 1960, a supersonic Bomarc missile caught fire at the base. The Bomarc was a ground-to-air missile intended to protect East Coast cities from Soviet nuclear attack. The Bomarc was tipped with a nuclear warhead. The warhead melted in the fire, and when firemen used water hoses to put out the fire, plutonium spread throughout the site.

A WHIRLWIND

At last the day of the reenactment of Washington's crossing that I had been waiting for arrived—the difficulties of state budget cuts having been surmounted with fund-raising, including a large donation from the local global weapons manufacturer and from volunteers from the community. I had a good feeling as I drove down from New York City, though it was cold, with a freezing rain, the snow and ice on the ground confirming the end of fall. I drove carefully along the narrow river road from Trenton, on the Pennsylvania side, imagining Hessian encampments—fires and posted guards. I wondered if any spectators would come at all, if the news of the visitor center closing and the weather would keep attendance down, but when I got there, the parking lot was full. I parked down the road and hiked back through snow and rainy slush to the visitor center. With the participants set, the river was now the only question. The water needed to be high enough for boats to cross—sandbars stood in the way at low water—but not so fast moving that the crews could not row their way across. If the boats, replicas of barges that carried iron ore, went off course, they could crash into the bridge, or into each other. "We need for it not to get any higher," Doug Miller, the site director, had said a few days before. I immediately walked to the river, a great collection of giant swirling sheets of watery glass—rains from the mountain's past, oceans of the future.

I checked in at a table in the temporarily reopened visitor center. Reenactors dressed as Continental soldiers, in bandages or not, excused themselves as they squeezed past laypeople; I bought a T-shirt from the local high school students selling sweatshirts and T-shirts emblazoned with the Leutze painting and the words "Midnight Regatta." They had run out of the authorized ID badges, featuring an art deco version of the Leutze painting, so a volunteer gave me hers, writing on the back in pen: "PRESS." I noticed Doug Miller chatting with the director of the Bucks County Visitors Bureau; Doug looked calm, relaxed. Jennifer April, the temporarily rehired park employee, was working the table, wearing a raincoat, communicating via walkie-talkie—looking harried but keeping it together. "It's going," she said. "What's supposed to be happening is happening. You know, it's different—it's not the way it's been done before. But it's happening. I think I saw Washington check in. No, wait, that's not Washington."

Would the river cooperate? It had not for the previous three years; the reenactors had walked across the nearby bridge. Prior to the Terrell reenactment period, the river was frozen over on Christmas in 1917, as it was in 1871, 1875, and 1893. (I can find no record of the river freezing over during Terrell's tenure.) In 1978, during the inaugural Kelly reenactment, the Delaware froze, the first time in a little more than half a century. Kelly called it off for ice again in 1980. Now, in 2009, water volume was also an issue. Prior to this crossing, it had been raining in the Catskill Mountains, a prime source of the Delaware, the longest undammed river east of the Mississippi, a river on which five percent of the nation relies for farming and industrial use, not to mention drinking—New York City drains water from the Delaware for its eight million citizens. The Delaware was expected to rise again. That Tuesday, the water level reached ten feet at Trenton, its flow velocity fifteen thousand cubic feet per second; the little riverside parks below the site of the crossing were half submerged. On the morning of Christmas Eve, the water was rising again, its speed increasing. But on Christmas morning, the river level went down, like a gift. The river would rise quickly after the reenactment, velocity nearly doubling in forty-eight hours, but for now, there was a little window in the river, a way through.

At around 11:00 a.m., Doug Miller went into a meeting with police and rescue officials, inspecting data from the National Oceanic and Atmospheric Administration (NOAA), a federal agency. Next, the boat crews were called into the back of the visitor center. The reenactors milling around were bright and upbeat. I ran into Bruce Cobb, commander of the Fifth Pennsylvania Regiment Rifles, also known as Oldham's Company. Cobb is the captain of a boat. It was his thirty-third crossing, or thirty-second, if you don't count the year when he was a teenager and broke his shoulder and couldn't row. He started in 1976, the year the fourth Durham boat replica arrived; his father had brought him along. "I didn't get to crew the boat," he recalled. "I stayed on the dock and caught the ropes, and stuff like that. I think they might have let me go back and forth on one of the trips. I *think* they did—I'm not really sure." He remembered the times the crossing had been canceled. "But the pageantry is never called off," Cobb said.

Now it was time for what felt like the locker-room speech. The man playing George Washington, a police officer from nearby Bristol Township named John Godzieba, entered the room. Godzieba had started making the crossing in the early nineties, as a lieutenant. Doug Miller stood beside him, and people quieted to hear them speak. In about an hour, Godzieba would reenact Washington's speech to the troops, in a display of what reenactors refer to as living history, signaling the commencement of the crossing. "All of you who have been holding my hand along the way, you have my thanks," Doug said.

At last, the decision. "I checked the NOAA information, and the river looks good, so we are a *go!*"

"*Huzzah!*"

Washington spoke, seeming less like a big-shot Virginian and more like a high school kid finally allowed to take the car out. "It's been a whirlwind actually," he said. "I mean, who would have guessed?" He had finally won the role of Washington earlier in the year. Suddenly I recognized him from the video that used to run in the visitor center—had he played Charles Willson Peale? Now he spoke, slowly and clearly, to the assembled reenactors. At least, I think it was Godzieba speaking; I couldn't always see clearly over the oarsmen; it might have been Miller.

"I know everyone here is going to work hard to create a truly great living history event today for the people who are here," he said. "I know I don't do this for myself. I do it to help people imagine what it was like here two hundred and twenty-three years ago. So let's make this happen. I have every confidence in you. Let's make this a great event."

There was an older guy walking in and out of the room. For a second, I wondered if he was an old man suffering in the cold, bundled up in old blankets. But it turned out he was Jack Jameson, a forty-year veteran of the crossing. When I spoke to him, he remembered first sailing with Jack Kelly. "He was Grace Kelly's brother," he said.

INVOLVED

And so the reenacted crossing began. The guys playing the regiment from Marblehead, Massachusetts, many of them from the Washington Crossing area, went to a replica barn in which the replica Durham boats and oars are kept during the year. Slowly, the oars were marched out to the river's high bank, where a staircase led down to the dock, the Durham boats prepared. The reenactment was cordoned off, and on the other side of the ropes nonreenactors stood, many with families, their raincoats and baseballs caps providing contrast to the buckskin and raccoon hats. Jennifer April was down near the old ferry house under a small tarp, wearing a bright yellow raincoat, her gloveless hands red from the cold. She had just talked to Doug Miller, but she wasn't sure where Washington was. It had begun pouring rain, the snow water-logged. "As soon as Washington comes out, we're ready to go," she said.

Eventually, I saw Godzieba meandering down the pathway, speaking to the troops as if he were actually their commander, answering the spectators' questions as if he were Washington answering questions from passersby during a military maneuver, nodding in a dignified manner to all the little children. He wore a dark blue coat, a sky-blue sash, a shirt ruffled like a cloud; his countenance was serious, reserved. He paused before the troops and spectators, and listened as the director of the Bucks County Visitors Bureau thanked the community, as well as Congressman Patrick Murphy, who would lose his reelection bid the following year to a Republican. The director also thanked Lockheed Martin, the local employer and global weapons purveyor. "Today's reenactment marks the two hundred and thirty-third anniversary of an event which was to become one of the most significant in American history," the director said.

The Visitors Bureau director then gave a version of the crossing—snow, ice, boats, dwindling enlistments, Hessians in Trenton, last chance for Washington and the rebel cause. The speech shifted tenses—or perhaps awarenesses of time—and suddenly we had all slipped back to a future in the past. "Soon, the army will gather along the banks of the Delaware River under the leadership of General George Washington," he said. "Designated areas for the troops have been marked by safety ropes. We ask that our visitors respect the roped areas in order to ensure a dignified reenactment of this event."

A cannon went off a minute or so later. The littlest kids jumped, as did I. Godzieba delivered Washington's speech, standing in the snow and cold rain, wearing a small microphone on his face the way pop stars wear them, discreetly, as if it were a medical device. Children eyed the cannons.

Looking around, I saw what Terrell's whim had wrought: the rain-soaked reenactors, the wet-to-their-socks spectators, the emergency personnel on the river, in Zodiacs and rescue craft, ready to snag the boats if they drifted too far downstream.

At that moment, it occurred to me that the spectacle was less like a reenactment than a parade, or some even older ritual, where people jump into rivers, or dive into them, or set things afloat. Even though the participants had spent a lot of time and money on their costumes, the crossing had even more to do with the river than I had imagined. As I was looking around, I saw Diane Breen. I recognized her from my first day at the visitor center, a laid-off reception-desk worker—also temporarily reenlisted—working crowd control. She saw me and gestured toward the visitors, maybe two thousand people in all. "If you think about it, this is something like the number of people who were here back then," she said. It was true—the crowd reenacted Washington's original contingent merely by showing up.

The troops marched down the stairs on the bank of the river, down to the boats. Washington sauntered along behind, inspecting the other reenactors as if he were buying furniture from a place with a decent return policy. After a while, I lost track of Washington in the little crowd of officers; he seemed beside the point, frankly. One by one, the boats rowed out—rowing not straight across, the way you might have painted the crossing if you had not been there, but heading upriver, to compensate for the downstream rush. Ten minutes later, the river was crossed, indicated by a roar of the crowd on the New Jersey side. The Pennsylvania side's cheer followed, a time lapse.

But as I sit here now and type this account of the crossing, the thing I most recall is a wreath that was put into the river just as the first boat pulled out into the center of the stream: it floated slowly, then was quickly grabbed by the raging current. After the crossing was over, I asked Bruce Cobb about it.

"That's for Lonzi Rinkler," Cobb told me. "He was the self-appointed General John Glover."

Rinkler was the person, in other words, who arranged all the boat crews, yearly emulating the Massachusetts general in charge of the Marbleheaders, the Massachusetts regiment.

The year before, Cobb had lain a wreath for his own father in the river. He recalled that his father had been enlisted to take part in the crossing after showing up at the visitor center and asking questions about local history; the elder Cobb had restored an old barn in the area. Cobb's father had never been a commander. "He was just a rower," his son said. "That's all he ever wanted to do. He just wanted to be involved."

ACCURACY

I was feeling the urge to cross the river myself, to march on Trenton and Princeton, and on to the Morristown winter encampment, but soaked and cold, my feet frozen, I realized the boats were coming back, the spectators were already headed to their cars. I went down to the dock.

"You just made a good run," Bruce Cobb announced to his crew as his boat pulled in.

"Yeah, excellent job, guys," another rower said.

The park maintenance worker was not in costume as he grabbed a rope. "Huzzah!" he said.

The crew marched the oars back to the boat barn, this time wearing their life jackets over their costumes.

Cars were pulling out of the parking lots, a couple of people stuck in slush and mud, police signaling traffic. I spotted Doug Miller describing the machinations of a cannon to a still-interested family. "Hey, this is the ground it took place on right here!" he was saying. "Cornwallis at Yorktown, after the British surrendered, in '81, they had a big dinner, and he said, 'You know, you beat us on the banks of the Delaware.' And Yorktown wasn't really a battle, anyway, it was a siege."

I kept looking back at the river. As I say, the idea of reenacting the Battles of Trenton and Princeton did not appeal to me so much as considering the river itself did. I was becoming more interested in resituating myself than in reenacting, in reconsidering the landscape's relationship to history. Before I went home, I walked over to the camp of the Marbleheaders. As best I can tell, the Glover reenactors date back to 1976, the Bicentennial. The original Marbleheaders were a regiment from Marblehead, Massachusetts, commanded by John Glover, a shoemaker and fishmonger, the kind of guy a patrician military officer like George Washington would have been wary of before the war, though not as much during. Glover commanded a regiment of black and white and possibly Native American sailors—a unit imbued with the practical social integration of the maritime trades—and throughout the war, in moments of do-or-die for Washington, Glover came through. He commanded a small flotilla against the British fleet in Boston, and he evacuated and saved the entire Continental Army in Brooklyn Heights, Brooklyn. In the Battle of Pelham Bay, which took place on the future golf course that I visited in the Bronx, Glover held off a British invasion by taking advantage of a hill and a stone wall.

When I inquired about the Marbleheaders at the Delaware Crossing, Bruce Cobb had said, good naturedly, "They are all the crazy ones."

The Marbleheaders were standing around under tents in the rain, eating pepper pot stew. They were with their friends, wives, and girlfriends. The stew was spicy and hot, delicious. I got to talking with the Marbleheaders, all in their New England Revolutionary garb, and at some point, I decided that if I were to have an opportunity to experience the crossing as a reenactor, I would want to cross as a Marbleheader. They seemed to take life easy, took crises in the reenactment camp kitchen in their stride. I was getting ready to head back to the city, and one oarsman, hearing me say so, talked about when he lived in New York and partied at Studio 54, in the eighties. He now lived in the area and was upset about development destroying historic homes. We talked about river flooding, and I learned that during a drought one summer in the 1980s, you could walk across the river.

I ate more stew, which they were saying was Washington's favorite. "It's cow's intestine with onions, carrots, and leeks," someone said. "We just had a roast chicken and a piece of roast beef. Some of it's traditional. Some of it's not. A guy last year, he made cod chowder."

A woman who was taking photographs of a friend who was a Marbleheader turned to me. "They're very interested in accuracy."

"We found the recipe on the Internet," the Marbleheader said.

A soldier from another regiment dropped by, tasted the stew.

"So what do you think?" a Marbleheader asked.

"I like it better than last year's!"

Hip, hip—huzzah!

THE MOUNTAINS

৵৶ ৻৻

AWAY TO THE MOUNTAINS! Off to the hills, to hole up for the winter, to
recover and prepare for a new year, to see if I could cross back in time,
or in thinking, and maybe discover something for myself about the
Revolution, or New Jersey! Studying the Delaware Crossing's reenactors
had served me well as an introduction to the landscape of the Revolution and all its iconic associations, its changing popular traditions. But
at this point, like Washington and his army, I was ready to charge back
toward the area in and around New York, to find some new strategic
vantage point. I was ready to head into the mountains that were as strategic to the Continental Army as they are forgotten today.

Time was changing for me. After the crossing, I felt as if I were
straddling two rivers in some ways, though I didn't go home and live in
Revolutionary War garb or anything like that. I felt as if phases of the
war were mingling, battles from the beginning mixing with surren-
ders toward the end, mixing even with more recent times, when people
reconsidered the Revolution. On a more tactile level, I woke in the
morning and felt differently about the wind and the cold. Walking
around New York City, I occasionally stepped into a park to look at the
earth, frozen and hard, grass brown, ready for another blanket of snow,
and I found myself more and more looking out across the harbor toward New Jersey. I was looking at my map and thinking about the
troops after the crossing and the Battles of Trenton and Princeton,

and at some point I realized that the Continental Army's march from the Delaware Crossing to the winter encampment was a long way. All of a sudden this march seemed dramatic, even though I could think of no painting of it, no famed iconic image of the post-crossing march. One January, I tried it for myself, a thirty-mile march from the post-crossing battles to the winter encampment spot in Morristown, New Jersey, on the flanks of New Jersey's Watchung Mountains—the place from which the newborn Americans observed and obsessed over New York.

The day I started out was clear and mild—the cold was on its way that evening—and when I left my apartment and walked to the subway, I knew immediately that my backpack was way too heavy. At our neighborhood produce stand, I passed Carmine, the guy who runs it, who is a history buff, and he acted as if I was the fifth person he had seen that day who was about to remarch the Continental Army's path from the crossing of the Delaware to its winter encampment. "Four miles an hour," he said, cryptically.

"What do you mean?"

"My dad was in the infantry, and when they marched in World War Two, he used to tell me, they went about four miles an hour."

I was pleased to know this initially, then realized that it was going to get dark and cold and that four miles an hour meant I was really late.

I took the train to Princeton, crossing the Meadowlands, New Jersey cities ticking by: Newark, Elizabeth, Linden, Rahway, New Brunswick. In Princeton, I quickly trudged over to the Princeton Public Library, to check my route to Morristown against the local histories. As I noticed people noticing me, it began to dawn on me that middle-aged men with backpacks and camping gear don't generally walk around taking in the sights in a pretty little town like Princeton. At the local library, where I arrived perspiring profusely just from the short walk, I was greeted warmly by the librarians, who directed me to the local history room, and regarded warily by the patrons looking at DVDs. In a book called *The Nine Capitals of the United States*, I read about Princeton being the capital for a short period of time, after the school's grounds had survived as a battleground, a bullet passing through a portrait of King George, according to tradition.*

I didn't quite believe the maps I had already seen of Washington's route—everything can seem so clear-cut about the history of the Revolution until you get on the ground, at which point everything gets muddier. The old maps had me in a quandary: the army seemed to loop too far west, instead of going on the old roads that would have taken them more directly to their destination in the north. I hoped I would understand the route as I walked it. Meanwhile, I was trying to determine where precisely to begin my march, for that frisson of historical accuracy, when I happened to read something interesting about the history of Princeton University's trees. The most famous tree in Princeton, the Mercer Oak, had recently died, the tree beneath which, according to tradition, General Hugh Mercer lay wounded by a bayonet. Most historians believe he was not wounded at the oak, that he was wounded elsewhere and carried there. Mercer was born in Scotland and fled to America in 1746, after being on the losing side of the Battle of Culloden, where the British routed the Jacobites on a moor. When strong winds finally blew down the Mercer Oak, in 2000, branches were handed out. People visited the site. Some people knelt and prayed, some wept. "Young and old remembered playing, flying kites or being read to with the Mercer Oak always a prominent part of the activity," said an official township press release. The tree died just four days after the death of Richard Baker, the town historian. Baker had worked to preserve the tree and the battlefield for decades. The president of the Princeton Township Shade Tree Commission said: "We're losing bits of history

---

*Some of the nine towns I recognized as being onetime capitals of the United States; some I did not. Princeton was the capital after Philadelphia but before Annapolis, Maryland. Perhaps because *The Nine Capitals of the United States* was published by a printing company based in York, Pennsylvania, the book had a lot to say about York being the capital in 1778, shortly after Lancaster was the capital. In 1966, W. W. Van Baman, a York attorney, argued in a book that was published on the occasion of the 225th anniversary of the incorporation of York that York was the first capital of the United States owing to the fact that it was where the Articles of Confederation were adopted, the basis of the first U.S. government: "In actual legalistic form, it is the first capital of the United States," Van Baman said. Another capital was Baltimore, which, as *The Nine Capitals* notes, was described at the time by Benjamin Rush as "the Damdest Hole in the world."

when guys like him and the oak pass away." The township planted saplings grown from the oak's acorns in the stump and around the battlefield, small grafts known to arborists as scions.

After I read of the Stamp Act trees at Princeton, I closed the book,
packed up quickly, headed back down to the campus gate, walked to
the two sycamore trees in front of Maclean House, and put my hands
out to touch them. According to campus legend, they were planted to
celebrate the repeal of the Stamp Act in 1766, making them the oldest
trees on campus. I placed my hands on the trees for an amount of time
that seemed least likely to attract attention from passersby and campus
security, and at that moment set off for the mountains. I would have
recited an incantation, but I couldn't think of one. It was early in the
afteroon, and I began walking to Morristown, thirty miles to the north.

WILL-O'-THE-WISP

In the graying afternoon, a cold breeze hit my neck, a chill that made
me shudder. I figured it would take me about two hours to get out of
town and get to a village called Griggstown, where I planned to make
camp the first night. Due to the weight of my pack and the cold front
coming in, the march had officially begun to seem like a bad idea. Still,
walking warmed me up, and it felt good to be leaving Princeton; a passing police car seemed relieved as well. It wasn't until a mile and a half
out of town that I turned back, realizing I had forgotten my sleeping
pad, the only thing between me and the cold ground. Sure, a reenactor
would have used borrowed blankets, or hay, or sticks, and I remembered something about sleeping on pine boughs my dad had taught me
when I worked on my Boy Scout wilderness survival merit badge as a
kid. But I did not want to reenact a freezing soldier. (The only reported
rebel casualties during the crossing of the Delaware were the two
men who froze to death.) I quickly hiked back to the Stamp Act trees,
where I had seen taxis, flagged a cab, put the backpack into the trunk,
and got a ride to a nearby camping store. As we drove north and a little
west and into rocky terrain, I understood why eighteenth-century settlers referred to the area as the Devil's Featherbed. Said Peter Kalm,
the Swedish naturalist, in 1748: "I saw several pieces of stone or rock so
big that they would have required several men to roll them down."

The driver, a talkative guy in his twenties, mentioned that he had been born in Taiwan, then come to New Jersey as a child. "My father says we young people don't know anything about the Revolution," the cabdriver said at one point. "That we don't understand what the older generation went through." I did a double take, then realized he was talking about China's civil war. "I guess he's right," the cabdriver said.

I got a good deal on a thermal sleeping pad, and the cab dropped me at a point just outside town, saving me a couple of miles. At a little bridge over the Millstone River, I recognized a spot from a 2008 reenactment associated with the 225th anniversary of Princeton's time as the new nation's temporary capital, in 1783. Chemistry teachers from nearby Rutgers University dressed as George Washington and Thomas Paine and poked sticks into the riverbed, lighting the resulting bubbles. It was an experiment first described by Paine and Washington, who were explaining a ghostly phenomenon called Will-o'-the-Wisp, light seen on the river's surface after sunset.

As I continued north, the Millstone River went off on its own for a while. Now I was walking along the Delaware and Raritan Canal, the old canal path that is today a state park. It was muddy going for a while, the weight of my pack sinking me, worrying me about the next day. I was looking east into a wide expanse of young woods—the big trees uncrowded, saplings deer-eaten—when two women walked past me, nodding hellos. Then a man training for the Appalachian Trail stopped me to inquire about my hike. "You are going to have a hard time when you get to the end of this thing," he said. By "this thing," he meant the canal path, I think. In a few minutes, there was no one; this was my personal version of historical reenactment, quiet and contemplative, less about what might have happened, more about the place. It was taking me away, anyway, from well-known moments in the Revolution and toward lesser-known ones, through the ripples of the war's impact, the local histories before and after.

In the boggy land between the river and the towpath, I saw a few deer running off ahead of me, as if signaling something, and on the canal, little spillways in the old locks would occasionally open, a rush of water startling me, a shift in the hydrologic balance. I imagined ghosts of the place—Welsh miners before the Revolution mining Ten Mile Hill, the Irish canal workers who died in a cholera outbreak in

1832. I pictured the staff of the Atlantic Terra Cotta Company, the largest terra-cotta makers in the world, who used clay from this valley that Washington marched through to make a terra-cotta Washington in the center of Perth Amboy, entitled *The Father of His Country*. A few miles on, across the canal, I spotted a big tree: a huge mottled trunk, bark like old flaking skin, the tips of its longest branches white, a leafless, arthritic canopy that resembled an old gray face. With binoculars, I saw a plaque beneath it: "By this route / Washington / with his army / retired after his victory at Princeton / January, 1777."*

---

*Trees are our stand-ins in the past. Trees that lived through the Revolution, trees that were planted after the Revolution in honor of its participants, trees that in some ways inspired the inhabitants of the colonies to revolt in the first place—they were there. In the 1600s in France, the *mai* was a tree that, with all but its uppermost branches pruned, was a rallying point, associated with fertility rights, or hung with the tools of dead laborers to entice wandering souls. And if a ship's mast or a collection of poles was placed before a manor house, wine sprinkled liberally about, the crowd awaiting its *dû*, or payment, the poles became a kind of community ransom note. By 1790, the *mai* had become the *arbre de la liberté*, and in cities, where trees were often unavailable, poles were used. In Boston, in 1765, on a summer market day, an effigy of the stamp agent and a large boot (to represent Lord Bute, the First Lord of the Treasury, who Bostonians mistakenly believed authored the tax) were left at the foot of a large elm tree. For royalists, the tree was, as one noted, "consecrated as an Idol for the Mob to worship." Long before the war, the elm had become a rallying point for the Liberty Boys, the Founding Fathers' fathers, generationally speaking, who decorated the branches with flags and bunting, filled the limbs with lanterns, and placed at the center an obelisk, specially designed for the protest, covered with poems and drawings declaiming tyranny, proclaiming liberty. Towns throughout the colonies began to adopt their own Liberty Trees, and in New York people adopted poles, which the historian David Hackett Fischer sees as related to a ship's mast, a more commercial version of the tree of liberty (their descendants still stand in squares around New York today—near City Hall, for instance). Thomas Paine wrote a poem called "Liberty Tree," and Irish Republicans sang a song with the same title. Toussaint L'Ouverture, the leader of the Haitian revolution, which began in 1791, said: "By overthrowing me, you have succeeded in cutting down the tree of liberty of the blacks in Santo Domingo, but have failed to destroy the roots that are deep and strong. The tree will grow again." In an essay entitled "Liberty Tree: A Genealogy," Arthur M. Schlesinger described the Liberty Tree as "silent propaganda" and wrote that "no single venture paid richer dividends than the Tree of Liberty." The last surviving Liberty Tree from the time of the Revolution was on the campus of St. John's College in Annapolis, Maryland. It died from damage suffered during Hurricane Floyd in September 1999. A scion replaced it.

In the quiet, peopleless night, I pictured Peder and Oluf Pederson sitting down one evening in 1925, drawing a circle with a fifty-mile radius of New York, reading an ad in *The Rural New Yorker*, driving to Griggstown, buying some cottages, swimming in the canal, founding Norseville, the village I was entering. "It was a beautiful day," one of them remembered, "a little cold, but sunny, and the foliage on the trees were in their brightest hues of yellow and gold and brown and red . . . It all looked good to us and like the Mormons of old when they came upon Utah, we said: 'This is the Place!'" They planted Norway maples and named the three new roads for Leif Erickson, Abraham Lincoln, and George Washington. In 1971, after a hurricane, the old Kunze store, at that point run by Sigurd and Alice Berven—with herring from Iceland, Gjetost cheese from Denmark, flatbread from Norway, and lingonberries from Newfoundland—flooded, a refrigerator floating near the ceiling.

But taken all together, the little canal-side passageway was like an empty stage after a big crowd had left the house.

I was maybe a mile from my camp when I saw that the moisture in the dusk was making the air seem like a kind of scrim or veil, so that as I looked ahead I doubted at first that I saw an old man on a bike with a small white creature on his chest. In another minute, I could easily make out the man and his cat, peering, semi-bored, out of a knapsack the man was wearing on his chest. I was impressed that the man was able to bike on the muddy trail, elbows out, pedaling slowly, clown-in-a-circus style. When he came to a stop beside me, he said, "When you think of it, the world is the most magnificent gift."

The man began to talk about the nature of time, and I was not completely following him for a number of reasons, several of them technical. On a practical note, he said I should not attempt to write anything about history in the United States. "I think it's a superficial enterprise," he said, "because Americans are superficial people. But in the future, when technology makes it such that work is over, you won't have aggressive competition anymore, and when there is no more aggressive competition, then people will think about history."

His cat was poking impatiently out of the knapsack now, making me nervous.

"That's when people will really start thinking about history," he said.

When I told him I was walking to Morristown along the path of the Continental Army in its march to Morristown, he said, "Why don't you just rent a truck?"

I turned around to watch him bike away, disappearing in the strange, thick air, and it was only after taking a few steps further that I realized someone was laughing and calling out. "*General Washington!*" the voice was saying.

It was the wife of the couple who lived in the old colonial property I was headed for, the former Black Horse Tavern. I went a little further and crossed the canal on a small road. At their home, a portion of which was a Revolutionary-era tavern, I was greeted by their dogs, who guarded me faithfully as I quickly set up my tent on the edge of a beautiful field, at the roots of an old tree, on a hill that was difficult to imagine as part of an underground septic system.

WEATHERWISE

Weather had a big hand in the American troops making it through Griggstown in 1776, and not in the manner that weather is typically recalled in relation to the Revolutionary War. Typically, weather comes in as a dramatic player at key moments, as an act of providence: a Continental troops–saving fog, for instance, a punishing-the-British storm, a meteorological cymbal crash, the highlights in the musical score of a made-for-history film called *America!* Someone who looked at Revolutionary War weather another way—as weather that was just weather but was then noticed in a manner that ended up in itself strategic and fate-making—was a meteorologist who grew up in the Watchung Mountains and as an adult lived in Princeton: David Ludlum, the founding father of American weather history.

Ludlum was the founder and longtime editor of *Weatherwise*, a journal for weather enthusiasts. In 1976, *Weatherwise* examined the weather at the Delaware Crossing, as well as at the Battles of Trenton and Princeton, concluding with the weather as it related to the troops' march to Morristown. It was a reverse weather report for the crossing, beginning, naturally, with some debunking—in this case, a criticism of Emanuel Leutze's *Washington Crossing the Delaware*. "From the meteorological

point of view, the very thick ice cakes, with their uneven upper sur-
faces resembling miniature icebergs, gave a false impression of the type
of ice in the Delaware that night," Ludlum wrote. "Being new ice of recent date and broken up only a few hours before, the floes must have
been much less thick and more even than what the artist pictured."

Ludlum, who was born in East Orange, a town in the Watchung
range, was obsessed with snow as a boy. He studied history at Princeton and was teaching high school history when World War II began.
He enlisted to avoid the draft, studied weather, and quickly rose
through the ranks of military weather forecasters, retiring as a lieutenant colonel. As a member of the Twelfth Weather Squadron, he led a
mobile unit to North Africa in December 1942. In 1944 his forecasting
postponed the air raid on Cassino, Italy, for a week; this attack was
eventually named Operation Ludlum. It was the only military operation named for a weatherman in U.S. history, a fact publicized during
the war by *Time* and *Newsweek*, making Ludlum, for a brief time, a
weather celebrity. After the war he sold weather instruments, and then
worked at the Franklin Institute in Philadelphia. He became Philadelphia's first TV weather forecaster, and, very likely, the first TV weatherman in America. He organized the Amateur Weather Enthusiasts of
America, which published *Weatherwise*, and met his future wife, Rita
Manion, while working at the headquarters of the American Meteorological Service. In Princeton, where he lived until his death, in 1997, he
operated a weather station at his home, predicting weather for the organizers of local community events.

Ludlum is thought to be the only person ever to have owned a personal copy of the records of the National Weather Service, and in the
1960s he began to research the weather prior to 1870, when the federal
government began keeping records. He wrote several books on the history of weather in America, including *Early American Hurricanes,
1492–1870, Early American Winters, 1604–1820,* and *Early American
Tornadoes, 1586–1870.* To do so, he combed through old newspapers
and the logs of weather-interested citizens. In reading Ludlum's books,
I have noticed that while he is thorough and exacting, he enjoys making puns that attest to his military background, frequently describing,
for example, a rainy situation where the ground gets soaked (and
troops cannot move very well) as General Mud.

I have also noticed that he has a special appreciation for people in history who have not just tracked the weather but become aware of patterns, who view a given day's weather in the context of previous weather. He refers to these people as "weatherwise." He calls Timothy Dwight, an early American minister, politician, theologian, and educator, weatherwise. He refers to Noah Webster as "the weatherwise Noah Webster." The same for Noah Webster's father. Another person he refers to as weatherwise is George Washington.

TYPICAL

A good deal of Ludlum's respect for Washington's weather awareness comes from the so-called Ten Crucial Days, especially Crucial Days Six through Ten. Ludlum described them in the bicentennial edition of *Weatherwise*. He takes the iconic versions of the crossing (and the battles following it) and flattens them out, referring to them less like an epic and more like a weather log, mundane. He begins, as do most historians, by orienting the reader with relation to the weather and the Leutze painting, proposing, first, that the Durham boats that were in fact utilized (as opposed to the boats pictured by Leutze) would have performed as "improvised ice breakers." From the records, and from his knowledge of area weather systems, Ludlow concluded that the march from the crossing to Trenton, begun after 3:00 a.m., would have passed through a storm surging at dawn, with sleet that, according to one of Washington's aides, "cuts like a knife." Like an alchemist working in reverse, Ludlum takes the knifelike sleet and transforms it into a weather map, the storm proving to be extraordinarily ordinary. "Many similar storms have swept this area about this date in early winter, when a northeasterly flow from the still relatively warm Atlantic Ocean prevails, bringing first snow, then ice pellets, and finally rain, often with alternate periods of each, or a mixture of all three," said Ludlum. Most significantly, from the point of view of the troops in 1776, he noted that by morning the blinding hail was at the backs of the Americans and blowing straight into the faces of the Hessians. Non-weather-interested reports tell us that hundreds of Hessians were shot or bayoneted by the Americans, while two Americans, as I have noted, froze to death.

After the crossing, there was a thaw. The British Army, stationed north of Trenton, had raced south to face the Americans' relatively small number of troops. At the end of a battle that neither side won, Washington was on a hill, with the Delaware behind him, a marshy creek called Assunpink on another side, and the more formidable British force in front of him. I think it is in the area of some large landfills I have seen from the highway. (Throughout U.S. history, marshy areas evolve into dumps, a bitter irony in light of the ecological importance of swamps.) Then it rained, a lot, making the roads muddy, trapping Washington. Next, the ordinary happened.

On January 2, a cold front moved in. This cold front is not usually celebrated. There is a fog that reportedly aided the American troops in their evacuation of Brooklyn, four months before they crossed the Delaware, and this fog is sometimes noted. This cold front in Trenton is not generally mentioned in the accounts, but it is this cold front that, Ludlum argues, Washington noticed. Specifically, he argues that Washington would have noticed the wind holding to the northwest. Ludlum maintains, further, that the Virginia planter and gentleman farmer would have recognized this weather from Mount Vernon. Mount Vernon, after all, is in the Chesapeake watershed, sharing an estuary with the Delaware—southern New Jersey and Virginia are climate kin. Thus Washington knew the roads were about to freeze; but, even more important, he recognized that the roads, when frozen, would be passable. Or then again perhaps it was a member of Washington's staff who recognized this, or several members, or a couple of farmers from the area who were attached to a New Jersey or Pennsylvania regiment and were able to confirm the general's weather-related hunch—the point being that weather knowledge is not exclusive to any one man, that the weather is of course available to anyone who takes it upon himself to notice. Ludlum emphasizes Washington, a leader of weather noticers.

"From his past weather experience at Mount Vernon, Virginia," Ludlum wrote, "Washington realized this meant a freeze that night, a freeze that would harden the roads into a tractable surface and permit the army, now immobilized by 'General Mud,'" to move.

The roads froze. Washington and his army traveled north to Princeton via what is now Quaker Bridge Mall and the Princeton Country Club. An American captain wrote: "The roads which the day before had been mud, snow, and water, were congealed now and had become hard as pavement and solid."

"It was a typical anticyclonic morning in wintertime," Ludlum noted two hundred years later, in classic Ludlum prose. The Battle of Princeton lasted about forty-five minutes, just south of Nassau Hall, on the Princeton University campus, with General Mercer dying somewhere near what would become his memorial oak. "The 15-hours-duration of the freeze from about 10:00 p.m. on January 2nd to about 1:00 p.m. on the 3rd," wrote the weatherwise Ludlum, "enabled Washington to disengage from a muddy confrontation with Cornwallis before Assunpink Creek, march 18 miles over tractable roads, maneuver to defeat a British contingent before Princeton on a solid-surface battlefield, collect booty in Princeton, and escape northward along the Millstone River before a thaw set in." To be sure, Ludlum uses the term "providential" in his writings on the Ten Crucial Days (a "providential 15-hour freeze"), but more frequently he uses the term "typical."

The next day, an American soldier who saw morning arrive in Princeton described the snowless but brittle battlefield as something beautiful: "bright, serene, and extremely cold, with a hoar frost which bespangled every object."

BESPANGLED

As darkness fell in the quiet, forested valley of the Millstone River, on the banks of the old canal, I dined at the former tavern, the former tavern owners concerned that I was actually planning on sleeping outside, given that the temperature was already dropping, me concerned about the former tavern owners being concerned. I was hyped up by the hike, in a strange state, such that I could easily imagine that some of the timbers of the house had absorbed the laughter or whispers or the huzzahs of Revolutionary War–era patrons. We had a drink by the fire and for dinner ate locally grown grass-fed beef, a detail that touched me, as it referenced the reputed Revolutionary War–era spy who lived a few houses down, his house still there—a man said to have used as cover his work as a butcher for the British military. We drank the state's oldest beer, the name of which I can no longer recall. I felt half like a luxuriating officer of some past war, half like a rude foraging soldier, for I had forced this visit on these poor people—the only people I know who live on the Continental Army's old route—and I was planning on sleeping in their backyard.

Naturally, this road was traveled continuously throughout the war by British and Continental soldiers alike, by Tories and rebels and people in between; but, fast-forwarding to the end of the war, when the French had come to North America with reinforcements, the Marquis de Chastellux also took this route on his way south, to Yorktown, in 1781—and at one point he, too, stayed at Black Horse Tavern, describing it as "an indifferent inn but kept by obliging people."* For the

---

*In fishing the stream of American history, there are, naturally, many things I don't like about Washington: he can't brook dissent, has a horrible temper, allows enslaved Africans to fight in the war, then reneges on a pledge to free them, despite respected advisers imploring him to do so. He ends up seeming not so terribly radical. There are, too, some things I inevitably admire: it seems to me that in some ways he managed to make his weaknesses his strengths, and instead of struggling to win the Revolutionary War, he eventually managed not to lose it. A moment at which I have great sympathy for Washington is when, after having won the aid of the French, he marches with them to Virginia, where the war would end at Yorktown, in 1781 (the trip on which Chastellux would have stayed at the Black Horse Tavern). Washington must have been feeling exhilarated and overwhelmed, at the end of a long project, financially tapped, excited to go home to Mount Vernon, to try to get back to a life at his plantation. He was also reluctant; Washington spent most of the war hoping to recapture New York, and that is where he wanted the war to end—as he repeatedly imagined, the war ended with the French capturing the port as he marched in with troops. The French agreed to that plan but then just set in motion their own (to beat the British in Virginia) without apology or explanation. The French also made him feel personally insecure. He was embarrassed about his disheveled army. The French, meanwhile, were impressed—or partly impressed, partly feeling a frisson that, I would guess, had something to do with the French feeling as if they were consorting with a group of guys from the wrong side of the tracks; they were slumming. "Whatever his shortcomings as a military strategist, the French understood that Washington's greatness as a general lay in his prolonged sustenance of his makeshift army," wrote the historian Ron Chernow in his 2011 biography of Washington. Even the Germans were impressed: "It is incredible that soldiers composed of men of every age, even of children of fifteen, of whites and blacks, almost naked, unpaid, and rather poorly fed, can march so well and withstand fire so steadfastly," wrote a German general. On the march to Virginia, Washington is described as expansive at meals, lingering at the table, presumably sometimes in the company of the Marquis de Chastellux. Washington may have even seemed confident. Meanwhile, the French wrote home, appalled at the manner in which Americans served food: "The table was served in the

record, I found the former inn to be sumptuous in its comfortableness and amiable tone, the hosts most excellent company, and, as a result, after dinner, I accepted an invitation to retire with the family to their sitting room. Christmas having just passed, their son recalled a line from *A Christmas Carol*, conjuring ghosts of the past, while the husband read a newspaper that reported on his trade. "There's not much happening," the husband eventually said. The wife watched *American Idol*, the TV show then in its ninth season, as did I, and finally so did the husband, peering over the trade paper to comment. At some point, I went out back with the dogs.

It was already cold, in the low thirties, as I walked up the hill to my tent. The moon was a waxing silver, the sky lush with stars. The former inn's owners repeatedly encouraged me to abandon my tent at any point, reminding me they were keeping a bedroom at the ready. The dogs, however, encouraged me to stay outside—Angus, once an Adirondack stray, off somewhere in the dark, and Jack, watching me excitedly, keenly interested in the tent. Jack is a miniature dachshund, unassailable. When I got into the tent, Jack followed me inside. I immediately kicked him out, and he stood at the flap looking at me as if I were a traitor to the cause. I zipped up tight in my sleeping bag, closed my eyes, and recognized immediately the scratching on the tent as Jack's. I suggested he leave me alone, and for a moment he did. Again, I closed my eyes, and this time I could hear something circling the tent, which I assumed was Jack, who eventually began scratching again. It seemed to be getting very cold, and I was concerned Jack might freeze to death. I was not interested in any casualties during my foray into the Revolutionary landscape. I let him into the tent, though refused him entry to the sleeping bag. I slept on my side, and he curled up in the crook of my legs. As Jack slept, I listened, dozing in and out of consciousness. The walls of the tent seemed suddenly delicate; it was as though I could hear everything in the Millstone River valley: the very occasional car on the canal road, and, farther off, a few more, maybe the occasional truck. Mostly what I could hear was

---

American style and pretty abundantly: vegetables, roast beef, lamb, chickens, salad dressed with nothing but vinegar, green peas, puddings and some pie, a kind of tart . . . all this being put on the table at the same time. They gave us on the same plate beef, green peas, lamb & etc."

a nothing, a thick silence punctuated by little indiscernible sounds, sounds from close, sounds from far away, the faraway sounds seeming echolike and, thus, as if they had originally been made who knows how long ago.

I fell asleep eventually but woke up in the middle of the night; Jack was standing alert, barking at the door of the tent. A little freaked out, I opened the tent, at which point Jack sprinted off, barking, growling at I had no idea what. Angus was nowhere to be seen, though I have to say I sensed he was around. It was freezing, and I began to shiver. I touched the tent—ice. I tried to go back to sleep, then became absolutely convinced something was outside, something non-dog. I screwed up the courage to open the flap again and did. I looked out for a second. Suddenly, out of the blackness and into the tent bounded Jack, nearly killing me by heart attack. I asked him what he had seen, but he was busy trying to get into my sleeping bag, as I zipped up the tent. I kicked him out of the bag again; veterans, we resumed our previous posts.

I woke early, in those coldest minutes of the night, the still seconds at the cusp of dawn when the thermometer bottoms out. I watched the sun slowly light the tent. When I stepped outside, I looked down the hill and saw movement in the former tavern. I could see the old road and the water of the canal. In the septic-tank-covering grass and in the big field between the house and the woods, a mat of brittle white spread out toward the trees, a hoarfrost. Maybe it was just me, but this was a crisp new day that still felt old, a tape rewound to play forward again, every object bespangled.

SPIES

I bid farewell to the owners of the former Black Horse Tavern, who embraced me warmly, and I set off, charged with the happiness inspired by a clear winter morning, by the semirural surroundings, by the fact that the muddy trail was now a hard pavement of frozen mud, and by the pleasure of having not died of hypothermia in my sleep. I also had the pleasure of a really good breakfast, made as the tavern owner said breakfasts were made back where he had been brought up, in a place called Armagh, in Northern Ireland. The dogs barked, as if to wish me well. I looked up to see a convoy of geese flying off in formation, and, within a minute or two, passed the former home of John Honeyman, also an Armagh man, or so it is frequently reported. Thus, I reflected on the argument as to whether or not Honeyman was a spy, a Homeric battle between a small number of Honeyman-interested intelligence historians and the Honeyman-interested relatives of Honeyman who hold fast under siege.

Was there a Trojan War? Was there a spy named Honeyman, or is his spy work a myth, a story concocted by his descendants, hoping to smooth the transition from colonists-not-so-supportive-of-the-cause-for-independence to Constitution-abiding Americans, a move that could sometimes seem like a rights-reducing move to citizens of the new nation, given the not-uncommon fear of outright democracy, of the dreaded mob rule, or given the concern that all property might be lost in an independent America? Recently, a historian writing in *Studies in Intelligence*, a journal published by the CIA's Center for the Study of Intelligence, wrote: "The problem is, John Honeyman was no spy—or at least, not one of Washington's." In analyzing the story of Honeyman as it has passed down through generations, the historian adds: "There is not a shred of evidence to this tale."

A descendant of Honeyman who responded to the *Studies in Intelligence* analysis said this: "There is NO evidence to say that my relatives are liars."

If you believe Honeyman was a rebel spy, then your belief is rooted in part on the opinion of a history written in 1898, when the president of the New Jersey Historical Society published the still-referred-to *Battles of Trenton and Princeton*. The book mentioned the "well-established tradition that the most reliable account of Colonel Rall's post at Trenton was given by George Washington's spy, John Honeyman." In the 1920s, Honeyman was referred to as the man "who made the first great victory possible." "'Loyalist' John Honeyman bought cattle, kept his eyes open—and may have made the surprise victory at Trenton possible," the journal *American Heritage* wrote in 1957. "Official documents of the war leave us in the dark," the magazine went on. "But in the records of a colonial village family and the findings of a New Jersey Supreme Court justice and a well-known historian of the Revolution, the mystery comes out of hiding." NBC broadcast a special on Honeyman in 1961, *The Secret Rebel*. But in recent decades, Honeyman has begun to slip from the histories, and in the seminal *Washington's Crossing*, David Hackett Fischer writes: "[The story] might possibly be true, but in the judgment of this historian, the legend of Honeyman is unsupported by evidence. No use of it is made here."

The story goes like this. Honeyman, born in Armagh, comes to America with the British army during the French and Indian War, and fights the Battle of the Plains of Abraham—Abraham, in this case, being a Canadian farmer in Quebec. He is an aide to General James Wolfe and carries Wolfe from the field when he is wounded in battle. He dislikes his treatment as a soldier, is honorably discharged, and makes his way to Philadelphia, where he works as a weaver, marries, and fathers seven children. He meets George Washington in New Jersey, as the Americans are about to be expelled from New York, and the two men secretly arrange for Honeyman to sell cattle behind British lines, as a camp follower. He travels the roads of Trenton, Princeton, New Brunswick, and the surrounding area, following the British, studying positions and routes. Immediately preceding the Delaware Crossing, Washington has Honeyman hunted down and arrested. Washington dismisses his aides and personally interrogates the Tory butcher, two French and Indian War veterans left alone. When Washington completes his interrogation, Honeyman is put back in holding, but then a fire breaks out on the grounds of the farm Honeyman is being held at and in the pandemonium he escapes. The fire, it is asserted, was set by Washington.

At the Honeyman house in Griggstown, when residents supportive of the American cause approached Honeyman's wife and children, she showed a letter written by Washington, which is quoted in the old accounts, though it is said no longer to exist: "It is hereby ordered that the wife and children of John Honeyman, of Griggstown, the notorious Tory, now within the British lines, and probably acting the part of a spy, shall be and hereby are protected from all harm and annoyance from every quarter, until further orders." The family is spared; Washington crosses the Delaware. Honeyman reappears later in the war as a weaver and farmer living north of Griggstown, near a place called Pluckemin, New Jersey. He keeps his intelligence work secret until his death, at ninety-three, in 1822. If there are weaknesses in the story that are immediately apparent, they double as strengths—i.e., he did not talk about his intelligence work because he was a spy.

Those who doubt the Honeyman legend say it is "almost wholly fake," as the military historian who authored the report in *Studies in Intelligence* wrote. Their version insists that Honeyman got in trouble, after the crossing of the Delaware, for being a Tory. The military historian looks at it from the viewpoint of the history of intelligence in America, arguing that Washington had not yet developed the idea of planting someone behind enemy lines to pose as a Tory sympathizer; there were not yet any moles. Skeptics point as well to the absence of Washington's letter. They charge that the legend itself comes down to one source, the grandson of Honeyman, A. Van Doren Honeyman, who was also a prominent New Jersey judge. "These historical explorations additionally will remind modern intelligence officers and analysts that the undeclared motives of human sources may be as important as their declared ones—particularly when, as readers will see here, a single source is the only witness," writes the military historian. I decipher "undeclared motives" to mean that A. Van Doren Honeyman, the prominent New Jerseyan, wanted his ancestor to come out looking good, in the long run.

The clincher in the *Studies in Intelligence* argument against Honeyman's secret heroics comes down to another Honeyman relative, the eldest daughter of John Honeyman, known to A. Van Doren Honeyman as "Aunt Jane." It appears that Aunt Jane told people about her father's spy work around the same time as the publication of James Fenimore Cooper's novel *The Spy*, the tale of a Revolutionary War spy named Birch, which is considered by intelligence experts to be the first American spy novel. In the novel, Cooper's spy takes his covert work to the grave, though Washington writes a letter of appreciation, revealed at the man's death. "*The Spy* was an enormous hit, and it wouldn't be outlandish to suppose that Aunt Jane read it sometime after her father died," *Studies in Intelligence* says. *Studies* then takes a shot at Aunt Jane: "Could she, in order to consecrate her father's silent martyrdom and hush those neighbors still gossiping about his wartime past, have merely plagiarized Cooper's basic plot and final twist?"

OUTRAGEOUS

As best I can tell, Deborah Honeyman, the descendant of Honeyman who most recently defended him, is not an intelligence expert or military historian—her expertise lies elsewhere—but she took it upon herself to publish a critique of the *Studies in Intelligence* report, starting with the attack on the single source of information for the story. "While this may be true it is also important to know that a single source may be your only witness in many cases, and a deeper analysis is necessary, not being brushed aside as lies, just because there is the only one source," she said. Regarding family history generally, she makes an indisputable point that also happens to relate specifically to Honeyman: "The fact is that family histories come through families." Looking closely at her ancestor's motives, she points out that A. Van Doren Honeyman, already a lawyer, judge, congressman, and bank president, would not need what she called a "social boost." And she criticized *Studies* for using as a source for its argument the very same family account that it simultaneously criticizes. In considering the case of Aunt Jane, Deborah Honeyman argues that Aunt Jane, who had two clubfeet, was likely not well educated and was probably taught by her parents to be a dressmaker as a result. Then, in a closing burst of what might be called serendipitous textual analysis, the defending Honeyman picked up a copy of *The Spy*, choosing one of Cooper's passages at random, which she describes as unintelligible.

"This is by far, not the hardest paragraph in this book either," Deborah Honeyman went on to say. "People who have a hard time reading the words in books are not likely to be avid readers. Did Jane read the book, maybe but it [is] more likely that Jane did not read Cooper's book. My opinion is just as valid as the author's opinion, neither are 'facts.' To brand Aunt Jane a liar on such flimsy evidence is outrageous."

I had once believed the Honeyman legend; then, as I saw historians I admired back away from it, I began to discount it. In 2009, *Studies of Intelligence* subsequently published a defense of the Honeyman legend. This second *Studies* piece came *after* the Deborah Honeyman defense. The author, a retired CIA caseworker and intelligence historian, said that Washington did in fact set up moles early on in the war, and that the spy Cooper reportedly based his fictional spy on was Enoch Crosby, a counterintelligence officer from New York City. "Obviously, a key aspect of conducting intelligence activities is to keep them secret," the retired CIA caseworker said. "All intelligence professionals know only too well that the failures become public while the successes remain secret. Thus, if Honeyman provided intelligence of value regarding the Hessian positions and activities around Trenton, his mission would have been a success and his involvement worth keeping from the public."

But in my case, something else turned me back toward an embrace of the Honeyman story: my march to the Watchung Mountains in Morristown.

As I looked at the documentary evidence of Honeyman's life—records of him living as a weaver in Philadelphia, and then in Griggstown, where he farmed up the road from Princeton—I saw that after Washington and the Continental Army successfully crossed the Delaware, Honeyman moved his family up the Millstone River to a town called Lamington, which is very close to Pluckemin, an old crossroads at the foot of the Watchung Mountains. I noticed that Pluckemin was around the place where Washington stopped the troops on the way to Morristown, and I slowly began to realize that my confusion about Washington's route north might be Honeyman-related.

Why, I had been asking myself since I stood with my backpack in the Princeton library, and even before, was Washington marching the army so far west on a trip from Princeton to Morristown that was essentially south to north? There were several answers, and I would face a backbreaking one at the end of that day's twenty-mile march, but as I passed by John Honeyman's Griggstown house, it suddenly dawned on me that my route north to Morristown, via Pluckemin, was a route that Honeyman would have surely known, and might very well have taken. If you take the indisputably documented points of Honeyman's life—his residences before, during, and after the war—you can connect the dots to see Washington's route to his winter encampment in the mountains.

PILLAR OF FIRE

In those first minutes of my march, I felt the modern-day sense of freedom that comes with a good map and a faraway destination across land that one has never set foot on before. The canal water was edged with ice, the sky clear blue. There were no walkers, only the occasional car rushing by on the canal road, and I squinted to see a heron on the edge of the water moving its spindly legs in the slushy shallows, wings spreading, flapping slowly, then faster, a blue-gray segue between Jersey earth and morning sky. If the other things I saw walking along the canal in the first seven miles or so were typed up into a brief scouting report for the benefit of my superiors, I would mention the following: a little herd of deer; an F-14–like formation of geese soaring above the leafless vine-infested canopy; little gold-plated plaques on canal-side benches, named for people who, presumably, enjoyed sitting in the area (e.g., Fred Brown); small trash eddies in the canal water, whirling circles of Styrofoam and lost lichen; another old sycamore, its white-tipped branches like graying hair; power line–interrupted woods; farm fields with hoarfrost now fading; and creeks, here called runs and taking their distances as names, Sixmile Run and Tenmile Run. On a tall, thin oak someone scratched "I ♥ Vicki." My hands were cold and numb, and to warm them I put them in my pockets, which made the huge backpack more awkward and slowed me as I lunged across a state highway, Amwell Road, a return route back to Washington Crossing, Pennsylvania.

I was learning some things about the canal, having read about ten miles' worth of historical markers. In Zarephath, I came to what looked like a university, and a plaque explained that Alma Bridwell White had come from Colorado, in 1906, to base her religious community on land donated by a widow in debt, calling the community the Pillar of Fire. The plaque did not mention that the church is said to be the only church that publicly supported the Klu Klux Klan, drawn by the Klan's anti-Semitism, anti-Catholicism, and anti-immigrant stance—markers can sometimes be too polite this way. Another plaque featured a photo of Zarephath in the 1920s, when the canal was used by yachts going from Philadelphia to New York, and, earlier, for the transport of a World War I submarine chaser, to counter German plans for an attack on Manhattan. A quarter mile later, where there were no houses, I saw charred sticks, dead coals, the site of what had been a small bonfire the night before. And then, just after noon, the Millstone River widened and, near a small man-made falls adjacent to what I guessed to be a sewage treatment plant, joined the Raritan River, on its way, as I could see on my map, to New York Bay. It was at that point that I got my first view of the Watchung Mountains, my destination a day or two hence.

In my notes I wrote: "I see hills!" Considering the amount of time I would spend in the coming weeks lying on the floor, inspired by pain to say dark and spiteful things about the world, I now lament my enthusiasm and wonder why didn't I go around the Watchungs, through Pluckemin, along the lines of the Honeyman–George Washington axis. Why didn't I go the way that Honeyman the spy might have gone? Alas, as is well known, there's no going back.

Beneath the interstate I had a crisis of confidence. I halted. It was no longer clear to me that the canal path would allow me to enter Bound Brook. Clouds rolled in as if on cue. I could not reach my wife at work, so I called in support from a friend in St. Paul, Minnesota, who was sitting in a coffee shop with his computer. He searched for an Internet map of New Jersey and then sent me straight ahead. Breathing a sigh of relief, I entered Bound Brook, taking the South Main Street Bridge. Large, brightly decorated plaques greeted me. Some highlights:

> To the casual observer there is little to indicate the historical significance of this particular bridge crossing.

and

> At this spot on January 4, 1777, General George Washington made the final decision to abandon any intention of attacking New Brunswick. He instead moved his army northward to winter quarters at Morristown. Thus ended the victorious Trenton–Princeton campaign, saving the Revolution.

Grabbing tight to the modern railing on the bridge, I stared down into the rushing water for a few minutes, until I realized I was perspiring profusely and getting chilled. I looked ahead. The pleasant flank of hills I had seen a few miles back was, up close, more threatening, and if I had not fully understood before why the American army had decided to go way out of its way to the west, toward the land of Honeyman, I now had a better idea. Unfortunately, I needed to go straight at this point, to spare myself five or so miles trudging. I would come to regret this action. To see a mountain pass on a map is one thing; to see it from your car, and perhaps hear the engine strain, is another. But to walk it with a too-heavy pack on your back, in the afternoon of an already long day, makes for a more resonant awareness, a deeper realization, an understanding of the landscape not offered in a sentence, or on a chart, but in your bones, which, on occasion, will be aching. Again, to think that I did not go the way of the Continental Army sometimes makes me a little angry.

A STRANGE DISORDERLY WORLD

I feel compelled here to briefly step out of the account of my march into the mountains that overlook New York City from New Jersey and explore, in a sense, the terrain of *liberty* and *freedom*, insofar as it relates to the Middle Colonies in the time of the Revolution. Please note that the area in and around Bound Brook—this stretch between Philadelphia and New York through which my canal route cut—was a mix of religions and ethnicities, an intertidal area of cultural and economic interests being pulled between Philadelphia and New York, between Crown-appointed colonial governors and local assemblies, between speculating landlords and under-pressure tenants, a place where the discussion of what exactly liberty and freedom meant was ongoing and happening in the streets and taverns, not just in the finest homes and schools. Newspapers printed extracts of John Locke, for instance, as the settlers of the colonies had become enthusiastic about the rights of British citizens by participating in the French and Indian War, in the English Civil War, in the Great Awakening. There were waves of immigrants from England, Ireland, Germany, and Scotland, as well as those already immigrated from Holland, among other places, who were forced to live here in a tolerant pluralistic society. Likewise, there were settlers on the western edge of the Middle Colonies who saw liberty as having to do with being defended from Indians. It was a markedly violent area before the fighting with the British even began. There was, in the 1760s, what historians have taken to calling "a rage for liberty."

Before and even after the war, New Jersey was the Times Square of the colonial populace, in terms of crowds as well as information. In 1763, there were twenty-one newspapers in the colonies; in 1775, there were forty-two, thirteen of them in the Middle Colonies. Newspapers were read in taverns and read aloud in coffeehouses. In 1765, several thousand Philadelphians protested the Stamp Act at the state house; in New York, at the same time, two thousand people threatened to attack Fort George, in lower Manhattan. Arguments over religious authority imposed by England in the 1760s led the Middle Colonies to link religious liberty to political liberty—"the liberty," wrote Aristocles (a pen name) in 1768, "every man ought to have, to think and act for himself, in matters of religion." Those who argued for a less expansive view of religious and political liberty tended to become loyalists, who were inclined to think liberty was good only for the people they considered good; a New Jersey Anglican said liberty applied to citizens "in so far as they are good Members of Society." Even groups we today consider radical could sound fairly conservative; in New York City, the Liberty Boys—sailors, ship owners, and other seaport merchants who routinely assembled in New York City to harass British officials—sided against the land rioters in the Hudson Valley for abusing liberty, excoriating the rioters for "an Exemption from the Payment of Debts and Rents, and a Discharge from the Obligation of all Contracts." Sometimes, liberty had everything to do with property; in Philadelphia, "Rusticus" wrote: "None can the Bliss of Liberty ensure, / But such who may their *Property* secure." Other times, liberty had to do with not being a slave—a slave to the freedom-restricting rule of absentee landlords. In Monmouth County, half a day's march east of Bound Brook, residents disputed land titles with landlords appointed by the king. In 1769, a pamphleteer in Monmouth titled his work "Liberty and Property, Without Oppression."

A recent analysis of the history of the Middle Colonies argues that what unified the colonies was their diversity—of religion, culture, and political beliefs; that the pastiche of ideals made for a unifying grayness, as opposed to a polarizing black and white. "Were these people ever motivated by idealism?" a historian of the Middle Colonies asks. "Yes, but it was typically colored by their own needs and interests." In the Middle Colonies, the push toward revolution came from a conception of the future, as opposed to a longing for the success of the past. In New England, a growing population tended a rocky, overfarmed soil, while Pennsylvania was known as "the best poor man's country in the world." The per capita wealth of Middle Colony residents was fifteen percent higher than that of New Englanders. In the Middle Colonies, there were Quaker pacifists, Scots-Irish tradesmen, wealthy landlords, and small farmers. The population was more diverse than in New England, which was marked by what one historian has called "a relative uniformity of thought," as well as "a model of consensus made possible by homogeneity."

The economic downturn moved New England colonists toward the fight for independence—a conservative reaction. In the Middle Colonies, motivations, mixed and messy, were less about holding on to the past than creating something new. Calls for a new American Constitution came from New Jersey as early as 1768. At the same time, because religion and ethnicity played a significant role in determining loyalty, the Middle Colonies were not unanimous in their aversion to British imperialism. In 1776, the Middle Colonies were the last four colonies to sign on to independence. And when they did sign, they could sound small-minded. Sam Adams, a Boston-based Liberty Boy, talked about government's role in preserving the common good, a community's common wealth being an old theme for New Englanders. Meanwhile, Isaac Sears, the Connecticut-born New York City merchant, wanted to make certain that a new government protected his individual rights in the new world, but the rights Sears had in mind had less to do with community than with his personal ability to make money.

To secure these various rights, the Middle Colonists lived in a perpetual state of violence. The historians Julius Goebel and T. Raymond Naughton have described provincial New York as a nearly continuous riot after 1763. Crime, by one account, increased faster than the population. Violent crimes are called a "hallmark of Pennsylvania society." In the tumult of economic and social change, groups and individuals turned to violence to restore or create order. Courts used violence as punishment and even recreation. Preachers preached violence, as in a 1735 tract by a Presbyterian minister, *The Necessity of Religious Violence in Order to Obtain Durable Happiness*. In New York City, after an alleged slave revolt in 1741, slaves were hanged and burned at the stake. And violence was not restricted to the lower classes; wealthy people maimed each other, and dueling was referred to as "a civilizing agent." Violence seeped into political discourse, often with references to the discharge of human bowels. "You are to carry your Excrements in your Breeches, unless you prove to be too Nauseous to the Nose of the common Hangman," wrote a pamphleteer who was against what were referred to as "Piss-Brute-tarians," in this case the Reverend William Smith, the provost of the College of Philadelphia. Tar and feathering, a medieval English practice, had slipped into the American countryside from the seaports, where it had been brought by sailors. Tar was roasted out of pine trees and feathers were applied, either via "two Pillows of Feathers" or, on one occasion at the urging of a crowd in Connecticut, by cutting open a bed and rolling the victim in it. (In Salem, Massachusetts, a goose was repeatedly hurled at a man.) In the winter of 1766, the *Pennsylvania Gazette* reported that when two men entered the home of a Major Thomas James (it had been gutted during the Stamp Act riots) they discovered a pillow case stuffed with a newborn infant. After the French and Indian War, the British army acted as a police force in the Middle Colonies, which the historian Bernard Bailyn has described as "the scene of continuous contention" and "a strange disorderly world."

Entering Bound Brook, I had what felt like a tiny glimpse back at the old rage for liberty. I passed the Bound Brook Hotel, with a sign advertising it as "Historical," and I passed a few Mexican markets ("*Ningunas bicicletas*"). Then, on the outside of a tax preparation office, there was a plaque celebrating Peter Harpending, a tavern owner, whose father, Henrix, had come from Holland in 1720 and started the tavern at the site where, in 1776, the Declaration of Independence was read by someone named Hendrick Fisher. "Upon completion of the reading," the marker said, "the crowd went wild with joy, carrying Fisher on their shoulders through the village, while the Presbyterian church bell rang loud and long, cannons fired and rousing toasts were drunk by the lusty patriots gathered there."

CRUNCH

A police car was patrolling the main street in Bound Brook as I entered town. At the deli I wound up in, I met two guys with British accents working for an organization called USA, short for United Soccer Academy. A police detective was ordering a special sandwich called the Turkey Crunch.

"Turkey Crunch?" the deli owner behind the counter said.

"Yeah, no crunch," the detective said. He was reading a newspaper at the lunch counter.

"No crunch?"

"Ah, crunch—what the heck."

In the front of the store, in the seating area, I attempted to put down my pack without killing anybody, including myself. I was relieved to be sitting. I ordered a sandwich. The woman at the counter looked at me the way that you look at a guy who has just taken off a huge backpack in a tiny sandwich shop—warily. I ordered a turkey sandwich.

"Turkey?" she asked.

"Yes," I repeated. "Turkey."

"Chips?"

"Please."

I limped back to my seat, stopping to inspect the snapshots on the wall: a deli regular alongside Derek Jeter, the Yankee captain; the Raritan River flooded up to the deli counter; a parade featuring Revolutionary War reenactors and a George Washington on horseback; and the Raritan flooding the town square. I had burned through my huge breakfast from the morning, which seemed like days ago, and the sandwich was great. I went back to the counter to ask for directions. My map did not include the streets in the town, and I was looking for the best route to walk across the first mountain of the Watchung range, called Mount Horeb.

"Are you driving?"

"No."

"You're *walking*?"

I thought I had made that clear. "Yes," I said.

"He should go by Mount Horeb. It's nice."

"Yeah, I know, but right is the way I used to go to my cousin's in Boonton.

"That's too far," the woman said.

"Okay, fine," the man said. "So you want to walk down this way until you come to an AT&T store that used to be a gas station—you'll be able to tell, if you know what I mean."

Before I left, I asked about the photo of George Washington on horseback. "Is that parade an annual event?" I asked.

A man said the parade had stopped, and he noted the influx of Hispanic residents.

"They don't care," he said.

I passed a Costa Rican restaurant down the street that looked good, too.* I passed a pedestrian getting a ticket from a policeman and wondered if the man was originally from Costa Rica, as I tried not to stare. As I moved on, I thought the cop was suddenly looking at me, potentially the only backpacker in town. I kept moving down the road, saw the AT&T store that looked as if it had been a gas station, and quickly found the road I needed to get into the mountains. I stopped at a giant discount pharmacy on the corner, to stock up on supplies—beef jerky, a granola bar, bottled water. The woman at the counter was bemoaning the fact that another branch of her pharmacy had begun to sell alcohol, something she did not enjoy doing, a descent into a discount pharmacy barbarity, as she described it.

"It was like being a bartender," she said to a guy who was picking up spilled breakfast cereal. "I had to cut people off. They would come in wasted."

I bought bottled water from Fiji, one for the trip, one for wherever I would make camp that evening. I knew this drugstore would mark my last stop before dark.

I took a photo of myself in the parking lot and set out to enter the portion of the Watchungs known to geologists as a subrange called the Newark Mountains, but to locals as Mount Horeb.

---

*I subsequently learned that Bound Brook has one of the largest Costa Rican populations in the United States. The majority of Costa Rican–born Bound Brook residents come from a town called San Isidro, named for Saint Isidore, the patron saint of both farmers and day laborers. When Hurricane Floyd hit the East Coast in 1999, six people died in New Jersey, three in Bound Brook, where the East Main Street businesses were under twelve feet of water. In a more recent flood, many of the Costa Ricans were left homeless: as low-income residents, they are inclined to live packed in the lower floors of buildings, the first to be flooded. "They tend to live in illegal basement apartments," Father Ed Murphy, of the St. Paul Episcopal Church, told a reporter. "You know, it's not uncommon in this town—you have a two-family house, the owner lives on the first floor, the mother-in-law lives up on the second floor, and you have a family of laborers living in the basement. So when the basement gets flooded, they end up in shelters."

MUTTERING

By the time I entered the Newark Mountains I was not feeling good about them, for a lot of reasons. They appeared afflicted from this distance, attacked, due to having been quarried for generations. After I walked out of the discount chain pharmacy's parking lot, after I started up the road, after the houses of Bound Brook faded away along with the sidewalk, I found myself walking behind two Spanish-speaking men on their way to work—the only two people I had seen walking for anything other than exercise the entire day. It occurred to me that Spanish-speaking men tend to walk the old routes of the Revolution, while everyone else is driving. They eventually turned in to the Chimney Rock Inn, known locally as The Rock. Chimney Rock is what mapmakers call First Watchung Mountain, a mountain that, as I approached, I could see was in the process of having its innards ground to gravel for the construction of roads and driveways. Combine the craggy, dismembered aspect of First Watchung Mountain with the gray sky that had darkened while I was eating lunch, then add the sudden incline, and you are in the vicinity of the desolate feeling I had as I faced traffic barreling down out of the hills on the sidewalkless uphill road, as over-the-steering-wheel drivers' eyes startled into a slight and sudden trajectory adjustment, a quick shift of rubber on stray gravel. I stared straight ahead, at the edge of the curves up the hill, and listened carefully, lest I die. To the right were woods, a saturnalian remnant that I did not dare study, though I had seen old postcards of what was once a forest cataract: Buttermilk Falls, silenced now by the reservoir on my fenced-in left.

After a dreadful mile and a half, with the sun racing low across the sky, I came to a small, hidden valley, and a plaque marking the Middlebrook Encampment, a spot to which Washington had moved his troops in the spring after the Delaware Crossing, just after winter in the Watchungs at Morristown. From the Middlebrook Encampment, he could see (literally) the British at their garrison in New Brunswick, protected as he was by Chimney Rock, the jagged prominence on the now thoroughly quarried edge of Mount Horeb.* It appeared to me like an

---

*In the 1960s, New Brunswick was home to a group of avant-garde artists at Rutger's University who, through classes at the New School in Manhattan, had come under the spell of John Cage: Robert Watts, who after painting objects such as dollar

oasis, and the things that historians tell us happened here include fighting in the valley below, dancing, and, in 1778, to celebrate the one-year anniversary of the Franco-American alliance, the building of a giant thirteen-column faux temple just down the road—set on the side of a hill and illuminated, with a model of Columbia at the center, a work of mountainside art, showered by gun-shooting and fireworks that in one account took off part of a boy's hand, for which Washington gave him cash. I was tempted to walk to a lookout point, but, again, time was weighing on me like a giant pack, and a police car stood at the entrance to the park—I felt like a fugitive.

And yet, despite my concern for time, when I came to Washington Valley Road and spotted a tiny old wooden library, I squeezed my pack into the few cozy stacks and picked up a copy of *North of the Raritan Lots*, a local history, and encamped for a couple of minutes—the building was just too interesting to pass. I was cheered on by the volunteer librarian, who worked computerlessly out of an old vestigial card catalog. She was also rest room–less. "That's why we are only open two hours," the librarians there are known to joke.

---

bills became known as the Father of Stamp Art, as well as a founder of the Fluxus movement (he made a film about the Revolution, replacing colonial soldiers with what were then referred to as beatniks); and Roy Lichtenstein, who painted a portrait of George Washington while living in Atlantic Highlands. New Brunswick was also the home of poet Joyce Kilmer, the author of "Trees": "I think that I shall never see / A poem as lovely as a tree." Critics charged that because he kept a large pile of firewood in front of his home in New Brunswick Kilmer could not in actuality be a poet who loved trees. In *Geography of the Imagination*, Guy Davenport notes that the poem's last line—"Poems are made by fools like me, / But only God can make a tree"—echoes a line that Kilmer, a Catholic poet, might have known, given his interest in social justice issues. In her book *Labour and Childhood*, published in 1907, Margaret McMillan suggested that trees were valuable to young children, from both a physical and an emotional-health standpoint. "Apparatus can be made by fools, but only God can make a tree," McMillan wrote. (In England a piece of playground equipment is referred to as an "apparatus.") Kilmer was killed while on patrol during World War I, where he served in the 165th U.S. Infantry, or the Fighting Sixty-ninth, under William "Wild Bill" Donovan, an intelligence officer who established what later became the CIA. (Donovan is sometimes called the Father of American Intelligence.) Kilmer, an advance scout, led the troops on the day he was killed, dying on a hill alongside the Ourcq River, in France. His fellow soldiers, unaware he was dead, assumed he was quietly observing, until they realized a sniper had shot him through the head.

"I should really keep moving," I told the librarian, who was kindly insistent on calling me later, with information about the history of the valley, named for Washington. She wanted to put me in touch with a local historian. At her urging, I gave her my phone number.

Racing from the library, I trudged carefully up Mount Horeb Road, shadows long, my hands in need of gloves, map reading difficult in the wind of the passing cars. When I reached the plateau, I was muttering, I think, as a private school was letting out, children in the stream of large, sumptuous cars perhaps noticing the frozen-looking man speaking to himself, perhaps not. Mount Horeb was a letdown, with no real shining peak to reveal itself; it was anticlimatic, as well as a hard, slow hike. I passed Mount Horeb Church, and soon after raced past a dog-loud glade. In about three miles, I descended into the valley of another interstate highway. From a pedestrian's standpoint, each interstate crossing is akin to a battle, and I was scouting this one when my wife called on my cell phone.

"It's getting dark," she said.

"I'm fine," I said, which was true for the most part. I was trying not to sound as concerned as I was.

"Are you going to stop soon?"

"Yes, soon," I said.

THE FORMER DEAD RIVER PUB

I told my wife I had to call her back. I hung up and carefully crossed the interstate, passing little wind-created piles of pine needles, some broken glass, shards of plastic, and a tattered American flag attached to the fence on the overpass, as is customary on such overpasses, as if cars were citizens. I considered a hotel a few miles and another interstate crossing away. I called the interstate-side hotel I was standing before. "*Booked on a Tuesday night?*" I said to the parking lot after I hung up. Were other people marching to Morristown? My wife called back with the number of the Somerset Hills Hotel, less than a mile away, at the corner of Independence Boulevard and Liberty Corner Road, an intersection filled with chain investment offices and chain restaurants, at a bend in the Dead River. When I walked into the lobby, at mile 19, I was relieved to come into a clean and quiet businessman's hotel, decorated in the style of an English country estate. A young man in his twenties greeted me at reception, and as I lay down my maps and compass on the counter and dug out my credit card, he made conversation with me, at which point I mentioned the Continental Army's march to Morristown in January 1777. I immediately wondered if there was a hotel rule against that, just my luck.

"You probably think that's crazy," I said tentatively, laughing.

He did not miss a beat. "Listen, you *have* to go to this lookout," he said, and gave me extended directions. "That's where Washington went, and he could see the city from there. At least that's what we always heard when we were in high school."

Feeling safe for the moment, I limped with my pack toward my room, nodding nonchalantly to the businessmen in the elevator; the hallway seemed twenty miles long. I set up my tent, to dry it out. I took a long, hot bath and walked slowly down to the restaurant, the Tap Room, formerly known as the Dead River Pub, after stepping into the parking lot to briefly inspect the winter constellations. The bar was crowded. I took a seat, ordered a New Jersey beer, the specialty of the house. Indeed, it was a New Jersey beer drinker's paradise, a heaven of ales, and people all around me were making serious, well-considered choices for their first beers, and less-considered choices for their second and third. I talked with the bar manager, who directed me to an excellent porter from a brewery I eventually jotted down the name of in my notes and now find is indecipherable.

One beer provoked another beer. I countered with a fish dinner, and then, *Sure! I'll have a glass of wine! Huzzah!* I became more talkative with regards to my plans in the hearing of my bar neighbors. Yes, I had come from Griggstown, and Princeton before that, I explained, collapsing a good deal of important march-explicating details. And, yes, I hurt, but now not so bad, my eyes starting to swim a little in my head, muscle pain softening. The fish came. More wine! Washington *loved* wine! Didn't he make a porter? And maybe a whiskey! *Huzzah! The Revolution!*

Sometime later, in the hotel lobby, while I was carefully heading back to my room, my cell phone rang. Initially, it seemed to be hiding somewhere. I managed to track it down in my pocket. Hello? Did I hang up?

Hello? I hadn't hung up, and it was the librarian from Washington Valley, who was home now, and had found the number of the local historian she wanted me to talk to. I was wondering what time it was as I fumbled for a pen, as I dropped the phone, as I picked it up, and scribbled on the back of a map, and as I stare at it now I can't for the life of me tell you what it says, a number lost to time. I made it to my room, eventually, where I took a bunch of aspirin, and called my wife and said something and went to bed, falling into a deep sleep, serenaded by news reporters who were talking about a golfer and his extramarital affair.

"I shall feel no pain from the Toil, or the danger of the Campaign," Washington wrote to Martha, in one of the very few letters to her that were not destroyed. "My unhapiness will flow, from the uneasiness I know you will feel at being left alone."

THE STREAM

Waking up to another dazzling frost, I was soon standing on the edge of the Dead River, marveling at a magical haze of ice over the bankside sewage treatment plant, and at a crazy, three-way traffic intersection, where I watched a goose stand alone on a traffic island. The goose was like a patient sentry, a guard at the last approach to Washington's winter camp in the Watchungs, and, considering the race of rush-hour traffic, the goose was also like a sitting duck. A few minutes later, while waiting to cross the intersection, I realized I had replaced the goose. I passed beneath the last interstate, an emotionally less taxing route: a quiet cavern beneath a crazy rush of machines on an interstate that Morristown residents, in the 1950s, protested: dressed as Revolutionary War soldiers, they sat on bulldozers, picketing. A few dozen yards later, I stopped into a YMCA, where I bought a muffin and coffee, and members of an exercise class that was starting up recognized me as the guy with the pack they had passed while driving to the class. With an escort of more men speaking Spanish, I entered Bernardsville, and then with a woman speaking English who said her car was in the shop, I walked up Anderson Hill Road. A crow laughed at me as I turned east off a main road toward Morristown. In a moment, I stood beside a pond, startling a heron. Off Hardscrabble Road, I passed through a beautiful houseless field, marked as an encampment for the Revolution's New Jersey Brigade, and picked up a trail marked Patriots Path, a through-the-woods line that felt ancient, like a reenactment. At one point, with no one around, I took off my shoes and imagined being a shoeless Continental soldier walking the frozen ground. Suddenly, an angry-looking dog appeared, barking. I stopped dead and fumbled with my shoes as the owner appeared, leashing the growling dog. "Sometimes he gets upset," she said.

In a few yards the woods thinned out, and I looked down the slope of the hill to the Passaic River, a wide stream here, sparkling in the winter sun, deckled by the leafless canopy, on its way to the Great Falls in Paterson, the wide-open Meadowlands, Newark Bay, and on into greater New York Harbor and the mighty stream that is the river Oceanus, or Ὠκεανός—the early Greeks envisioned it encircling the world. Near the little footbridge, I knelt down and touched the stream, cold and fresh, at the army's mountain refuge. I was so tired. I sent a text message to my wife: "Made it!"

Close to, or perhaps beyond, exhaustion, I came upon Morristown National Historical Park's visitor center and saw a man in a Revolutionary War uniform together with a number of what appeared to be much smaller men with weapons of some kind. As I came out of the woods and crossed the parking lot, I realized that it was a school group doing a little reenacting with the park ranger. The school group was leaving as I entered the gift shop, the ranger changing out of his Revolutionary War–era garb and into a National Parks uniform. I was bursting with the news of my completed march, but the feeling I was getting from the ranger was that he did not want to hear about it, and who could blame him? I wondered if there was a rule against large backpacks in national historical parks. I perused books, bought some replica Revolutionary War–era paper currency, and called a cab, for I could not travel any farther under my own power, with thirty-three miles' worth of sore bones.

When the cab did not come after a while, I called back, asking the ranger for the address, a more complicated question than I had imagined—the ranger seemed more displeased by my request. The dispatcher, too, now sounded more irritated with me; she said the cab had come and gone. She said she would next be sending a driver who was not part of their company but affiliated, a reinforcement. His name was Junie, and though I was concerned he would have the attitude of everyone else I had dealt with at the cab company, he turned out to be easygoing. He was excited, as a matter of fact, to have entered the park by an entrance he had never previously used, despite having grown up in Morristown. "You know, I've never been this way!" he said.

On the ride down from the hills, he recalled being a kid in Morristown, wandering through woods that were now housing developments, and as he continued to reminisce, he became more animated. He was tall, with a warm, friendly voice, and he drove luxuriously, one hand on the wheel, one arm outstretched across the front seat of the old station wagon. He was the first person who asked what I was up to, and when I talked about the hills and the troops, he immediately recalled riding on horseback in the hills, which put me in mind of George Washington, who would have arrived in Morristown on horseback. "But I'll tell you what. I've been all over these hills on horse—*all over*," he said.

I was feeling as if I had been all over, in a way. I'd lived near Morristown in my high school years, and now I had approached it, the old way, from Princeton, entering Morristown as the Continental Army did, with the intention of using the town as a vantage point, a safe spot from which to ponder and observe the city of New York. I mentioned to Junie that at some point as I entered Morristown, back at the little stream in the woods, I had felt for a minute that I was back in time. He took that to mean that the character of the hills had changed. "All these developments come in, and they just cut down the woods, and it's all gone," he said.

He dropped me off at my parents' condominium, where I thought I would stop on the way to the train station. I thought I would surprise them. Their kitchen had just been painted; they were thinking about moving. The moment I sat down at their kitchen table was the moment I realized my back was essentially destroyed—a month later I would be limping to a rehabilitation facility. I ate a sandwich. My mother reacted just the way a mother whose forty-seven-year-old son had just hiked thirty-three miles with a giant pack on his back would: concerned. My father put down the history book he was reading and observed me closely.

"I hiked Washington's hills," I said.

"The hills with the signals?"

I wanted to explain how different marching into the hills of the winter encampment made me feel, but I couldn't really. I was too tired and needed to catch the next train back to New York. On the way home, I realized I had a completely different understanding of the hills than before—that something had happened. As that winter passed, I began to see the Revolution in the calendar. I would have mentioned this to my father, but it sounded a little wacky, to say the least; and besides, the thing about your father is he likely knows exactly what you mean, though slightly differently, given that he is looking back at you from an earlier time.

"Yes," I said, in response.

PART THREE

⁓

THE SEASONS

OF THE REVOLUTION

SPRING

꜀꜀

AFTER CROSSING THE DELAWARE, after traversing the rarely noticed Watchung Mountains, the little water- and cellphone-towered peaks of which quietly observe New York City like a long row of almost secret sentries, I returned to the city with a newfound awareness of the history of the place. As I left behind winter, and (for a moment) the semiforgotten mountains, I found myself stumbling into less-touted Revolutionary histories, into the less-celebrated moments in the founding of what would become known as the United States. Specifically, I met the founding fathers of New York's Revolutionary War history, the first historians, and I soon saw the city as it came out of the war and then hosted the first president, in 1789—the new nation born in the spring.

In the spring, the harbor calls to water-interested citizens, to walkers on the shore, to people who buzz out of their office buildings to gaze upon the river as if it were an oracle, an answer-giver, the secret source, somehow, of the near-unison burst of green in the plants and trees along the now people-filled streets. Except for its shoreline and for all the things dumped in or dredged from its bottom, the harbor—half water and seemingly three-quarters wide-open sky, a Jersey-edged bowl of white or blue, of Connecticut-destined clouds ushered through quickly by winter's departing blasts—has not changed since the Revolution. Or it has and it hasn't; in the spring it's a worked-over green-brown ledger, river water writing on ocean currents, on tides and flows, and the face of the bay is a record of passages. If you look, you can see the wake of the just-passed Staten Island Ferry as it crisscrosses the fading paths of tide-wary container ships. If you look harder, you can see the now-gone ripples of the great steamships replaced by the more recent waves of their municipality-sized cruise ship cousins. At the foot of Broadway, in Manhattan, ripples stirred up by the April breeze seem related to those drawn by the old sloops of the Hudson or the Hackensack, the way ancient Sumerian scripts are related to our modern alphabet. On the landing approach to LaGuardia, looking down, you can imagine whaleboats off the coast of Westchester and Connecticut, darting into British strongholds on Long Island, taking Tory prisoners, setting fires, rowing away secretly through the night-darkened chop.

Sometimes, walking along the coast of the Upper East Side of Manhattan, or looking out from the edge of Long Island City in Queens, I watch the tidal commotion at what remains of Hell Gate. Hell Gate is the notoriously wicked intersection of the Harlem and East Rivers, the former a true river, the latter a misnamed tidal strait; Hell Gate is the place where, in 1776, amid small, rocky islands and treacherous tides, the British commander, Admiral Richard Howe, masterfully managed to maneuver his fleet, in the dark, in the fog, through the watery commotion. The islands are gone now, eliminated: in 1888, the Army Corps of Engineers planted dynamite in the shoals of a small island called Flood Rock, and blew it up, what is pointed to in histories of New York as the largest planned explosion in America prior to tests of the atomic bomb. The geyser that resulted was nearly a football field high, the rumblings felt as far away, it was reported, as Princeton, New Jersey.

BATTLE SCENES

In that spring of 1789, the war was only just barely history, its ramifications (a new Constitution and Congress, a first president) were still current events. Who knows how the time went for all those involved? Did it seem like yesterday that the conflict had begun in New England, with riots and demonstrations, with farmers eventually firing at British military units, culminating in the Siege of Boston, a big battle for small hills and control of the harbor, ending when the British sailed to Halifax—a fermata for all involved? The Americans had caused the British anxiety in the north, attacking Montreal and Quebec, and the British did likewise for the Americans when they attacked in the Carolinas, until, at the end of the summer of 1776, the largest naval fleet in the world sailed into New York Harbor, controlling the waters there for seven years. In the summer of 1777, with Washington marching in and out of New Jersey, General Howe took Philadelphia, but the Continental Army remained intact, and, after rebel successes in Saratoga and then in Vermont, the Americans managed to prevent the British northern flank from descending into New York City, a move that impressed the French, who eventually signed on against the English, thwarting the British fleet at Chesapeake Bay and in the end containing them in New York.

In the summer of 1778, when General Howe was replaced by Sir Henry Clinton, the British gave up Philadelphia and raced to Sandy Hook, New Jersey. Washington intercepted them at Monmouth (also New Jersey), such that the British retreated: the last major battle in the North was a victory for the Americans. And yet, even when the fighting went south for three years, when Nathanael Greene, the Quaker-private-turned-general, wore down the seasoned British troops in hand-to-hand combat at times, even when the British, low on supplies, headed to Yorktown, Virginia, to wait for reinforcements from New York, General George Washington was reluctant to leave the orbit of Manhattan, as the French urged him to. After the British surrendered at Yorktown, when Washington could have returned to Mount Vernon, to await what would be the Treaty of Paris, he went instead to the Hudson Highlands, to those mountains that Henry Hudson's sailors could very well have seen from New York Harbor. From a hilltop, Washington looked down the great river toward the city, awaiting his triumphant war-ending ride to Wall Street, which occurred at last on November 25, 1783, the formerly celebrated Evacuation Day.

And so, on April 16, 1789, as he set out from his home in Virginia, the battle scars still fresh on the land he rode across toward his First Inauguration, Washington duly noted the departure in his journal: "At ten o'clock I bade adieu to Mount Vernon, to private life, and to domestic felicity," he said, "and with a mind oppressed with more anxious and painful sensations than I have words to express, set out for New York."*

Perhaps the landscape of New Jersey appeared to the about-to-be president as full of memories, of battles endured, accounts of skirmishes, of raids and plunderings, reminders of reports by the hundreds he had pored over. There across the Delaware from Philadelphia was Haddonfield, where there were battles in 1777 and 1778, in every season of the year, as well as the site of the Battle of Fort Mercer, where, at the fort named for the general who had died in Princeton after cross-

---

*Naturally, Washington, fifty-seven at the time, expressed reticence. "For in confidence I can *assure* you," he wrote to his friend and former general Henry Knox, "with the *world* it would obtain *little credit*—that my movements to the chair of Government will be accompanied with feelings not unlike those of a culprit who is going to the place of his execution; so unwilling am I, in the evening of a life nearly consumed in public cares, to quit a peaceful abode for the Ocean of difficulties." He was in debt, trying to borrow money, trying to sell land. He wrote to a lender to borrow money in order to pay off debts, as well to pay for the trip to New York. "Never 'till within these two yrs have I experienced the want of money," Washington wrote to a potential creditor on March 4, 1789. "Short Crops, & other causes not entirely within my Controuls, make me feel it now, very sensibly. To collect money without the intervention of Suits (and those are tedious) seems impractical. And Land, which I have Offered for Sale will not command cash but at an under value." The note is written more clumsily, from a grammatical point of view, than his official correspondence; you get the feeling that he might not have asked his young aide, David Humphreys, to write it. (Humphreys, also a poet, came with Washington to New York City, though he would later set up a woolen mill in Connecticut.) Debt was thought to be unmanly in the eighteenth century, a moral failing, despite its prevalence. "Debt was an inescapable fact of life in early America," wrote Bruce H. Mann, in *Republic of Debtors*. Only when a number of upper-class debtors landed in prison (where they set up lavish chambers, and received guests and business associates) did Congress create bankruptcy legislation to assist the greater number of citizens, though the Bankruptcy Act of 1800 died shortly after the Jeffersonians presented it. The historian Woody Holton noted that in 1785, Thomas Chandler's body lay rotting for weeks in prison due to Vermont's anti-jailbreak laws, which ascribed a prisoner's debt to anyone aiding his escape; friends and relatives were afraid to assist in burying the body, until the sheriff used a chain to technically extend the grounds of the prison to a cemetery, the "putrescent mass" carried out at midnight in a "rough box-like coffin." In New York, Washington rented a lavish house on Cherry Street in lower Manhattan, and lived in an opulence he could not afford, to make an impression. At one point he got sick from a carbuncle on his leg, so sick that people strewed hay in Cherry Street to muffle the wheels of passing carts, assuming Washington was about to die.

ing the Delaware, rebels had repelled a Hessian assault. In 1945, a member of the New Jersey Society of the Sons of the American Revolution counted fifty naval battles ("fights & other events") off the shores of New Jersey, as well as various lists of American vessels taken by the British (*Lady Washington, Three Sisters*), and of British transports seized off Egg Harbor. At Princeton, the about-to-be first president would have seen the old road to Monmouth, site of a summertime battle in 1778 on a day so hot (over one hundred degrees) that horses died while officers rode them. A woman, Molly Pitcher, was said to have drawn water from a well for soldiers to drink; the well is still visited by schoolchildren today. Washington, enraged at his commanders, took direct command himself, and in the end forced the British army to march a twelve-mile retreat, over an old trail through Freehold and Colts Neck (now known as Dutch Lane Road), then following the ridgeline of the Mount Pleasant Hills. They eventually crossed a pontoon bridge (anchored, planked-over boats) on a small inlet near Sandy Hook that is no longer there. Near what is today referred to as the largest nude beach on the Atlantic Coast, the British shuttled ships to Halifax, to the Caribbean, to England. Inside the hook of land that shields lower New York Bay and the mouth of the Raritan River, the British fleet likewise fought off privateers and skiffs and whaling boats, little boats harassing the British at night like relentless insects.

Farther north in Jersey, between the American winter encampment at Morristown and the British garrison in New Brunswick, troops skirmished in the lowlands: in the Dismal Swamp, in May 1777, Americans lost two dozen prisoners and had two of their own men killed. Along the route from New York City to Morristown, Washington's winter encampment, the two sides battled near the grounds of what today is the Mall at Short Hills and at a town that was once called Bottle Hill but is now called Madison, where my father, after he retired as a printer in New York City, got a part-time job as a printer in New Jersey, near the site of what my high school history teacher described as more of a moment of confusion than a battle (an American got shot in the buttocks, as I recall). In July 1779, in the so-called Minisink Massacre, Tories and Native Americans destroyed the village of Minisink. Writing in *Battles and Skirmishes of the American Revolution in New Jersey*, David C. Munn cites the beginning of the war in New Jersey as being a Tea Party demonstration on December 22, 1774, in a town called

Greenwich, on the banks of the Cohansey River; a group calling itself the New York Mohawks threw tea into the waters of what was at that time one of the three official ports of New Jersey. Munn cites the end of the war in New Jersey as the attack by Americans on the British sloop *Katy*, in March 1783, long after the British had surrendered in Virginia (but just prior to the war-ending Treaty of Paris), somewhere off the Jersey coastline. "The actual number of violent events that occurred in New Jersey can never be determined," Munn wrote. He notes that in the so-called neutral ground in areas such as Elizabethtown, "violence became a way of life."

Connecticut saw fewer large-scale battles. There was one at New London and Groton—in 1781, the British forces arrived on the Thames River, under the command of Benedict Arnold, a Connecticut native—and the British eventually raided and burned Danbury, New Haven, Norwalk, and Fairfield, as well. Connecticut was known as the Provision State, for the supplies and men it sent when Washington asked: during the winter at Valley Forge, soldiers drove herds of Connecticut cattle down through New York and New Jersey to Pennsylvania. At the very outset of the war, in the summer of 1776, a mob took down the gold-plated lead equestrian statue of King George in Bowling Green, the park at the bottom tip of Manhattan Island. The statue was beheaded, the head eventually smuggled back to England. The lead body of the king, as well as that of the horse, was carried by barge and transported upriver to Litchfield, Connecticut, where, in a shed in an orchard owned by General Oliver Wolcott, an assortment of family and friends cast, it was later reported, 42,088 bullets. What remained of the statue was thrown into the nearby Davis Swamp, where pieces of it have subsequently been dug up over the years. In 1822, a piece of the statue was sold to Riley's Fifth Ward Museum Hotel, in Manhattan. In 1874, two hundred pounds of tail, flank, and saddle were sold to the New-York Historical Society, and in 1972, Lou Miller, a Wilton resident, used a metal detector to discover a twenty-pound hunk, which he sold to the Museum of the City of New York for fifty-five hundred dollars, until the landowners sued and the money was transferred to them, the lead remaining in the museum. When I went up to Litchfield and looked for the swamp not too long ago, it had been replaced with a housing development. In 1997, before the development went in, a regiment of local historians combed the area with metal detectors, to no avail.

New York City before the war was a hive of preparations, beginning in the winter of 1776, when it seemed clear the British were coming back to take the city, their object being to split the northern and southern colonies by controlling the Hudson. In the weeks before the first big battle, in Brooklyn, Pennsylvania soldiers patrolled the edge of what is now Bay Ridge, to prevent loyalists from consorting with the British soldiers stationed initially across the Narrows, in Staten Island. During the war, the city, which was promptly lost by Washington, was under martial law. Place names were changed: Brooklyn's Ferry Horse Tavern became the King's Head Tavern and a racetrack in the Flatlands became Ascot Heath. Residents of Brooklyn and Queens were forced to tip their hats and bow their heads to British soldiers; they were required to wear red badges, which proved their allegiance to the British, and to swear an oath to the crown, a measure the British commanders did not entirely trust. "They swallow the Oaths of Allegiance to the King, & Congress, Alternately, with as much ease as your Lordship does poached Eggs," a British officer wrote to his patron.

Slaves, offered freedom by the British, left Brooklyn farms and headed to Manhattan, leaving the Dutch farmers in Brooklyn without labor. Crops were commandeered. For several years the city suffered under severe famine. Raiders came east from New Jersey to try to snatch prominent Tories, in hopes of trading them for rebel prisoners, while bands of Cowboys (loyalists) and Skinners (rebels) based in Westchester roamed the northern hills of the city, acting less in concert with their respective military forces and more like armed mobs. Out on Long Island, the Continental Army established a headquarters for its spies, known as the Culper Gang, meeting at a tavern in Setauket, where a woman named Anna Strong is said to have arranged clothing on her clothesline in a kind of code to advise of meetings. Whaleboats could read her laundry from out on Long Island Sound.

When the war was over in the city, wells had been filled with garbage, houses used as stables, and orchards axed. Soldiers returning to New York for the first time since the summer of 1776 were shocked by the overall deforestation. The first time Washington returned, when he was still a general and the British had at last evacuated in 1783, the Brooklyn village of Bushwick threw a party: "Our sincere congratulations, on this glorious and ever memorable era of the sovereignty and independence of the United States of America," they wrote. They roasted an ox over a fire that could be seen across the East River, in Manhattan.

AFFECTING MOMENT

Washington stopped on his trip from Mount Vernon in Elizabethtown, New Jersey, where a barge eventually took him across New York Bay to a pier at the foot of Wall Street in Manhattan: as he was rowed into New York Harbor, ships and cannons greeted him. This was, as noted, after the war, after the Treaty of Paris, which formally ended hostilities, and after the Articles of Confederation had failed and the Constitution was drawn up and adopted, a first president chosen, and a first capital, New York City, established. "Salutes were fired from ships at anchor and from the Battery," according to one historian. "It was one of the most animated and festive spectacles ever seen in the harbour."

The inaugural procession marked Washington's first time back to New York since he bid farewell to the troops after the British evacuated the city, and it was in some ways a first reenactment. On this again-triumphant return, Washington had passed through Philadelphia, where he was greeted by crowds, and he then proceeded on through Trenton, near where he had crossed the Delaware thirteen years before. He is reported to have left his carriage and mounted his white horse, as was his habit upon entering a town or settlement of any size when traveling. From there, accounts of the visit have him being greeted by a retinue of Trentonians, including a group of women wearing white dresses and standing beneath an archway of flowers, singing: "Welcome, mighty chief once more—welcome to this grateful shore . . ."

At this point in the accounts, Washington is invariably described as being overwhelmed by the display. He dismounts his white horse, walks alone along the Delaware, effecting a small solo reenactment on the banks of the river he had crossed. In terms of establishing a way in which Americans would go on to remember the Revolution, Washington's steps along the Delaware are like Neil Armstrong's first steps on the moon. As soon as he leaves Trenton, Washington, writing in the third person, sends back a letter, thanking the women: "General Washington cannot leave this place without expressing his acknowledgements, to the Matrons and Young Ladies who received him in so novel & grateful a manner at the Triumphal Arch in Trenton, for the exquisite sensation he experienced in that affecting moment." The former general then proceeds to note "the astonishing contrast between his former and actual situation at the same spot."

When he got to Elizabethtown, Washington went to bed and got up early the next morning, to have breakfast at a place called Boxwood Hall before boarding a boat—a forty-seven-foot barge, powered by thirteen rowers, all dressed in white—for the trip across the harbor to New York.

JUSTLY ESTEEMED

The city that Washington saw before him as he was rowed into the harbor in the spring of 1789 still looked as if it had just been through a war. It had undergone two disastrous fires—the first on September 21, 1776, the second on August 3, 1778. The tallest landmarks had been destroyed. Trinity Church and the Middle Dutch Church were still being rebuilt. The Lutheran Church was rechristened Burnt Lutheran Church. (During the war, the Dutch and Presbyterian churches had been used as prisons to hold the rebels, while the Church of England buildings had been protected by British troops.) Broadway was in ruins, the primarily wooden houses burned, only about a dozen ships in port. A visitor in 1787 described New York as being in a state of "prostration and decay." "In short there was silence and inactivity everywhere," a resident wrote. "Many of our new merchants and shopkeepers set up since the war have failed," another wrote. "We have nothing but complaints of bad times." Shipbuilders were not building ships. Rent was high, and the price of labor was high, as was the cost of goods, though a handful of merchants lived in opulence. "Law in abundance, the Trespass Act is food for the lawyers—yet we say there is no money," a diarist wrote. "Feasting and every kind of extravagance go on—reconcile these things if you can. Gloomy joys."

But things were picking up. New York was still smaller than Philadelphia, but refugees from the war—rebels who fled the British occupation—were regularly arriving in the city, as were immigrants. The population had gone from 23,600 citizens living in 2,300 houses in

1786, shortly after the war, to an estimated 29,000 citizens and 4,200 houses in 1789. The houses that remained were in the triangle of settlement at the bottom of Manhattan Island; a few were scattered up the Hudson River shore road, Greenwich Street, ending in the village of Greenwich, near what would become Washington Square Market, today the Meatpacking District. Prior to becoming Greenwich Village, the market was a Lenni-Lenape settlement, Sapokanikan, perhaps meaning "wet," or "field of plantation." A few old Dutch-style houses remained, with their high-peaked gables, but most homes were built English-style—framed, with brick fronts—the better to prevent fire. The city directory listed the following occupations: carpenter, washerwoman, grocer, breechesmaker, chandler, hairdresser, attorney, gunsmith, and painter.

Except for Broadway and Broad Street, thoroughfares were mostly narrow; Water and Queen streets were in some places too cramped for sidewalks. For the most part, the city did not permit the planting of trees south of the large pond that was the source of drinking water, called the Collect Pond. (The pond's banks are still visible today along the western edge of Chinatown at Columbus Park and on the eastern edge of Foley Square.) Streetlamps had been installed in 1762, but were used sparingly, in accordance with the phases of the moon. As a result, citizens repeatedly fell in the night, often against posts. After the war, laws were established to ensure that night soil would be brought out to the gutter in front of a house every evening. Brissot de Warville, a young Frenchman who visited the city and would return home to be a leader of the French Revolution, had high praise for New York's sewage system, which consisted primarily of black slaves carrying buckets to the river, tubs on their heads, in procession at the end of the day. The hospital stood empty when Washington and his family arrived. It had been ransacked by an angry mob in April 1788 in an incident known as the Doctors' Riot, which began when passersby spotted medical students cutting up cadavers dug from city graves and dangling body parts from windows.

There was a swamp in the northeast corner of the city, along Greenwich Street. There was another north of the Collect Pond, its streams flowing out into the Hudson via a channel that would eventually become a canal and ultimately Canal Street. People skated on the Collect Pond in the winter and washed their clothes in it during the warm months. A small reservoir was designed in the year before the Revolution by an Irish immigrant named Christopher Colles; it was served by a steam engine pumping water in, but the war shut it down. Beekman's Swamp, on the East River, was the only place animal hides were allowed to be kept for more than twenty-four hours in the lower city—the swamp and subsequent neighborhood were the traditional site for tanning, even when my father was a young man, working in the area and noting the stench. Street names that existed in 1789 and are gone today include: Verlittenberg Street, Saint George Street, Jew Street, and Princess Street. Liberty Street was called Crown Street, and, where it touched the Hudson River, around the modern World Trade Center site, a bathhouse advertised itself as having cold and warm water "of sufficient depth for both gentlemen and ladies." Ferry Street was known as the dirtiest street, and Wall Street was the most fashionable, as well as, according to a history written on the one hundredth anniversary of Washington's inauguration, "the centre of the political life of the United States."

Federal Hall was the old city hall renovated for the incoming Congress, Supreme Court, and chief executive; it was described as "the most pretentious building in the city." The ceiling was decorated with a sun and thirteen stars and would be demolished, along with the rest of the building, shortly after the government left New York for Philadelphia. One of the fanciest town houses in the city was a two-story brick building at number 1 Broadway that escaped damage in the 1776 and 1778 fires. It was home, after the war, to Isaac Sears, or "King Sears," a merchant and the leader of the Liberty Boys, who avoided arrest for debts he claimed to have incurred as a result of his Revolutionary War leadership and sailed to China, where he died in Guangzhou, then known as Canton. When Washington arrived in town, 1 Broadway was the home of Don Diego de Gardoqui, the Spanish ambassador. Although Washington eventually rented a house on Cherry Street, the city had built a house for the first president near 1 Broadway, but it was not finished in time for Washington's inauguration, and was thought to be vulnerable to an attack by water. The builders digging at the site discovered Dutch coins and Dutch graves.

Traffic was considered bad in lower Manhattan, the streets full of carts and carriages. The first time Washington appeared before

Congress to seek its constitutionally mandated advice and consent, the president walked over to Federal Hall with his secretary of war, General Henry Knox. These were the formative moments of enacted legislative and political power; they were also comical. At the first meeting, Knox gave a sheet of paper to Washington. Washington then handed it to Adams, the president of the Senate, who read it aloud. As Adams read, carriages passed by. Senators couldn't hear. A couple of them thought they heard the world "Indian." The senators asked to have the point read again. Adams complied. They began to debate, which irritated Washington; as he stood there, impatiently, his face was, like his hair, red. "This defeats every purpose of my coming here," he said to his staff. He went away in a huff.

In New York, Washington greeted citizens twice a week, men on Tuesdays, women and men at a tea on Fridays. He bowed; he did not shake hands. People referred to him as Mr. President, a title settled on after long debate. (The Senate, led by John Adams, who leaned toward pomp in establishing governmental traditions, voted for "His Highness the President of the United States and Protector of the Rights of the Same," but the House of Representatives voted that title down, and many representatives subsequently referred to Adams by the nickname "His Rotundity.") Washington considered many of the men who stopped by on Tuesdays freeloaders, there for the food. Washington enjoyed charming the ladies, being a so-called ladies' man, or at least a man with, as Abigail Adams noted, "a grace, dignity, and ease that leaves Royal George far behind him."

In the morning, Washington might ride his horse. Once he boarded a barge to Flushing, in what is today Queens, to inspect some gardens and, on the way back, to see a barn he had heard a lot about. He did not care for the gardens. "These gardens, except in the number of young fruit trees, did not answer my expectations," he wrote in his journal. "The shrubs were trifling, and the flowers not numerous. The inhabitants of this place shewed us what respect they could, by making the best use of one cannon to salute." He did not like the barn either. "It was not of a construction to strike my fancy—nor did the conveniences of it at all answer their cost." He enjoyed lunch in the village of Harlem, where he met Martha Washington and Abigail Adams, both on a country outing, at a tavern run by a man named Captain Marriner. Marriner was a whaleboat captain during the Revolution who, with his partner, Captain Hyler, ran covert missions in the waters of New York, New Jersey, and Connecticut, kidnapping soldiers and Tories, burning British ships, causing general havoc. When I think of the newly inaugurated President Washington in or along the harbor, I imagine him seeing ghost ships—British warships or American sloops, as well as the rebels in whaleboats. I think of a crisscross of new commercial and old war interests. I think of a farmer and veteran enjoying the particularities of a summer's day on the waters of New York.

Washington's diary notes numerous walks, sails, and horseback rides, all to enjoy the morning or afternoon air. New Yorkers considered their climate to be especially healthy, due in large part to the harbor. "New York is justly esteemed one of the healthiest cities on the continent," notes John Bard, an eminent physician, in 1789. Dr. Bard listed its attributes: close to the ocean; a "spacious bay"; the "influx and reflux" of two great tidal waterways; the terrain of various heights, a topographical attribute that to him meant trash was washed away in the rains. Bard praised the fresh water and all the markets filled with produce, and he believed that the winds worked in concert with the nearby farms and orchards to mist the city with a perfume of bounty. Fields and orchards, he wrote, "often in their season salute the inhabitants settled on the west side of the Broadway with fragrant odours from the apple orchards and buckwheat fields in blossom on the pleasant banks of the Jersey shore in view of their delightful dwellings."

Then, as now, of course, the air could be very hot, especially in July and August. In August 1789, twenty people died during a heat wave; people blamed the absence of winds.

NOTORIOUS REFLECTIONS

For entertainment, there was the theater. "There was but one theatre in New York in 1789 (in John Street), and so small were its dimensions that the whole fabric might easily be placed on the stage of one of our modern theatres," remembered George Washington Parke Custis, son of Washington's stepson, who lived with George and Martha after the inauguration. Washington was an enthusiast of the theater to the extent that amateur troops sometimes even performed in his home on Cherry Street. Some of the plays appearing at the theater on John Street were

The Rivals, High Life Below Stairs, The Deserter, Roman Father, School for Scandal, Love in a Camp, The Tempest, Man and Wife, and *Provoked Husband.* Sometimes the stage sets themselves were the thing: a play about Captain Cooke's voyages included elaborately painted screens of natural vistas in New Zealand, as well as, on one occasion, a view of the Passaic Falls, in Paterson, New Jersey. Over the cascading falls, as the lights slowly came up, a figure of Columbia arose from the man-made mists. Then Columbia waved her wand and the finally refurbished Federal Building ascended on a cloud supported by the Temple of Concord. Through a transparent scrim, theatergoers could see that the temple was supported by columns marked *Wisdom, Fortitude, Virtue,* and *Justice.* While critics disliked *Darby's Return,* the play, a riff on current events with ribs aimed at Washington himself, is remembered now mainly thanks to the fact that it is thought to be the one play during which Washington laughed. "Our beloved Ruler seemed to unbend and for the moment give himself to the pleasures arising from the gratifications of the two most noble organs of sense, the Eye and the Ear," the *Daily Advertiser* reported.*

Popular science exhibits also drew crowds. People went to look at insects under a microscope at the home of Christopher Colles, who, after his war-thwarted attempt to build a reservoir, became an early Ameri-

---

*Another play that Washington attended repeatedly was Joseph Addison's *Cato,* a play loved by the generation that fought the war. Nathan Hale was alleged to have quoted the play as he waited to be hanged, or a line from it was ascribed to him. Hale: "I only regret that I have but one life to give for my country." Addison's Cato: "What a pity it is that we can die but once to save our country." Patrick Henry worked "Give me liberty or give me death" out of *Cato,* and Washington echoed the play or referred to it in numerous letters and speeches; *Cato* permeates America's founding performances. Washington had it performed for the troops on several occasions. In the play, written in the style of a classical tragedy, Cato, in a vain attempt to save the Roman Republic, commits suicide (and the Republic falls). In a modern forward to the play, the historian Forrest McDonald says that the play was popular because it suggested people sublimate their personal interests in favor of public interests. "In his public life, Washington followed Addison's advice, and so did Hamilton, and so did a host of other founders; and in the doing they overcame their private shortcomings and behaved virtuously enough in public to establish a regime of liberty that would perdure." I wonder, though, if, in addition to striving to sound selfless in public, they didn't find Alexander Pope's words—Pope wrote the play's prologue—inspiring in some sense: "Dare to have sense yourself; assert the stage / be justly warm'd with your own native rage."

can mapmaker, and exhibits of curiosities were often announced at the homes of other men of science. A Dr. King arrived from South America, opened a room at 28 Wall Street, opposite the Tontine Coffee House, and exhibited "a Male and Female of the surprising species of the Ourang Outang or the Man of the Woods," as well as a sloth, a baboon, a monkey, a porcupine, an anteater, a tiger, and a buffalo. A moose from St. John's in New Brunswick was exhibited in 1789—"very tame"—and there were horse races and shooting matches, and boat races off Sandy Hook. Balloon launches were a relatively new public spectacle. Joseph Decker sold advance tickets to a public balloon launch, after having first privately flown a balloon nine miles away, landing in the Harlem River. On the day of the launch, the balloon burned.

One of the books people were talking about around the time of the inauguration was by Dr. William Gordon, entitled *History of the Rise, Progress and Establishment of the Independence of the United States of America*. An article printed in several newspapers panned the book: "Much has been said and much still remains to be said concerning the inconsistency, the partiality, the notorious reflections, the mistakes, the redundancies, the manifest errors in grammar, the absurd conclusions, the odd conjectures, and the repetitions which appear in almost every page of Dr. Gordon's History of the American Revolution." The book's New York publisher went ahead and, according to one account, "published a long advertisement lauding the book to the skies, and doubtless made money through the interest aroused by the criticism of it."

OLD POMPOSITY

When it comes to the history of New York, anniversaries are like springtime, moments at which the past returns, buried objects rise to the surface, like arrowheads in a farmer's field. It was the three hundredth anniversary, in 1909, of the entrance by Henry Hudson into the harbor of New York that inspired the most frequently cited work on the history of the city, a six-volume work entitled *The Iconography of Manhattan Island*. Whenever I read a book about the history of early New York, I poke around and eventually find bits and pieces of the *Iconography*; it holds the genetic material of New York's Revolutionary War history. If I stumble on a piece of the city's history I've never met before, then I go to the library and see that the *Inconography* has been there. The *Iconography* is a compilation of other histories, of maps, illustrations, drawings, journals, directories, lists, receipts, and, especially, newspaper accounts—all compiled between 1915 and 1928 by one man, Isaac Newton Phelps Stokes, who was born in 1867, on George Washington's birthday. His goal, as he wrote in his introduction, was "to produce a book dealing with the physical rather than the personal side of the city's history, which shall be at the same time useful and interesting to the student of history, the antiquarian, the collector, and the general public."

I. N. Phelps Stokes was the oldest son of Anson Phelps Stokes, president of the Phelps Dodge Corporation, a company that began importing textiles in 1834 and ended up a mining corporation. Stokes grew up in the house that was bought by J. P. Morgan, Jr. and then became an extension of the Morgan Library. Stokes sledded as a child on Fifth Avenue before it was completely Fifth Avenue; he spent his summers on Staten Island, enjoying his mother's pet monkeys, one of which, playing with matches, nearly burned down the Staten Island house. After Harvard, and studies in Paris at the École des Beaux-Arts, he became a prominent reformer, working with immigrants and settlement houses. "I came to the conclusion," he later wrote, "that better housing for the working classes was one of the crying needs of the day, and that the designing and promotion of better housing, especially in our large cities, furnished as good an opportunity for useful service as any other profession." He often investigated the living conditions of the poor by going undercover, like a spy, a habit that continued when he returned to New York, where on one occassion two unemployed trackwalkers asked him if he had ever worked on a railroad. "I told them that I had," he said, "which was true, as I was at the time president of the Nevada Central R.R."

Stokes won a contest to design the University Settlement House on the Lower East Side, then thought to be the most squalid urban area in a city in the United States. He helped write the Tenement House Law of 1901, requiring tenements to have, for example, large side courts, deep backyards, and larger rooms. He oversaw a renovation of Central Park, having discovered Frederick Law Olmsted's original plans; a strict constructionist in terms of historic preservation, he was adamant about the designer's original intent and opposed to the addition of, say, the ballparks that populist groups championed. During the Great Depression, he commissioned WPA murals, frowning on what he called modernist art, thus disallowing a set of murals the artist Ben Shahn had planned for the jail on Rikers Island, fearing they would depress the inmates. He imported a sixteenth-century Tudor manor from England and had it reassembled in Greenwich, Connecticut, where he worked with Olmsted to plan a community around it. (After his death, the house was demolished.)

Stokes married Edith Minturn, the daughter of reformers who frequently posed in tableaux for artists. She herself was the model for the twenty-four-foot-tall *Statue of the Republic*, at the 1893 Columbian Exposition in Chicago. Minturn is often described as being like a character out of a Henry James novel. "I have known one or two women as beautiful; one or two women as interesting; one or two women as spiritual; but for the combination of the three I have never known her equal," the reformer who married her and Stokes said. In the painting of Minturn by John Singer Sargent that hangs at the Metropolitan Museum of Art, Stokes is in the background, a satisfied shadow.

As a reformer, he supported Mayor Fiorello Raffaele Enrico La Guardia, though they initially despised each other: tall, thin, delicate in manner, Stokes was a member of the so-called Top Hat crowd, while the mayor, short, heavyset, and loud, was the son of Achille La Guardia, an immigrant from Cerignola, in Italy; his mother, Irene Luzzato Coen, came from a Jewish family in Trieste. It is said that the two men came to appreciate each other because of their wives. La Guardia had nursed his wife through the year and a half it took her to die of tuberculosis; his disdain for alcohol is said to have been the result of a year of binging after her death. During the Depression, Edith Stokes suffered a series of strokes that paralyzed her and took away her ability to speak; Stokes read to her, told her jokes, wheeled her through Central Park, convinced she could still hear him. When La Guardia learned about Stokes's wife, the relationship between the two men changed. Stokes may have been the first person to call La Guardia "Little Flower." La Guardia called Stokes "Old Pomposity."

On the tricentennial of Henry Hudson's entrance into New York Harbor, in 1909, historical prints and images of the city began to surface all over, things found in drawers and cellars and attics, as well as in the old bookshops. Stokes ran around collecting and collating. The first volume of the *Iconography* was published in 1918, the last in 1928. "The thing that first strikes any user of the *Iconography* is how utterly improbable it is that a man should have gone to all this effort," wrote the architectural historian Frances Morrone. It is the kind of book that people plan to write and don't. It wasn't until after the *Iconography* was completed that Stokes himself recognized it was improbable. "I now realize," Stokes wrote late in life, "that it involved an expenditure of time, energy, and money, which was probably out of proportion to the results achieved, and consumed many hours which should have been devoted, not only to my office, but to my family, and to social amenities, so that, on the whole, I suspect that it has proved a rather selfish, perhaps even a narrowing, influence on my life."

After the *Iconography* was completed, Stokes lost a lot of money in the stock market crash. By the end of his life, he lived alone in a small apartment, taking his meals at a lunch counter, or at Schrafft's, a place he loved. One of his last jobs was as a curator of views of the city at the New York Public Library: ancient panoramic prints, views of the various aspects of the harbor. He remained an expert in a kind of time travel; he could see the city as pasts in layers.

"I have long specialized in dreams of old New York, and they are the most delightful of all my dreams," he wrote.

> I usually start from some point in the modern city, and on my way—
> perhaps to keep an appointment at some other well-known point—I
> am tempted to try a short-cut. I wander over the hills and valleys, and
> often through virgin forests, and sometimes come out on the shore of
> the Hudson or the East River where I recognize the topography from
> the old maps, and take great pleasure in searching for landmarks
> which I know exist—or at least existed at the time pictured in my
> dream.

A CRISIS

A story relating to the history of the history of New York that is *not* in the *Iconography* concerns a rescue mission that I. N. Phelps Stokes organized after the great fire in Albany in 1911, the one that destroyed the

New York State Capitol Building. The New York State archives were thought to have been completely destroyed in the fire as well, and the New York Public Library sent Stokes to see if anything could be salvaged, a special tactical assignment. He was at what might be called the height of his historical power, with his wealth intact, the *Iconography* in progress, his wife still alive and well.

When Stokes arrived, the building was smoldering, water from fire hoses everywhere. Witnesses said that flames from the windows of the archive room had crossed the street. Stokes entered the building with A.J.F. van Laer, the Dutch-born state archivist. The stairways had burned away, and the area of the building in which the archives were located had been declared unsafe. Stokes and van Laer borrowed ladders from firemen. Stokes examined plans of the building and determined to climb into the room from the floor above; he carved a hole through the floor of the Senate clerk's office and descended into the area of the archive that housed the state's colonial history. Inside, he found that everything was indeed burned; shelves and desks destroyed, water streaming from the ceiling and in puddles. "Here and there little fires were starting," he said. They slogged through debris four feet thick. "The sight did not encourage us that anything could be saved," he said.

Van Laer headed straight for early Dutch records, which appeared burned. "Still, knowing the power of resistance to fire that compressed paper possesses, we made the attempt," Stokes said. These were the original documents that had been stored by the colonial governor on a ship in New York Harbor when revolution seemed imminent; they had survived the war in the Tower of London. The two men carried the Dutch records to safety. They discovered that beneath a layer of destroyed documents the original Dutch records were intact and decipherable. The records would be retranslated in the 1990s to reveal a new and radically different understanding of the Dutch influence on the formation of New York and America. (See especially *The Island at the Center of the World*, by Russell Shorto.) When Stokes and van Laer returned to the building, the governor put soldiers under Stokes's command; a chain was formed, men carrying out baskets full of records. Inside, Stokes used a hose to douse and then grab still-hot volumes off the shelf. "Although I had assured the men that everything was safe, whenever there was a noise as of something falling, they would be startled and anxious to quit work, for which nobody could blame them," Stokes said.

They worked late and returned the next morning to rescue even more of the past. Small fires had broken out overnight, after a cold snap, the temperature dropping the way it does from time to time in April (as it did the year I wrote these sentences, when late snow covered the first trout lily in the Upper Hudson's woods). Even though it was the beginning of April, the water froze in the capitol building; winds whipped through the broken windows, carrying away the occasional historic document. The two historians believed that they had saved twenty percent of the archives, including some early Dutch land patents, from 1630. They saved the manuscript records of the War of 1812. They saved the papers of Major John André, the British spy. "The only wonder is that the wind, rushing through the gutted building, did not whirl away more of them," Stokes later recalled.

On the second day of the rescue mission, word made it to Stokes that the fire had taken an important piece of the collection, George Washington's sword. The day before, Stokes had seen two firemen with a twisted piece of metal, one fireman hesitating, the other shaking his head, then tossing the metal aside. He had filed the moment in his mind. The next day, he returned to the spot. The soldiers dug. At the bottom of the debris, they found Washington's sword, twisted but repairable.

Later, when a newspaper reporter discovered that Washington's sword had been lost then recovered, when the reporter subsequently put questions to Stokes, the author of the *Iconography* neglected to mention the additional fires, as well as the debris falling from the ceiling. Van Laer later pointed all of these things out to the reporter and suggested that Stokes had exhibited a strong presence of mind in the midst of tremendous destruction.

"In short, this is a good man to have around in a crisis," the reporter wrote.

WATERS REJOICE

One year, as March blew into April, as mackerel clouds dispersed and the first striped bass fishermen were taking chances near Sandy Hook, I was itching to get out on a boat, so I hired an actual boat captain. He was, of course, more used to finding schools of bluefish than retracing the watery excursions of old generals, but I told him what I wanted—a forty-five-minute trip from Elizabeth to Wall Street, and a return to his pier in Brooklyn—and he gave me a price, four hundred dollars. This seemed high, but, as I understood, it had to do with fuel. He was moored in Brooklyn, at nearly the opposite end of New York Harbor, and it would take him an hour to get to Elizabeth to pick me up. I said I would get back to him after I studied the inaugural route to see if it was even possible.

In the accounts of the first inaugural, there are no clouds, the sky is clear. In Elizabeth, church bells ring and crowds cheer as Washington leaves Boxwood Hall and proceeds to the ferry. The forty-seven-foot barge is decorated with red-white-and-blue bunting, and has seating for the president and the three senators and five congressmen who were accompanying him. A canopy protects the representatives from the sun; the boat is powered by thirteen rowers. The water is calm, or as Elias Boudinot, a former president of the Continental Congress, wrote in a letter to his wife back in Elizabethtown: "The Waters seem to rejoice in bearing so precious a burden over its placid bosom."

In the morning, they set off into the wide tidal strait called the Arthur Kill, shots fired in celebration along the shoreline. They see the hills of Staten Island on the right—during the war, Staten Island had been a loyalist stronghold—and the spring-green meadows of Jersey on the left, breeze-blown salt marsh hay waving gently, where today there are concrete bulkheads.

As they enter New York Harbor, they can see the small, war-injured skyline ahead. A sloop pulls aside the inaugural barge as a chorus of men and women sing an ode to Washington, to the tune of "God Save the King": "Let ev'ry heart expand, / For Washington's at hand, / With glory crown'd!" The passengers on the presidential barge wave their hats. Closer to Manhattan, a Spanish packet, decorated with flags, fires thirteen guns. As the inaugural barge approaches Manhattan, more guns are fired, more boats appear, a long chain of vessels. At Wall Street, cannons fire from shore as the about-to-be-president steps on land. Washington walks into a swarm of people waving flags and hands and cheering, into what one newspaper called "an immense concourse of citizens."

"It is impossible to do justice in an attempt to describe the scene exhibited on His Excellency's approach to New York," the *Gazette of the United States* reported. "Innumerable multitudes thronged the shores, the wharves and the shipping, waiting with pleasing anticipation his arrival." There were a lot of strained references to ancient civilizations: "The voices of the ladies were as much superior to the flutes that played to the stroke of the oars in Cleopatra's silken corded barge, as the very superior and glorious water scene of New York Bay exceeds the silver Cydnus in all its pride," the *Gazette* said.

NOT A PROBLEM

The particular detail that stood out for me regarding Washington's inauguration, as I set out to experience the inaugural waters at their season-appropriate moment, was a line from the diary of Elias Boudinot, the New Jerseyan: "At this moment a number of Porpoises came playing amongst us, as if they had risen up to know what was the cause of all this joy."

When I contacted the boat captain and agreed to his price, he asked me if there was anything special I might need while on the boat. Naturally, there were jokes made about tricorne hats and powdered wigs, as one might expect there to be when in conversation about investigations related to the first U.S. presidency and New York City's role in the American Revolution, and I may have said something myself about wooden teeth, and how I would not be wearing them.* But when the captain asked me, I suddenly thought of Boudinot again. This in turn caused me, first, to make mention of Boudinot's reference to porpoises, and then to attempt a joke, which was, as you will see, not much of a joke, really.

"Well," I said, "do you think you could have a school of porpoises greet us?"

"We have a whole bunch right now," the captain said.

I didn't comprehend what he was saying. "No," I said—I thought he didn't understand my joke—"there were porpoises *then*, in 1789."

"*No*," the captain replied, "there are porpoises and dolphins *now*, just this week. They are out off the runways at JFK, right now."

---

*As I mentioned already, Washington's teeth were more likely made of numerous things—gold, ivory, lead, horse and donkey teeth, as well as the teeth of his slaves.

As a result of this conversation, my excitement about the boat trip was growing. I was concerned only with one issue. "Are you sure you are going to be able to pick me up in Elizabeth?" I asked the captain.

"That's not a problem," the captain said.

TEA PARTY

In the early days of the commemoration of Washington's inaugura-tion, there do not appear to have been reenactments, and so the spring-time remembrance of the inaugural is like the commemoration of other events related to the Revolution, as well as to the Civil War: peo-ple commemorated differently when the soldiers who survived the ac-tual battles were still around.* For the fiftieth anniversary of Washington's inauguration, in 1839, John Quincy Adams came to New York and, during a long commemoration, sat in what was Washington's chair while Washington was president; crowds of people were turned away from the ceremony. Philip Hone, a socialite and former mayor of New York who was known for his anti-immigrant views, his parties, and the detailed diary he kept from 1828 to 1851, was a member of the

---

*For a little more than a decade, the Gettysburg battlefield in Pennsylvania has been undergoing restoration, park managers cutting trees, planting orchards, and demol-ishing buildings to re-create a nineteenth-century vista, the intention being that, once the restoration is completed, visitors will "almost feel the bullets," as a National Park Service director put it. One of the complications involved in restoring Gettysburg is that there are very few photos that show how the battlefield looked *before* the battle. There are also differing versions of exactly how the battle went. The battle's first histo-rian interviewed participants in 1880, and even then the collective memory of the battle was varied and contradictory. General Abner Doubleday wrote: "It is difficult in the excitement of battle to see every thing going on around us for each has his own part to play and that absorbs his attention to the exclusion of everything else." Recently, the historian John Summers, who grew up in Gettysburg, wrote in *The New Republic* that "historical suffering must be regarded from a distance if tragedy is to make us humble—or even be understood at all." Summers describes the growth of trees on the Gettysburg battlefield as akin to writing on a palimpsest, "offering the closest we may come to communing with the lost souls." He also quotes Stephen Crane's *Red Badge of Courage*: "As he gazed around him the youth felt a flash of astonishment at the blue, pure sky and the sun gleaming on the trees and fields. It was surprising that Nature had gone tranquilly on with her golden process in the midst of so much devilment."

committee in charge of the celebration. Four years before, he had been to a commemoration of the sixtieth anniversary of the Battle of Lexington and Concord, in Massachusetts, and, with veterans of the battle, walked to a granite tablet marking the site of the first bloodshed near the Lexington Common, processing next to the area of the battle itself. Hone had been concerned about New York's inauguration commemoration, describing himself as "extremely anxious and nervous, from an apprehension that sufficient interest had not been excited, and that the distinguished guests of the society from other States might witness a failure."

"But my fears were groundless," he noted afterward. "It could not have been better."

As Ralph Waldo Emerson had written an ode to the Battle of Lexington and Concord that was set to music and performed during the commemoration in Concord, so William Cullen Bryant was similarly commissioned in New York, though Hone was disappointed with the end result.

"The ode, in my judgment, is very so-so, considering it is the production of the crack poet of New York," he wrote.

Adams offered his own history of the formation of the U.S. government, including some harsh words against his old political opponents, and he recalled details from the original inaugural day, as a witness.

"All this," Hone reported, "together with some touching and interesting details of events attending the triumphal journey of Washington, his reception in this city, and the administering of the oath in front of the City Hall, —this day fifty years ago, —were given in a voice and manner eloquent and animated, but tremulous and feeble."

The invited group retired to a dinner in the saloon of the City Hotel, a posh place in a downtown that Hone fretted was disappearing before his eyes: New York was becoming unrecognizable from the city that George Washington had lived in. The banks were building large headquarters on Wall Street, the fashionable houses being demolished, the well-to-do moving uptown. Hone's own childhood home was being razed; the neighborhood looked to him as if it had been hit by an earthquake. Hone gave a speech noting that Federal Hall, where Washington had taken his oath, was still there, though it, too, was about to go, just as the original Federal Hall had been taken down in 1812. "The spirit of pulling down and building up is abroad," Hone said. "The whole of New York is rebuilt about once in ten years."

For the one hundredth inaugural anniversary, in 1889, a large but temporary wood-and-plaster arch was installed over lower Fifth Avenue, in Greenwich Village. In 1895, a permanent arch was designed by Stanford White, and large sculptures of Washington were attached for the 125th anniversary. Shortly thereafter, the arch was lit by Thomas Edison's new electric company, on the quadricentennial of Christopher Columbus's arrival in America. On the night of January 23, 1917, some editors and artists from the revitalized *Masses* magazine climbed the staircase inside the arch, carrying food and hot tea. They were artists who had contributed to the groundbreaking Armory Show, as well as the Paterson Strike Pageant in Madison Square Garden, a group including John Sloan and Marcel Duchamp. In a few months, World War I would break out. Sloan, and others, believed that socialism was the only antidote to what many Greenwich Village radicals saw as the growing might of international financiers, a class they believed was pushing nations to war for corporate profits and oil. The artists hung red balloons and Chinese lanterns. They declared Greenwich Village a new nation, and asked that President Woodrow Wilson recognize the "Free and Independent Republic of Washington Square." The declaration was read by a village poet who went by the name Woe. (When he gave poetry readings, he introduced himself by saying, "Woe is me.") Woe said the group was seceding from "big business and small minds." They fired toy cap guns. They drank tea as a reference to the Boston Tea Party.

TWO GEORGES

Two reenactments of George Washington's inauguration that stand in contrast are the 1932 reenactment, on the centennial of Washington's birth, and the 1939 reenactment, on the 150th anniversary of the inauguration itself. They are two Georges straddling the Great Depression, one re-created inaugural barge trip on the nation's economic way down, the other on the beginning of the way back up.

In the 1932 reenactment, Kenneth M. Murchison portrayed Washington. Murchison took a boat from Elizabethtown, which was by then known as Elizabeth, to Wall Street. The day of the replica inauguration was, like the original, picture perfect. The replica barge, which had an outboard motor attached and was more like a boat, made the trip quickly. As it motored by, steamships signaled—"a shrieking tumult," one newspaper said. Leaving the Port of Elizabeth, the boat entered the Kill Van Kull, the tidal strait separating Staten Island and New Jersey. Leaving the kill and entering Upper New York Bay, the replica barge picked up a caravan of police boats and Coast Guard cutters. It was one of the worst years of the Depression; Prohibition was still in effect, and the Coast Guard was patrolling for rum runners. President Hoover, in his last months in the White House, had begun to support government spending, despite the refusal of governors in his own party to use federal money for construction projects; for his efforts, Hoover was described as a "second Washington."

"A Depression," Hoover said, "is, indeed, like a great war, in that it is not a battle on a single front but upon many fronts."

On Wall Street, Murchison got in a faded yellow carriage, which took him to midtown, and to a replica of Federal Hall built in Bryant Park, which was surrounded by crowds. (A full-scale replica of Mount Vernon had also been built in Prospect Park, in Brooklyn.) Mayor Jimmy Walker was waiting to meet Murchison. Walker was a few months away from fleeing the country to avoid corruption charges. Murchison was an architect who had, like I. N. Phelps Stokes, studied at the École des Beaux-Arts in Paris, but he had given up architecture and devoted himself to throwing lavish for-profit themed balls, for which he wrote and conducted all the music. "He is what you might call 'Beaux-Arts,'" a reporter said. Reporters also noted that drunkenness was a theme at the for-profit balls, where women unexplainably lost all or some of their clothing. The list of performers at the balls was drawn up by Pierpont Morgan Hamilton. In 1932, the balls were bringing in about half as much as they had before the stock market crash of 1929. Murchison claimed to have the same measurements as George Washington. He also said he had high blood pressure.

Before the replica of the Federal Building, there was a long speech from a historian, recounting the history of the Revolution, saying that Washington was nervous when he took the oath. A band played while

Murchison waited for a radio show to end before taking the oath, which was broadcast live. "Long live George Washington!" the crowd cheered. Ticker tape fell from the surrounding skyscrapers.

When he arrived at the faux Federal Hall, Murchison posed with Mayor Walker. "Hey, George," a photographer shouted. "Shake hands with Jimmy Walker!" The two shook hands and tossed off wisecracks.

"That's the first time George Washington was ever followed by rum chasers," said Walker.*

---

*W.E.B. Du Bois's pageant "George Washington and Black Folk" appeared in the 1932 edition of the NAACP's magazine *The Crisis*, founded by Du Bois. Pageants had been popular in the United States during the Progressive Era and were revived in 1932, the bicentennial of Washington's birth, one more effort to distract Americans from the Great Depression. African Americans were not often included in pageants, and if they were included, portrayed slaves or buffoons. In 1913, Du Bois (who noted that he was born the day after George Washington's birthday) had staged "The Star of Ethiopia," describing the contributions of African Americans to the world. "George Washington and Black Folk" began with Crispus Attucks, the runaway slave who was first to die in confrontation with the British, in the Boston Massacre. It also featured Paul Laurence Dunbar's poem "Black Sampson of Brandywine," about the Revolutionary War battle at Brandywine Creek, in Pennsylvania: "Was he a freeman or bondman? / Was he a man or a thing? / What does it matter? / His brav'ry Renders him royal—a king." The pageant referred to black soldiers winning battles and fighting throughout the war. Du Bois's Washington looks ambivalent about ending slavery in the scene entitled "Emancipation," and Du Bois's real hero ends up being Toussaint L'Ouverture, who led the revolution in Haiti, paving the way for the first black republic, in the 1790s. Writing in the journal *Callaloo*, Rumiana Velikova notes that Du Bois, at his high school graduation, gave a speech on Wendell Phillips, the Boston abolitionist. In the speech, Du Bois cited this remark by Phillips: "You may think me a fanatic tonight, for you read history not with your eyes, but with your prejudices. But fifty years hence, when truth gets a hearing, the muse of history will, . . . dipping her pen in sunlight, write in the clear blue, above them all, the name of the soldier, the statesman, the martyr, Toussaint L'Ouverture." Velikova continues: "Washington is a traditional symbol not simply of citizenship, but of white citizenship. One's belonging in the United States may be signified through the symbol of Washington. One's belonging to a minority culture involved in the struggle for racial equality that does not coincide completely with the goals of a conservationist patriotic culture, bent on preserving the racial status quo, seems to require the rejection of Washington. This is why Du Bois may alternatively accept the U.S. foundational documents (like the Declaration of Independence) and reject the Founding Fathers, or acknowledge Washington's birthday and place it at the beginning of his own personal history, and then substitute it, replace it, and eclipse it with an alternative line of foundational texts and

Seven years later, the re-creation of the inaugural barge trip was much more grand, tied, for instance, to the opening of the 1939 New York World's Fair, the largest international festival ever at that time, the United States on the verge of mobilization for World War II. This time the barge had an engine *and* it was towed down the Arthur Kill, the towline being disconnected just before the craft pulled in sight of newspaper cameras. This time, the George Washington impersonator had set out not from Elizabeth but from Mount Vernon, stopping in towns along the way—it was an all-out reenactment, with backing by the federal government. The trip took the 1939 Washington eight days.

Children threw flowers at the 1939 Washington as he boarded the barge in Elizabeth, à la the original inauguration. *The Grapes of Wrath* had just been published, and Hitler was annexing territory, expanding his naval fleet so as to invade England; Marian Anderson, forbidden by the Daughters of the American Revolution to sing at Constitution Hall, in Washington, D.C., sang before seventy-five thousand people on Easter Sunday from the steps of the Lincoln Memorial. In contrast to the boats used in 1932, the 1939 boat was less rowboat and more barge, with a canopy and a superstructure made of iron sheets. There were eight rowers, and the boat was towed for a distance from Elizabeth, yawing in the current. The towline was cut as the boat neared Manhattan, rowers commencing. The actor playing Governor DeWitt Clinton was Austin Strong, a playwright who had written a stage version of "Rip Van Winkle" that concentrated mostly on the part of the story wherein Rip wakes up in the Catskill Mountains after having seen Henry Hudson and his crew, the sad and eerie transformation scene; Strong called it *Rip*. There were a million people in town for the World's Fair, which the acting Washington would open, along with President Franklin D. Roosevelt, who was taking a train from his home up the Hudson River. But as opposed to the crowds that greeted this George Washington along the way, when the reenactor arrived at Wall Street, New Yorkers were described as clapping but otherwise blasé. The Sanitation Department Band led a short parade.

---

historical predecessors. Acknowledging Washington reassures the guardians of patriotic tradition that change can be kept under control; doing away with Washington, then, sends the emphatic message that change is inevitably going on."

"This symbolic trip brings back in a flash the history of our young republic," said Mayor La Guardia, who had won the election of 1933, after losing to Jimmy Walker and a Socialist candidate in 1929.

The Washington stand-in went by car to lunch at the Metropolitian Club; visited the Jumel House in Washington Heights, where the actual Washington was headquartered in the fall of 1776; drove through the Washington Square Arch, in Greenwich Village; and then went to the observation deck of the just-completed Rockefeller Center, to take in the commanding view. Another impersonator took over for a few days, until the World's Fair opened, a short time later, when the original impersonator returned to open the fair.

The 1939 Washington impersonator was Denys Wortman, an artist who drew cartoons for the *World-Telegram*. Wortman had studied with Robert Henri, the social realist, and artists such as Edward Hopper and George Bellows, a member, like John Sloan, of the Ashcan school. His subjects were people talking on the subway or across fire escapes, married couples at the breakfast table, and, very often, women talking to women. (Until she had their son, Wortman's wife took photographs for her husband to draw from.) The year before the inauguration, Wortman drew a cartoon that featured two dejected-looking men standing on a crowded street. "They call this a 'recession,' not a 'depression,'" one man says to the other, "but I don't feel any difference." Another caption also featured two dejected-looking men on the street. "If you're going home, I'll give you a lift."

"Thanks Bill, I'd rather walk. It'll kill more time that way."

A newspaper photo of the 1939 inaugural barge trip shows Wortman standing in the bow of the boat, facing Manhattan, a hazy skyline before him, the water rough, the impersonator looking possibly a little overwhelmed. It is said that when the boat was released from the towline, the rowers found the rough water difficult going, due to the chop.

AWARDS OF EXCELLENCE

My own personal inaugural barge plans went like this: on a spring day similar in its Aprilness to the April day in New York Harbor on which Washington took his boat trip, I would meet a couple of friends on a close-to-the-harbor corner, two fathers who, after dropping off their children at school, were enticed by the idea of a boat trip on a nice day. We would then take a train to Elizabeth, New Jersey; walk to the water's edge, a mere two miles; meet the captain I had engaged for the inaugural purposes; then proceed via the water to Wall Street. To facilitate the transition from land to water, another father from the neighborhood—a guy who was at that point in time dividing his off-work time between soccer games with his sons and reading a lot of ancient history, particularly the Greeks—would keep in contact with us from the fishing boat. This last father's code name for this trip was "Herodotus." All I wanted to do was see the water, to be in the same place a Founding Father had been in the seasonally appropriate moment, the words of the captain as they pertained to all of us fathers being picked up in Elizabeth echoing in my brain: "Not a problem."

And so it was that on a sunny spring morning we three fathers stood in the center of a circle, at an intersection of old roads at the Elizabeth train station: south to Princeton, east to the old ferries for New York, west to a pass in the Watchung Mountains, me noting the Watchungs with a slight twinge in my by-then-repaired-after-climbing-them spine. We had maps, a compass, coffee, and assistance from a commuter who pointed us toward the center of Elizabeth. In a minute, we were on the streets of downtown Elizabeth, in the shadow of a bedraggled art deco skyscraper as we walked past pawnshops ("We Buy Gold!"), discount stores (Bargain Man), and a bodega window decorated with family photos.

Within ten minutes, we were standing before an old wooden building, Boxwood Hall, a two-story Georgian structure built in 1750 and, as of 1772, Boudinot's home, and temporarily the home of Alexander Hamilton when Hamilton was studying to enter college. The hall faced a quiet grassy square filled with monuments. And there weren't just a couple of monuments in the square. We were bombarded by monuments: a pyramid-shaped monument to General Winfield Scott, who, the plaque said, lived from 1786 to 1866 and was a "Hero of the Mexican War"; a gravestone-shaped monument to the astronauts who died in the Space Shuttle *Challenger* disaster in 1986 with engraved photos of each smiling astronaut who died when the ship exploded on reentry into the earth's atmosphere; a two-tiered pedestal-shaped monument, crowned by a gold-painted bust of José Martí, the Cuban poet and leader of the 1895 Cuban War of Independence, donated, according to the markings, "as an enduring memory of the Cuban American immigration experience in the U.S." by groups such as Club Cubano de Elizabeth, Freedom Loving Cubans, Masones Cubanos, and the Independent Order of Oddfellows. There was a rock-shaped stone monument in commemoration of the United Singers of Elizabeth, who had sung, in 1915, at a Sängerfeste, a German American singing festival, as well as a tall obelisk, marked with a stone-white sculpture of a sword that said: "To our honored dead, who gave their lives in our wars to uphold the noble principles set forth by our founding fathers." On a telephone pole there was a poster with a description of a man being robbed and beaten in front of the José Martí monument. "There was laughter as the man wailed to the cops for help," the poster said.

It was a node of remembrances, though of the most significance to our procession was a large, boat-shaped granite monument, featuring a fancy etching of the following: George Washington, Boxwood Hall, a carriage, and a barge. The monument marked the success of the 1989 bicenntennial of Washington's inauguration. "Recipient of the International Public Relations Association's Golden World Awards of Excellence," the back of the monument said. We walked across the street to the front of Boxwood Hall. It was closed. I used my cell phone to call the hall's number. A woman inside happened to pick up.

"We're closed," she said. When I asked her if she knew the route Washington had taken to walk to the waterfront to ride a barge to New York, she answered with alacrity.

"He went right down Elizabeth Avenue, and that's how we did it in the bicentennial inauguration in 1989," she said.

ON THE WATER

We three fathers set out for Elizabeth Avenue, passing a large Vietnam War memorial, what the monument described as "America's longest war,"* as well as a cannon that was cast in Strasbourg for the army of

---

*In June 2010, USA Today measured the Vietnam War's length, beginning in 1964: "The formal beginning of U.S. involvement often is dated to Aug. 7, 1964, when Congress passed the Tonkin Gulf Resolution, giving the president a virtual carte blanche to wage war. By the time the last U.S. ground combat troops were withdrawn in

Louis XV, used against the British by the French in Canada, taken by the British, used against the Americans in 1775, taken from the British, and finally given to the Elizabethtown militia by Washington, in commemoration of their service in the Revolutionary War. Looking through the sight of the cannon, its metal smoothed by weather and hands, I saw a cell phone store and the office of a lawyer whose sign reads "*Aprenda Inglés.*" We refreshed ourselves in the Union County Courthouse, where, in accordance with the long list of things not allowed inside, I left my camera with a guard.

From there we crossed over the Elizabeth River, a concrete-walled trickle, and saw in a tired strip of stores along its banks a shop selling Texas Wieners, a New Jersey–specific style of hot dog. In a dark, pigeon-dung-lined underpass, we crossed under the Elizabeth Viaduct, "a pioneer Superhighway," according to its plaque. Another plaque beneath the highway described Elizabeth, the first capital of New Jersey, as a place that during the Revolution "suffered terribly," due to being occupied, alternately, by the British and the Americans. On the other side of the viaduct, we landed in a suddenly vibrant, people-filled commercial avenue, a long row of Columbian restaurants and Portuguese bakeries. In the center of a square was a statue of a Revolutionary War soldier, and I don't remember what the pedestal said, because as we were standing there with our maps and camera, a cop pulled up, looked at us, dropped off a woman in the square, and drove away. Once again, like many things done in public without an automobile in the twenty-first century, walking Revolutionary War–significant paths was feeling vaguely illegal.

At around that time, I received a message from the boat. Herodotus, using his cell phone, had sent me a text message: "On the water."

THE HARBORMASTER

As I say, it was good to be with a bunch of fathers while thinking about the inauguration, a communal exercise in historical remembering,

---

March 1973, the war had lasted 103 months." The newspaper then noted that U.S. forces attacked Afghanistan on October 7, 2001. "By June 2010, the war in Afghanistan had completed is 104th month."

though my particular strengths do not include leading others, and there was a certain responsibility that came with enlisting aid from other fathers. I was hoping things would continue smoothly as we passed beneath the New Jersey Turnpike and entered the last stretch before the marina, my chief fear being stranding one or all of the fathers in the midst of a Founding Father's long-ago trail when they had their own fatherly duties to attend to that afternoon. After Pete's Hairstyling—a sign outside the homelike store read "Pete Is Back"—we passed a big old tree in an empty field marked by the ruins of a home, and then saw the marina, adjacent to the waterfront Veterans Memorial. We next received word that our captain had docked his craft at the Port of Elizabeth. When I stepped up to the docks, I spotted Herodotus. He was pacing back and forth, on the cell phone, trying to work out something having to do with his son's soccer team. It sounded complicated. He stopped talking on the phone to speak to me.

"We've got a problem," Herodotus said. "They're not gonna let you get on." He motioned toward the harbormaster's house. "The guy's in there." Herodotus resumed his soccer negotiations.

I looked toward the captain of our vessel, who was fueling and watching me—sheepishly, I thought.

The harbormaster did not get up from the chair he was sitting in while watching TV. As I looked at him, I had the crestfallen feeling of not being able to travel the harbor in spring on the oft-traveled route of Washington's inauguration, as well as the disappointment that would come from being out something like four hundred dollars. Add to that my desire not to break any laws in a corridor of oil refineries and airports while living in a country that implores me to always be on a military-like alert. I have to admit, I was a little miffed at the captain. *Not a problem!* I thought. His arms folded, chair tilted back, the harbormaster had an air that suggested he had been in many previous conversations that involved him listening to someone making a point on which he disagreed and would long continue to do so.

I recognized this as an important confrontation, a point of decision, a kind of personal Delaware Crossing. As a first volley, I decided to go with the truth, explaining in hyperventilated detail our three-father march and the coordinated moves of the captain and Herodotus. I had been going only a few seconds when I began to add frantic and unanticipated hand gestures. Maybe it was the detail about the porpoises that showed up in 1789, but within thirty seconds, the harbormaster put his hands up, as if stopping traffic, or surrendering. "Just go ahead," he said. I thanked him and waved the others on board. We got out of there quickly, like whaleboat runners in the Revolutionary-era night.

EVANESCENT

We ripped out into the Arthur Kill, sped north, the green hills of Staten Island on our right, the Port of Elizabeth on our left, and all around us the great estuary of New York and New Jersey, the blue sky decorated with industrial-fringed green. For a few minutes, it was smooth sailing. No chorus-laden sloop serenaded us with songs; no salutes were offered by guns ashore. I recall sensing that the fathers expected me to do something at this point, to make an announcement of some sort, being, in the broadest possible sense, in charge, but there was nothing I wanted to do; I just wanted to follow the route: it was spring as it had been spring in 1789, and I was on the water, in the first inaugural's wake. I was now officially relieved that we were actually on the boat, after having been forbidden to board. I had encouraged Herodotus to bring along a passage from the works of his namesake to read on the boat; finished with soccer negotiations, he read aloud from a new translation of the ancient Greek writer sometimes referred to as the Father of History. The opening line: "Herodotus of Halicarnassus here presents his research so that human events do not fade with time." When I eventually returned home from the boat trip I am herein describing, when time had passed and I wrote out these words, I saw that the Greek word translated as *fade* in this new translation of Herodotus's history was ἐξίτηλος, more literally *faded*. Touring each alternative definition was like sifting through resonances relevant not just to the construction of a book considering a historical incident or a day on the water, but relevant to fatherhood in general. From my Greek dictionary: "losing colour, fading, evanescent." From a lexicon: "of a drug or wine that has lost its power."

As the captain hit the throttle, we passed beneath the Bayonne

Bridge, and then Shooters Island, a heron rookery.* We passed along-side the ruins of boats, old shipyards and dry docks, a tugboat pier, and Bethlehem Steel's rusting shipyards, where dozens of World War II–era naval destroyers were built on Staten Island's shore. We soon looked up into the mile-wide mouth of Newark Bay, a huge inland sea

*I first came to Elizabeth to look around on the shore of the Arthur Kill, in 1990, when the Exxon Bayway Refinery released 567,000 gallons of oil into the tidal strait—it was an amount equivalent to what was spilled, more notoriously, by the *Exxon Valdez* in Prince William Sound, Alaska. As opposed to Alaska, the Arthur Kill was assumed to be lifeless, a dead place. When New York City and various environmentalists moved to litigate, Exxon argued that it was not obligated to provide reparations because the waterway was of no ecological value. In retrospect, this would prove to be the ecological equivalent of saying that New York City and its environs are devoid of Revolutionary history. A branch of the New York City Parks Department called the Natural Resources Group (NRG) worked with the city, joining state and federal bureaucrats in pursuing damages against Exxon. After the government won a 15 million dollar settlement, the NRG began to restore wetlands there. They planted spartina, a salt-marsh grass, specifically in the area of the Arthur Kill, protecting what turned out to be a heron rookery on Shooters Island. East Coast spartina marshes are wildly productive: the fish, crabs, mussels, copepods, and bacteria together produce ten tons of organic matter per acre per year, more than ten times the amount that a desert produces, and about twice as much as a typical forest or farm. NRG hoped the spartina grass would pump oxygen into the ground, thus re-aerating the marshes so that the bacteria in the peat would ingest the oil. The plan worked: after about two years, tests indicated that the total amount of petroleum hydrocarbons in the marsh had fallen. In retrospect, it was a moment of radical change in the consideration of urban ecology, and the work at the Arthur Kill has since been used as a model for similar remediation efforts in London and Beijing. All of a sudden, the Hudson River estuary was not dead, but a place of great ecological output; abused dumping areas and polluted marshes were replanted with marsh grass, and in a way "remembered." What was considered the "historic estuary" had returned or, it was discovered, not disappeared, and, most important, it returned not as a beautiful and scenic place that looked like a landscape from long ago, but as a beat-up-looking industrial swamp, still productive. The idea that these forgotten landscapes had value despite their apparent un-scenicness was pioneered in part by the land art movement of the early seventies. In what would be his last article before he died in a plane crash in 1973, Robert Smithson took on a *New York Times* critic who had attacked the so-called Earth Artists as land destroyers who "cut and gouge the land like Army engineers." The *Times* wanted an artist to "make these places visible—communicate their spirit." "There is no going back to paradise or nineteenth-century landscape," Smithson said.

that I think of as a secret: if you are not operating as a stevedore offloading containers from overseas or bringing in fields and fields' worth of imported automobiles, then you know little of Newark Bay, the destiny of the water that passes over the Passaic Falls. If we had been on a fishing boat during the Revolution, we would have been in the militarized zone between loyalist Staten Island and not-so-loyalist New Jersey, Arthur Kill being the anglicized version of the Dutch words *achter kill*, meaning "back channel." I pictured the British on Staten Island, looking across the kill to New Jersey, where, for the majority of the war, the Americans were sort of sometimes in control. I also put on sunblock.

Now, just past a hill on the edge of Staten Island and a little sailors' cemetery, we entered the Upper Bay of New York Harbor, considerably more crowded, from a marine traffic standpoint, with Staten Island Ferries off to starboard. On the maps, we were passing over symbols for shipwrecks.

The setback at the docks had caused me to be concerned about maritime rules and regulations that I could only imagine, but I was pleased to be making progress. I was a little shocked when the captain slowed the boat down near the Statue of Liberty; I had not requested that he do so. I felt as if my order had been disobeyed, not that I had the nerve to explicitly order him. But the spot we paused at was like a panoramic landscape painting, the maritime equivalent of the view from the Empire State Building's observation deck, a postcard print of the Statue of Liberty and the harbor.

"I can do whatever you want," the captain was saying.

We were in the Grand Central Station of New York City water traffic. On the Arthur Kill, we had seen very few boats, but now, at the Statue of Liberty, tour boats came close to the island—people waved, cheered, saluted us, and five guys who were not fishing in a fishing boat waved back. Helicopters hovered above us. The captain now faced us, leaning casually against the boat's console, the depth sounder behind him indicating that the water was not deep at all, just two or three feet between the boat and the bottom. The captain talked about the quality of fishing in the area; bluefish schooled, he was saying, in the area just behind the statue, in the vicinity of the historic oyster beds. But a problem I was having was that we were stationary when I had hoped we would be moving forward—how to express my anxiety?

The debate going on in my head was like the Constitutional Convention wherein one guy was shouting for order and another delegate was telling him to relax. I tried to relax and take in the view, like the other fathers. But not heading to Wall Street was frustrating.

It was at that moment, as we floated near the Statue of Liberty, that one of the fathers, Dave, who had been watching the water depth indicator, said something, or perhaps the captain noticed on his own, but in any case, the captain suddenly grabbed the controls, and with a split-second adjustment of course and speed, prevented us, in the nick of time, from running aground on the sandy flats off Liberty Island—the blade of the propeller had only gently touched the sandy bottom. A few moments later, when we were back in deeper water, the captain stopped the boat and raised the engine, nervous since the prop had just been refurbished. Upon inspection, it was found to be undamaged, a near miss.

NAKED GUY CREEK

Our captain was a good captain, a seaman of high standing who came with only the best recommendations, and so I now felt sure I had brought a certain amount of bad luck to his ship. I also believed that he was thinking as much. Additionally, because I was telling him to head to Wall Street, and he was not, I began to feel that I was in the midst of a leadership crisis.

"What do you want to do?" the captain was saying, again. "It's up to you. I can do anything you want."

I kept saying that I merely wanted to go to Wall Street, or somewhere just off the street in the East River. I no longer had any hopes of actually landing on Wall Street, since that seemed likely to initiate some kind of national security crisis, given all the police helicopters darting like cormorants in and out of view. At last, the captain complied, pulling back into deep water, heading toward lower Manhattan. We arrived in a short time. In view of the heights of Brooklyn and the glass towers of lower Manhattan, we stopped to look at the base of Wall Street. A water taxi passed; the Staten Island Ferry pulled out from its pier in lower Manhattan; on the Brooklyn–Queens Expressway, traffic moved smoothly in the now noonday sun.

By this point, I had a good idea of the water route taken by

Washington during the inaugural; I was pleased. I felt the joyousness of the harbor in spring—an actual historic fact that still pertains—and thus, with the afternoon coming on, with increasing concerns about the fading enthusiasm of my comrades and their various upcoming professional and parental duties, I directed the captain to head home to his marina in Brooklyn.

"I can head back, no problem," he said.

The captain hit the throttle, and we left the flat, faceless towers in lower Manhattan, raced through Buttermilk Channel and the lower bay, and headed out to Brooklyn, toward the Narrows and JFK, gentle just-green hills on the other side. The Arthur Kill and Newark Bay are the secret back channels of New York Harbor, but we were now headed to the front gate, the wide-open mouth that marks the entrance to the lower bay, what mariners refer to as the New York Bight, with the Rockaways of Queens the upper jaw, the lower jaw being New Jersey's Sandy Hook.

It was a pleasant trip, to say the least—happiness prevailed—and I looked back to see the rough white wake of our boat quickly fading. In a few minutes, we would come to the mile-wide stretch that separates two forts as old as the colonies and older than the Verrazano-Narrows Bridge: Fort Hamilton and Fort Wadsworth. And as we passed through the narrows, something incredible happened: the air changed, immediately, clearly—the Atlantic Ocean announced itself. The horizon shifted, too, from green hills and docks and city skylines in the upper bay to the wide circle of the lower bay, the dark blue horizon and cloudless sky-blue ceiling. It took about twenty minutes to dock at the captain's marina in Brooklyn, on Dead Horse Bay. As we entered, we looked down Gerritsen Creek. Often, the captain told us, an older Eastern European man could be seen sunning in the reeds in that spot, nude. I believe the captain referred to the waterway as Naked Guy Creek.

But just before the Narrows, before the trip ended and Herodotus drove all the fathers home, while we were still in the midst of Buttermilk Channel, the captain was trying hard to extemporize. Again, I appreciated his sentiment. Even now, I take this as an essentially positive gesture—he seemed intent on adding valve to the trip in some way, aware, perhaps, of the more than one-hundred-dollar-an-hour charter fee. He suggested that we stop for lunch in Red Hook, Brooklyn. At one point he had me scurry up a ladder to test a gate on a locked pier in Red Hook. By this point, the lunch-finding trials were making me impatient—I wanted to get everyone back.

Then, just off the pier in Red Hook, while the captain was suggesting yet another lunch possibility, the boat suddenly hit a submerged jetty. There was a loud crunch and a brief panic. Immediately, the captain shut down the engine. Once again, he slowly pulled the outboard motor up out of the water, though this time slightly more desperately, due, I imagine, to the more severe sound. This time, as we could all see, the rotor had suffered significant damage. I felt bad for the captain, but I eventually revised my view of the incident. In the end, I returned to feeling a little miffed, because on the way back to Naked Guy Creek, the captain kept telling me how much it was going to cost to fix his boat.

MOST AGREEABLE TO MY FEELINGS

Being in a library, I have often felt, is a little like sailing along a coast and choosing unknown rivers to explore, sometimes dead-ending, sometimes discovering new and unexpected lands. One day, I was at the New-York Historical Society, reading about New York in the time during and surrounding the Revolution, when I happened upon a couple of large leather-bound ledgers lying out on a shelf. Inside were pages and pages of handwritten script, mostly dates, with a few words. Upon inquiring, I discovered that these ledgers were used in the creation of *The Iconography of Manhattan Island*; the ledgers, I learned, were as Lake Tear of the Clouds is to the Hudson, the highest pond source. "Stokes used them," a librarian said. The handwriting was that of Thomas F. DeVoe, New York butcher turned historian.

"For several years, the *unemployed hours* from my business, or rather profession, had hung heavily on my mind, and to fill them up satisfactorily, was a thought I had often indulged in," he wrote in the introduction to his masterwork, *The Market Book: A History of the Public Markets in the City of New York from Its First Settlement to the Present Time*. DeVoe was a street historian, a guerrilla culler of old journals and papers, presenting the New York you would have run into on Broadway, late for work. "I knew I had some knowledge, which business and observation had given me; but I also knew that I was very deficient in *learning*, or at least of knowing how to express myself, satisfactorily to *myself*," he wrote. "I had the disadvantage of not knowing which end to begin with, but went headforemost into what appeared to me to be the most agreeable to my feelings."

Born in 1811, DeVoe moved to the city, as a boy, from Yonkers. He was a butcher at the former Washington Market, as well as a colonel in a New York City militia. As a butcher, he was chosen by the other butchers to represent them before the city; the *Evening Express* called him "a prince among the butchers." "To be a good butcher is a good thing; but to be a good butcher and a good author at the same time does not often happen, even in New York," the paper said. DeVoe described himself as having a history problem. "I found there was no remedy for this *dreadful* disease, but by taking, in allopathic doses, sundry *piles* of old musty records, in various forms and at various times," he said.

Thus, in his history of the markets, he gives us the records of the Dutch markets, of the British taking over, and we see the Revolution as a kind of economic crisis, with an attendant scarcity of food, with markets shut down—we read lists of forgotten disasters. In 1778, lightning hit an ordnance ship lying in the East River, with 248 barrels of gunpowder on board: "a tremendous explosion." "A number of houses were unroofed, many windows broke, and some furniture demolished," says DeVoe. He notes that in the spring of 1776, induced perhaps by the British offer of freedom for military service, a slave runs away. In a column called *Run a Ways* in the *Continental Gazette*: "He is a likely, well-set fellow; understands butchering very well; was late the property of John Beck, of this the City of New York, butcher; speaks Dutch and English tolerably well."

Today, the *Encyclopaedia Britannica* dates the American Revolution from 1775 to 1883, but in DeVoe's *Market Book*, the Revolution comes slowly, lingers, changes the pace of the city but not the markets themselves—the Old Slip Market; the Fly Market, near the steps to the Brooklyn Ferry; the Meal Market, at the foot of Wall Street; the Fish Market, on what was Dock Street, where before and long after the Stamp Act or the Peace of Paris, clams were tied to strings, little ears flapping in the breeze to dry.

The newly inaugurated president makes his appearance in New York, and briefly he is the center of attention in a city where, historically, attention is scattered. The first president lives in a house on a street that no longer exists near what is now an off-ramp to the Brooklyn Bridge, a skateboard park. Washington had servants who shopped at Peck's Slip Market, at the base of a now-forgotten rise called Cowfoot Hill. DeVoe notes Washington's punctuality: eating daily at 4:00 p.m., allowing five minutes "for the variation in time pieces." Samuel Fraunces was the first president's chef. He went by Sam. Sam bought a fish at the Fly Market, a shad, the first of the spring season. Sam served it for Washington's breakfast. Washington asked what it was.

"A fine shad," Sam said.

"It is very early in the season for them," the president said. "How much did you pay for it?"

"Two dollars."

"Two dollars!" the president said. "I can never encourage this extravagance at my table. Take it away, I will not touch it."

PARTICULAR OBSERVATION

As Virgil in his *Georgics* extols the products of the fields, the moods and tempers of the streams and the skies, so DeVoe catalogs the harbor city and its natural history—its meat markets and poultry stands, the fruits and vegetables that come in by cart and ferry, the fish arriving by boat, the infinity of off-loaded apples and oysters.

From the 1753 edition of the *Independent Reflector*: "Tho' we abound in no one kind of fish sufficient for a staple, yet such is our happiness in this article, that not one of the colonies affords a fish-market of such a plentiful variety as ours. *Boston* has none but sea-fish, and of these *Philadelphia* is entirely destitute, being only furnished with the fish of a fresh-water river. *New York* is sufficiently supplied with both sorts."

From the *New York Gazette*, in 1752, describing the whales on Staten Island, near Fresh Kills, what would become, in the 1970s, one of the largest municipal garbage dumps in the world: "Last Saturday a whale, forty-five feet long, ran ashore at Van Buskirk's point at the entrance of the *Kills* from our bay, when being discovered by the people from Staten Island, a number of men went off and killed him, and may now be seen at Mr. John Waters', at the Ferry-house on Staten Island."

From an April 1756 newspaper report: "On last Tuesday, 5,751 shad were caught at one draught on the west side of Long Island." (DeVoe exclaims: "Enormous!")

From a newspaper at the time of the Stamp Act, when "oyster" was another word for "New Yorker," when the New York bivalves went by an encyclopedic list of names, from all along the Middle Colonies—Cow Bays, Blue-points, Chingaroras, Virginias, Delawares, East Rivers, City Islanders:

> Nor ought our vast plenty of oysters to pass without particular obser-vation; in their quality they are exceeded by those of no country what-ever. People of all ranks amongst us, in general, prefer them to any other kind of food. Nor is anything wanting, save a little of the filings of copper, to render them equally relishing, even to an English palate, with the best from *Colchester*. They continue good eight months in the year, and are, for two months longer, the daily food of our poor. Their beds are within view of the town, and I am informed that an oyster-man, industriously employed, may clear *eight* or *ten* shillings a day.

FRESHWATER HILL

DeVoe was a lister, a compiler, a noter of notes, with one eye on colo-nial New York and the Revolution and another on everything else, es-pecially food and the seasonal cycles of the public markets. After *The Market Book*, he published a companion volume, *The Market Assistant: Containing a Brief Description of Every Article of Human Food Sold in the Public Markets of the Cities of New York, Boston, Philadelphia, and Brook-lyn*. It is a book-length snapshot of all the goods sold in an East Coast market, a kaleidoscopic epic of the quotidian in New York's late nine-teenth century—a time, incidentally, when the idea of Founding Fathers was born, at the moment the founders themselves were dying away.

See his notations on fish, fowl, and meat: American wild geese, wild turkey, cattle's feet (six dollars per hundred), ox eyes (for sauces and medical students), ox teeth (for dentists), loin of lamb, brisket of pork, caribou (from Maine), northern hare ("The flesh of an old hare is tough, dry, and insipid; but the leveret, or young one, when in good condition, is very fair eating"), lamprey eels, sturgeon ("This jumping fish is also often seen, by almost every passenger in the summer season, when go-ing up the North River, leaping clear out of the water some eight or ten feet"), blackfish ("A fine large blackfish, weighing nearly twenty-eight pounds, was caught at McComb's Dam, on Thursday last"—September 29, 1855), yellow pike perch (a.k.a. glass-eyed pike, big-eyed pike, pike of the lakes, or Ohio salmon), spring mackerel ("one of the most beautiful of all fish"), robins ("I, however, think that these birds are more useful to man living than dead"), the soon-to-be-extinct passenger pigeons ("One day last week, upwards of seventy-five thousand pigeons were brought to the market, insomuch that fifty were sold for one shilling"), lake mooneye, river mooneye, shredder crabs, saltwater terrapin, soft-shelled crabs, hawksbill turtle.

See the yield of the fields and farms along the Hudson and Hackensack, of the orchards up through the valleys of the Raritan and the Passaic, as well as in gardens in the city of New York: cabbage, colewort, cress, dandelion ("In 1856, Messrs. Hills & Stringer, of New York City, introduced 'dandelion coffee,' made of the roots of this plant, which I found a very pleasant drink"), milkweed (tied up in bunches, appearing in May), cardoons (September to March), patience dock ("The root is much used as a purifier of the blood"), pumpkins (the *New Jersey Journal*, 1839: "a pumpkin raised in a garden in Elizabethtown, which weighed, when taken from the vine, one hundred and eighty seven and a half pounds, and measured seven feet in circumference"), rhubarb (from a garden on Fifth Street and the Bowery in May 1830), tomatoes (formerly known as "love apples"), blood-root, brooklime, horehound, hops, and marshmallow ("but it should be procured by *one* or from *one* who is well acquainted with the plant").

See the apples, a longer-than-now seasonal catalog that ranges from spring to fall: summer pippins, autumn pearmain, seek-no-further, Jersey sweet, maiden-blush, Gravenstein, Newtown pippins, golden russets, Wagner, northern spy, and Roxbury russets.

Occassionally, DeVoe makes a point beyond his list, and when he does so, it is like scripture commentary. "The Spitzenberg and Baldwin are fine table-apples," says DeVoe, "but I might name fifty varieties, and each would have as many admirers as being the best." Always one feels the rhythm of the season, the eternal rhythms of the old city, as, for example, when summer pushes aside spring in the market—or when corn is harvested closer and closer to the city, corn harvest proximity being directly proportional to the summer's heat.

"[Corn] begins to arrive" says DeVoe, "from the South (Charleston), about the 1st of June; then from Philadelphia, say from the 10th to the 15th of July; from New York, about the 1st of August; and continues, by a succession of crops, to be soft and good until the 15th of October—although I have eaten it in a good condition on the 1st of December (1855)."

It is written that DeVoe's most treasured list was the list of all the butchers who ever worked in the City of New York, alphabetized. The list is five hundred folio pages, handwritten, and includes the name "Thomas F. DeVoe, butcher." My own favorite list of DeVoe's is the pages of notations he made while looking at the city's old newspapers, marking anything of interest, the first list of his I stumbled on. It is, to me, a founding document in New York's historiography. Stokes used the newspaper notations in the making of the *Iconograpy*. When I read this list, its pages and pages, I read it as if each listing were a frame in an old film, flickering by. Some examples:

1706, Cold weather
1722, Brooklyn crossed on the ice
1736, Boats, oysters—seizure of
1736, Fresh Water Hill
1767, Watering place, Staten Island
1771, Flying Machine
1773, Fresh Water Hill
1773, Weather very cold
1775, Golden Hill
1775, Earthquake
1776, Windmill
1783, Meteor luminous
1785, Eagle, bald
1789, Turtle caught
1791, Kissing Bridge
1793, Wood, scarcity of
1799, Well, Washington's

SHADOW

My inaugural excursion, the boat trip from Elizabeth to Wall Street, had left me vaguely unsatisfied, especially given the incident involving the damaged propeller. It left me hungry for other kinds of reenactments, which I would eventually find. In the meantime, on the actual day of the anniversary of Washington's inaugural, April 30, I went out alone, on the Staten Island Ferry, for free. It was a lo-fi version of my inaugural boat trip, featuring me, a couple hundred tourists, and a small number of sleepy commuters—reenacting merely the Staten Island–to–Manhattan portion of the 1789 inaugural barge trip, skipping the Arthur Kill. After a promising dawn—a bright star on the rust-colored horizon over the hills of Queens—I took the subway to the Bowling Green station. I walked through a sea of people coming off the ferry and heading into work in Manhattan; at the end of rush hour, I was moving against the tide of people. On the boat on the way over to Staten Island, as we neared the Statue of Liberty, the tourists raced starboard with cameras. I went to the port side, to escape the press of the crowd and balance the boat. I stared at the water for a while, then asked a crew member about porpoises, still remembering the spring-in-the-harbor detail from accounts of the original inauguration. "We see them all the time," she said.

We docked in Staten Island. I got off and got right back on. On the deck, leaning against the railing, I looked ahead toward the city, and, near the Statue of Liberty, as I slowly studied the horizon, I suddenly realized that I could see a panorama not just of the harbor, but also of the Revolutionary War, a water-level before, during, and after. I could see the Narrows, and the view to the open ocean. I could see the hills near Sandy Hook, where the British fleet came in one summer. I could see Brooklyn, and the hills on which the Battle of Brooklyn had been fought. Moving around tourists, I could look up the Hudson, past Manhattan's bristle of real estate, to see the George Washington Bridge, the modern steel structure that traces the start of the ancient escape route to New Jersey where the Continental Army, trounced by the British, began the long retreat to the Delaware. I could maybe even see the beginnings of the Catskills, seventy-five miles away, not completely impossible— Henry Hudson's crew saw them, after all. And then when I looked west I saw clearly the Watchung Mountains. I saw the edge that descended to the Raritan River and the Millstone, both of which, after my own crossing of the Delaware, had led me from Princeton to the Morristown winter headquarters. I could see it all, in other words—the history of the war in the view of the land. It was the opposite of a moment of decision. It was a moment of topographic retrospect, an epiphany of place, through which the past looked different, or else it was an unexplainably heightened awareness, or else I was getting hot, hanging off the side of the boat in the warm about-to-be-summer sun.

Now I looked down onto the sunlit brown-and-green, breeze-rippled surface of the harbor. I got my camera out of my knapsack and took a photograph of the water—just, I thought, the water, though when I got home I realized that I had photographed the water with a ghostly shadow of the ferry's flag.

HOT DOG

When I disembarked from the ferry on that perfect spring day, I walked a few piers over to Wall Street, to stand where Washington would have stood on his entrance into New York. I looked out at the water where our fishing boat had been, in a happier time prior to the propeller damage and, as I turned to face land, I accidentally walked into a bunch of memories at the foot of Wall Street—here was a place my father had worked as a printer in the city. I looked around and remembered all sorts of minutiae: rain pouring down in sheets from the elevated highway, stacks of freshly printed business forms and financial papers on wooden pallets, the smell of printer's ink, and a guy in the high window of a bindery off Water Street, looking down at the kid-aged me with a big toothless smile, waving. I remembered eating hot dogs as a kid near that corner, things pulled from the warm murky water, the tangy mustard, the skin snapping, the way my father held the two dogs at once in his hands, noble. I remembered the stink of the fish market, now gone, and, at a time when the old seaport buildings were being replaced with a mall, my father leading me into about-to-be-abandoned buildings, searching for relics, a clock, an old block and tackle that I still have in the bottom of a closet somewhere. I was having a small personal reenactment of my past, playing the son.

On the corner, I bought a hot dog, and the hot dog arose from hot dog water that looked good, as far as hot dog water goes. The vendor, in his early twenties, was cordial. I asked him how long he'd been at the spot. "A long time," he said. I pressed him. "A couple of years." Walking slowly up Wall Street, I noticed a slight incline, the idea of an old hill, and I marveled at all the people passing me by. When I stopped to take notes, my arm was jostled, my notes scribbled—I was in a stream of people, an old pedestrian channel in the midst of a spring freshet.

Across from Federal Hall, I stood with my back to the old J. P. Morgan Building, scars in the marble.* On the day I was there, there were New York City cops with gear and munitions more appropriate to a National Guard unit or a SWAT team than what I would have seen when I was growing up, when a cop had a revolver and a nightstick, and in warm weather wore a sky-blue short-sleeve shirt, a style frozen in 1970s detective movies, the preserving amber of my prehistoric youth. I guessed that this heavily armed policeman was part of an antiterrorism unit, defending the adjacent stock exchange. As I stood alongside

---

*Areas of the Morgan Building are still noticeably scarred from an explosion in 1920, blamed on an anarchist, though never proven; the explosion killed thirty-three people and injured more than four hundred, making it New York's worst disaster at that time since the Triangle Shirtwaist Factory fire of 1911, when 146 women died or jumped to their deaths, the doors of their sweatshop locked. Until the World Trade Center attacks, the Triangle Shirtwaist fire was the second-largest loss of life in a disaster in New York (after the fire on the *General Slocum*, in 1904). At a memorial for the Triangle victims, held at the Metropolitan Opera House in the spring of 1911, Rose Schneiderman, president of the New York Women's Trade Union League, spoke: "Public officials have only words of warning to us—warning that we must be intensely peaceable, and they have the workhouse just back of all their warnings. The strong hand of the law beats us back, when we rise, into the conditions that make life unbearable. I can't talk fellowship to you who are gathered here. Too much blood has been spilled. I know from my experience it is up to the working people to save themselves. The only way they can save themselves is by a strong working-class movement." A labor mural including an image of Schneiderman was taken down by the Republican governor of Maine, in 2010, and brought to a secret location. Schneiderman, an architect of the New Deal, coined the term "Bread and Roses," which became the theme of the 1912 Lawrence, Massachusetts, textile strike by women and immigrants. (According to the encyclopedia of the Jewish Women's Archive, Schneiderman—a Polish woman who was four feet nine inches tall, with "flaming red hair"—taught Franklin and Eleanor Roosevelt "most of what they knew about working people.") "The worker must have bread, but she must have roses, too," she said. A radio report I heard about the Maine mural ended with the reporter saying this: "Labor leaders say the governor may be able to remove the mural, but he can't erase Maine's labor history."

him, I looked across the street and up the stairs of the old Federal Hall, at the statue of George Washington. One after another, tourists posed for a photo with the likeness of the first president. I noticed a nearby wreath, and wondered if it could be inauguration-related.

I went into the hall—my first time—where a man dressed as General Henry Knox, the Boston bookseller-turned-general-turned-first-secretary-of-war (until personal debt brought him down), was giving a talk. I quietly circled the interior of the hall's rotunda. In the back corner, I came upon a giant slab of stone, barely contained in an old frame, and etched with this inscription:

STANDING ON THIS STONE

IN THE BALCONY OF FEDERAL HALL

APRIL 30, 1789

GEORGE WASHINGTON

TOOK THE OATH

AS THE FIRST PRESIDENT

OF THE

UNITED STATES OF AMERICA

I was ecstatic; I had never imagined the stone where Washington stood would be there, much less still exist. I wanted to touch it but did not; a big crack ran though it. I stepped outside, and one of the cops from across the street was at the top of the Federal Hall stairs, appearing to observe the tourists, who were still posing, one by one, before the statue of Washington. I attempted to share my enthusiasm with the cop, mentioning the anniversary of Washington's inaugural. "You just missed him," the cop said. He seemed unfazed.

"What do you mean?"

"George Washington—you just missed him." The cop nodded toward the entrance to Federal Hall. "The whole thing ended a couple of minutes ago. He's upstairs now, having a hot dog."

SUMMER

PROBABLY IT IS THE HEAT that does it, that slows things down when it attacks, that offers us a heightened sense of merciful ocean-borne breezes, of old routes covered with modern and suddenly molten asphalt—but in the summer I can feel as if I am at war, or about to be. In terms of the actual chronology of the American Revolution, summer in New York could mean the summer of 1778 and the Battle of Staten Island, an American raid, or the summer of 1779, when, after the American victory at Stony Point, British soldiers fled to the city. It could mean the summer of 1788, when trade unions marched in support of the Constitution in New York, or even the summer of 1790, when, in August, shortly after a banquet with the Creeks, a Native American tribe who had just signed a treaty with the U.S. government, George and Martha Washington left New York for Philadelphia, New York's brief reign as first U.S. capital complete. But in terms of my own inner historical clock, summer is inevitably associated with 1776. The British had left Boston the winter before, resupplying in Halifax. The fleet returned that summer, with the largest invasion force ever seen. New York City prepared for war.

During a particularly hot summer a few years ago—when people perspired just standing around, when the underground breeze from subway trains racing into their stations was like the air from a hair dryer on its highest setting—my summer became the summer of 1776, so that while I read of the preparations in the old books (in Stokes and

DeVoe, in Washington Irving's portrait of the general that was his namesake) it was as if their pages were the pages of my daybook. I lived in a perpetual calendar. A recurring thought was an image of George Washington himself, during that Revolutionary summer, as he prepared for what he knew would be a difficult battle. In those summer weeks, as men dug trenches and built battlements on all the city's hills, Washington toured the vast area of the harbor, with maps and a spyglass.* I found myself acting similarly, finding little hills in the modern boroughs of New York, and even in New Jersey, looking out to see what I could on the horizon, thinking of the date as it lined up with summer days past.

From General John Glover, writing a report in the midst of the pregnant heat: "The Sentinels on Fort George, and on the Batteries are to keep a sharp look out towards the narrows, Staten Island, Red-Hook, & etc—to observe if any signals are given from thence, and acquaint the Officer of the Guard immediately therewith."

From a newspaper report from the summer of 1776: "Every Tide we expect an Attack will be made on this City from the piratical Fleet at Staten-Island."

A letter from Nathan Hale, the young Connecticut officer, to his brother: "For about 6 or 8 days the enemy have been expected hourly, whenever the wind and tide [are] in the least favored. We keep a particular look out for them this morning."

---

*Washington asked for no salary for his service as commander of the American military; he asked only that he be reimbursed for expenses. (When he offered to take no pay as president, Congress protested, given the size of his wartime expenses.) His receipts from the days before the start of the war, in the summer of 1776, are a tour of the city from the vantage point of vantage points. "April 15. To the expences of myself and party reconnoitering the several landing places etc. on Staten Island. . . . May 11. To expences of a tour on, and reconnoitering Long Island. . . . June 26, To expences in reconnoitering the channel and landings on both sides the [Hudson] river, as high as Tarrytown to fix the defences thereof. . . . To a reconnoitre of the East river and along the Sound as far as Mamaroneck. . . . July 15, To my own and party's expences, laying out Fort Lee on the Jersey side of the North river. . . . July 23, To the expence of reconnoitering the country as far as Perth Amboy." The receipts describe a circle centered by, say, the Empire State Building. Meanwhile, the Americans, as the *Saint James Chronicle* reported in London, "were throwing up Entrenchments, and otherwise strengthening Posts already by Nature very advantageous and defensible."

On the streets of my neighborhood, people disappeared. Families left town to escape the heat, and the people remaining stayed shut up inside, beseiged by high temperatures and defended by air-conditioning units they had posted in July. The evacuation was an echo of an old migration, as seen in an old diary: "Nineteen twentieths at least of the inhabitants with their families & effects had left that city between the latter part of the year 1775 & the month of June 1776."

I heard foghorns in the early morning and read old reports of British warships arriving at Sandy Hook—the *Phoenix*, the *Mercury*, the *Lively*, the *Dutchess of Gordon*, according to the *New York Packet*, dated June 6, 1776. I watched container ships line up in the narrows between Staten Island and Brooklyn, huge ships from overseas, waiting to moor at the local docks. I read another order given by General John Glover, from June 26: "The quartermaster-general is ordered to procure all the Row Boats and light Pettyaugres in and near this City, and . . . to station them, with all other boats belonging to the army, & not in use, in the dock between the Exchange Slip & Albany Pier."

A loyalist writing in August: "The Number of Transports now at Sandy-Hook, we hear amounts to 113 Sail, and we have not the least Reason to doubt, that General Howe is in this Fleet. From the Number of Troops now here, and those on their Way, from different Parts of the Country, it is computed our Army will soon amount to 25000 Men."

That summer, as I mentioned, was particularly hot, with modern records broken, and near the middle, I came down with a fever, so it was with great effort that I dragged myself into lower Manhattan, to the site of an eighteenth-century ship that had been suddenly revealed. Surprises are typical at New York City construction sites; archeologists are often dispatched when something is serendipitously dug up. I made my way over to the World Trade Center (a giant construction zone at that point, a decade since the buildings had been destroyed) to see the ship unearthed by workers on the site. What I recall: subway ride, woozy walk down blistering Wall Street, a giant dragonfly in the street below the cemetery at Trinity Church that was flying off toward the river, and, in an abandoned lot on a hidden-away stretch of Washington

Street, a sumptuous, rain-forest-like patch of forgotten and overgrown green. When I ran into two construction workers and asked about the uncovered ship, they downplayed the significance of the accidental archaeological find. "Broken fucking wood," one of them said.

There were security guards and barriers and walls surrounding the site of the boat's unburial, no viewpoint to be found. I walked for about twenty minutes, stopping, resting, dragging, Lazarus-like, a day away from visiting the doctor who would prescribe the drugs that would revive me. Finally I found a staircase where I could see the skeleton of the ship, the ribs of a wooden whale in a portal of gray, pre–World Trade Center muck. The ship's remains were in an older place, probably pre-Revolutionary—down near a bulkhead dated at 1899, and almost exactly at the spot where a 1797 map described two now-gone docking points, Lindsey's Wharf and Lake's Wharf. I stared. "It's sad sad sad," the man I realized was standing next to me said to the boy he was with, and I thought at first that he was talking about the boat, but I was mixing things up. He was talking about the destruction of the original World Trade Center buildings.

PATRIOT

A guy I know named Duke Riley lives on the edge of the harbor. Unofficially, Duke is known as Duke; semiofficially, Duke goes by a title: Duke Riley, Artist and Patriot. In using the word "artist," he is referring to any number of methods by which he makes a living. He is a tattoo artist, specializing in nautical designs. He also makes drawings and paintings, some of which remind me of old scrimshaw, some of which are phantasmagorical waterfront scenes, many of them filled with references to colonial or sometimes even Civil War–era America. He is also an artist in that he creates what you might call spectacles. During the 2004 Republican National Convention, Duke rowed to U Thant Island in the East River, a tiny speck of rock adjacent to the United Nations that is sometimes said to be New York's smallest island, the result of subway-tunnel construction debris. On arriving on U Thant's shores, Duke declared the island a sovereign nation, unfurling a glow-in-the-dark flag. On his way back, he was detained by the Coast Guard. When I think of Duke as a patriot, I think often of his commitment to the idea that people in New York should be free to be on the water, a place owned by no one. He has discussed this in various interviews: "New York City has this strange way about it. Manhattan's an island and it was at one time this major port city. If you go to pretty much any country in the world, to a major port city, you'll see all different shapes and sizes of vessels out on the water, intermingling with commercial ships. It's totally normal to see people commuting on small sailboats or rowboats or junks or anything, right alongside commercial traffic. Here in New York, they're not aware that Manhattan's even an island."

In his ongoing battle for harbor awareness in New York, Duke once built a replica of a Revolutionary War submarine, the *Turtle*, which he then launched in the harbor.

PRESENT CIRCUMSTANCES

The original *Turtle* was built by David Bushnell, who grew up on the family farm in Old Saybrook, Connecticut, a town on the seacoast, at the mouth of the Connecticut River. When he was thirty, his father died, thus freeing him to attend Yale, from which he graduated in 1775. While at school, he spent the time between classes designing ways to explode things underwater, then a difficult thing to do. He was thirty-five when the war began, and when it did, he quickly built a submarine with his brother, fashioning it in secret on an island in the mouth of the Norwalk River. It was quietly transported by boat to New York Harbor. The submarine was a bulb-shaped wooden craft that fit one man, judging from the sketches that still exist (all drawn after the sub disappeared). The pilot, looked at in profile when sitting inside the submarine, appeared to be riding a stationary bicycle, though instead of pedals and a handlebar, he worked a bilge pump, a small corkscrew-shaped propeller to move the boat forward and backward, another one for moving it up and down, some tubes for air, and another corkscrew-like device that was supposed to attach an explosive cask to a British ship. Early on, people referred to it as the Water Machine.

"His plan," a Connecticut physician, Dr. Benjamin Gale, wrote to Ben Franklin, on August 7, 1776, referring to Bushnell, "is to place the Cask containing the Powder on the outside of the Machine. It is so

Contrived that when it strikes the Ship, which he proposes shall be at the Keil, it Grapples fast, and is wholly Disengag'd from the Machine. He then rises off. The Powder is to be fired by a Gun Lock fixed with the Cask, which is sprung by Watch work, which he can so order as to have that take place at any Distance of Time he pleases."

Dr. Gale noted that Bushnell had tested the *Turtle* in Long Island Sound, towed there by a whaleboat. "He then sunk under Water, where he Continued about 45 minutes without any Inconveniency as to Breathing." Gale described a device for measuring water depth and "a pair of Glass Eyes by which he sees Objects Under Water." Bushnell seems to have preferred to operate in the dark. To see his compass in the submarine's dark interior, he used what was then known as foxfire, a fungus that grows on rotting wood and glows in the dark. He put foxfire on the points of the compass. Anchored underwater, the *Turtle* could await a change in tides and currents.

"This story may Appear Romantic but thus far All these Experiments as above related have been Actually Made," Gale wrote.

The *Turtle* traveled from Connecticut by sloop as far as New Rochelle and was then transported on land to the Hudson River. "The Machine designed to attempt blowing Up the Enemy's Ships is to be transported from the East to the North River, where a Small Vessel will be wanted to transport it," one American general wrote to another in New York City. The Americans had high hopes for the machine. "Tho' the Event is uncertain, under our present Circumstances it is certainly worth trying," he added.

The "present Circumstances" alluded to consisted of the Continental Army and the militias being completely overwhelmed by the invading British forces.

VASTLY PLEASED

Duke Riley, it seems important to mention, grew up in Boston, where his uncle was a fishmonger, like John Glover and his Massachusetts-based Marblehheaders, whom I think of as can-do watermen. As a teenager, Duke ran away from home, working at various jobs until he enrolled at the Rhode Island School of Design, where he studied painting and drawing. "Most cities are built on their relationship to the water," he has said. "That's where the crazy stuff goes on, and that's where you find a level of tolerance in mainstream society." Duke is not a big guy, but he is tough and wiry, with a wise-guy grin. He will swim almost anywhere in New York Harbor, and he keeps a truck parked in front of his apartment, in an old dockworkers' neighborhood, two kayaks strapped on top, ready to go. Duke is not a reenactor; I would say he reemploys old ideas. He looks at something that has happened, studies it, and then tries it again, or a version of it, taking liberties with the facts. In Queens, on the site of the 1939 World's Fair, he staged a Roman-style naval battle, or *naumachia*, entitled "Those Who Are About to Die Salute You." When he begins to work on something, he makes trips and reads and digs up old newspaper clippings, as if he were researching a book, though he is fact making an event, as happened in August 2006, when he built a Revolutionary War submarine replica and set out to meet a British ship, the *Queen Mary 2*.

During his investigations into the *Turtle*, Duke had talked to a historian and read a bunch of books, all of them describing the night at the end of the summer of 1776 when the *Turtle* attempted to blow up a British ship and didn't. In the case of the *Turtle*, things went badly. Bushnell had trained his brother to operate it; his brother got sick. As a replacement, Bushnell chose Ezra Lee, a twenty-seven-year-old sergeant with the Fifth Connecticut Regiment. Whaleboats towed the *Turtle* in the harbor, the British boats lying at anchor toward Staten Island. Lee set out in the dark. The tides were wrong. He waited. He noted that the moon was two hours up in the sky and then set out again, toward Bedloe's Island, what is today Liberty Island, home of the Statue of Liberty. Lee got close to the HMS *Eagle*, the largest of the British ships, and attempted to attach the bomb. "I could see all the men on deck and hear them talk—I then shut down all the doors, sunk down, and came under the bottom of the ship—Up with the screw against the bottom, but found that it would not enter," Lee said.

He had apparently struck a piece of metal, or something, anyway, that prevented him from attaching the explosive. By Lee's own account, he decided to get out of there. He zigzagged across the harbor, trying to pass Governors Island, which was closer than he thought. At one point, when he was convinced the British were chasing him, he released the explosive device, thereby accidentally inventing the depth charge, and "throwing up large bodies of water to an immense height," as he recalled. When the bomb exploded, the Americans spotted him, General Israel Putnam watching from a pier at the bottom of Manhattan Island. According to Ezra Lee's account, General Putnam was watching from the Battery at dawn at the end of the first failed attempt, when the water gushed in the air. Putnam was, in Lee's words, "vastly pleased, and cried out in his picular way—'God's curse 'em, that'll do it for 'em.'"

Bushnell took the *Turtle* out again, in October, leaving from Fort Washington in Washington Heights—a failure. At another point several of his underwater explosive devices were released in the Delaware River, causing the British in Philadelphia to fire at them and anything that looked like them, an incident the Americans facetiously described as the Battle of the Kegs.*

---

*Though you would perhaps never imagine it from the popular portrayal of her, Betsy Ross was involved in the Battle of the Kegs. That she is remembered as the flag maker is in many ways representative of how America processes its Revolutionary history. The one thing that we think we know about her—that she designed the first flag, helping Washington cut a five-cornered star, designing the Stars and Stripes—is in fact one biographical detail that we absolutely do not know about her. "Her legend looms so large that her life has been overlooked," writes Marla R. Miller, in the only scholarly biography of Ross, née Elizabeth Griscom. (Ross's personal records were burned, mistaken for trash, and previous biographies were mostly children's literature.) The things we do know about the woman, who was certainly one of Philadelphia's leading flag makers, include that she was politically active (women in Philadelphia had been asked to participate in political discussion for the first time in the colony's history); that she also made mattresses, sofa cushions, bolsters, and blinds, in a colonial culture that valued the amassing of luxury; that she worked with a team of men and women, skilled artisans in Philadelphia, which was at the time the furniture-making capital of America; that the star that ended up on the flag probably was not a matter of Washington's taste but was easy to produce in quantity. "The Betsy Ross story is usually treated as a matter of design, but it is not—it is a matter of production," Miller writes. The communal details of her life in Philadelphia for sixty years as an upholsterer are disregarded—as opposed to the single (and possibly false) moment with Washington that her family recollected long after her death. And yet, those overlooked details paint a picture of the Revolution that is more like a tapestry or quilt than a silk star. For instance, Joseph Ashburn, a sailor who was one of Elizabeth Griscom's three husbands, was captured by the British on a boat off Ireland, was marched seventy-two miles across the country (appalled at the poverty in Ireland, another British colony), and imprisoned in the notorious Old Mill prison. Meanwhile, the Griscom family, while living in British-occupied Philadelphia, was involved in

THE ACORN

There have been a few replicas of the *Turtle*. A high school shop class in Connecticut built one, and, a few years ago, an architectural education organization built one and had it tested in the Hydromechanic Laboratory at the United States Naval Academy in Annapolis, Maryland, making complicated water-tightness and drag-test calculations. Duke did comparatively less planning; he just started building. He would work late, then go out for beer. By 2006, Duke had noticed that after the World Trade Center was destroyed, police security all over the city had increased to a level that a lot of people thought was, if not overdoing it, then misdirected—subway searches of immigrant laborers, for example, while fund managers could pay for time-saving special security inspections before boarding JFK-bound helicopters on Wall Street. Police were more likely to be hassling you if you put a canoe in the water, or if you went for a swim, something Duke does frequently. Meanwhile, as citizens were searched, a cruise ship like the *Queen Mary 2* slipping in and out of the harbor unharassed appeared to Duke an irony.

As he recounted it to me, Duke's initial plan was to approach the *Queen Mary 2*, videotape himself alongside it, and then return. "I was hoping to document getting up close to it, and getting away, proving the ridiculousness of the whole Homeland Security system," he said.

Duke began thinking about his *Turtle* replica in the winter of 2006. He called it the *Acorn*, and portrayed it as a long-lost twin of the *Turtle*. It took him a few months. He built the *Acorn* in Red Hook, where he lives. Red Hook is a neighborhood in Brooklyn that feels like a little port city in Connecticut, or somewhere else in New England. Once it was an island-like point of red clay–colored land; the Dutch settled there in 1636, calling it Roode Hoek. Just prior to the Civil War, the construction of the Atlantic Basin, a large shipping facility, made Red Hook a hot spot for shipping, with large silos for storing the grain that had been shipped east from the Erie Canal. The Statue of Liberty was constructed

---

the construction of chevaux-de-frise, large sunken logs covered with spikes employed to upset British shipping in the Delaware. Elizabeth herself treated several boys after they were wounded by an exploding keg while in a boat on the Delaware.

to face France, and, as a result, first faces Red Hook. In the 1920s, J. P. Morgan dry-docked his yacht, *Corsair*, there. Red Hook has always been a tough place, too—a waterfront home to Al Capone, the site of various mob battles in the 1950s. By the 1960s, when trolleys had disappeared and no subway replaced them, the neighborhood declined; then a highway cut it off from the rest of Brooklyn. Shipping jobs moved away. In 1992, the principal of the local public school was killed in drug-related crossfire. Artists began moving in in the 1980s, around the time that a retired cop began renting warehouse space, and there was a short-lived attempt to rename the area Liberty View.

Duke put together his boat in an area that contains artists' studios, a parachute maker, and a well-known manufacturer of key lime pie. Construction on the *Acorn* began in the spring, with plywood; a friend helped him to fiberglass the hull, another helped with the metal hatch. Eventually, Duke would appear on TV news, helicopters filming him as he piloted his little submarine into the harbor to "attack" the British ship, police with automatic weapons intercepting.

In the first hours of his capture, a news radio station described the *Acorn* as a World War II replica; another called it an "orb." "Sub Moron," said the front page of the *New York Post*. "Sub Moronic," said the *Daily News*. The *New York Times* described the submarine as "something truly strange." The *Times* also said it "resembled something out of Jules Verne by way of Huck Finn, manned by cast members from 'Jackass.'" Also, the *Times* called Duke "a man with an obsession." In journalism, "obsession" can be a kind of code word for *passion*; it can also be a code word for *freak*. When he was captured, I remember thinking that Duke was on to something, as did many people I know who live near the water in Brooklyn. I remember, too, noting the wildly different descriptions of what he did and why.

Duke was arrested on charges that had to do with violating something the police described as the *Queen Mary 2*'s "safety zone," as well as for operating an unsafe vessel. The police commissioner referred to Duke's action as "marine mischief." Duke was quickly released, and later he exhibited the *Acorn* as part of an art exhibit.

People who were searching for an explanation as to why anyone would build a replica of a Revolutionary War submarine and take it out in the harbor to meet the *Queen Mary 2* found this statement on Duke's website: "I am interested in the struggle of marginal peoples to

sustain independent spaces within all-encompassing societies, the ten-
sion between individual and collective behavior, the conflict with in-
stitutional power. I pursue an alternative view of hidden borderlands
and their inhabitants through drawing, printmaking, mosaic, sculpture, performative interventions, and video structured as complex
multimedia installations."

"I would not say the scare was overblown, but I also don't believe I
was doing anything illegal," Duke told the *Post*.

A TRUE ACCOUNT

On a humid summer day in July 2010, on the anniversary of the *Acorn*'s
launch, I went to Red Hook, in Brooklyn, for a True Account, a remembrance by a key participant in the seizing of the *Acorn*, Duke himself.
Around the time I talked to him, Duke had been working on a project
involving the sewers in Cleveland, Ohio, and he had recently staged a
mock takeover of an island in the Delaware River, near Philadelphia.
Duke and I had been planning to meet for a while; it had been a couple
of years since the voyage of the *Acorn*, but I wanted to talk to him about
it before it was ancient history. I followed Duke's motorcycle over to the
site of the launch, a little sandy beach in Red Hook near the entrance to
Buttermilk Channel. The launch site was just around the corner from
where, when it is docked, the city-sized *Queen Mary 2* towers over Red
Hook like a menacing iceberg of white steel and hidden buffet tables.

We stood at the very place where the *Acorn* was launched, facing
the Statue of Liberty. The tide was going out. "I remember first being
attracted to just the shape and the design—it's almost like a da Vinci
drawing," Duke said. He remembered thinking about the achievement
of the original sub. "Everything was just so much more dangerous back
then," he was saying. "A simple cut could kill you. And then you could
go out in this boat, which goes underwater, and, really, it was just having no idea what would happen, a total unknown. This idea back then
was the equivalent of getting into a space suit."

He remembered working on the *Acorn* day after day, finishing late
most nights, going into a bar at two in the morning, covered in fiberglass, people saying, "How's the submarine going?" Initially, he felt
confident, but he soon developed second thoughts. "Would I pull it off,

I was thinking. It's not my area of expertise, or strength—I'm not an engineer," he said. "I was really kind of winging it, in terms of budget and plans. There really were no plans. There's a letter to Bushnell, I think, from Ben Franklin or somebody, which says, 'Thank you so much for your contribution, and could you tell us how you did this?'"

In addition to substituting fiberglass for pine tar, Duke did not steam wood.* "I just decided to bend plywood, 'cause I don't have time to steam-bend oak, and the money, especially if it sank . . ." he said.

I asked him if he thought about risks.

"Yeah, drowning," he said.

At some point after construction began, Duke realized the *Queen Mary 2* was coming, and he connected the project to the boat's arrival. "I think I needed a mission," he said. He knew he was going to meet the *Queen Mary 2*, though he did not know precisely how. He missed a self-imposed June deadline, then a July deadline.

"I was like, 'This sucks. I'm running out of time,'" he said. "I knew the *Queen Mary 2* was coming on August 3 and then on September 11, and I really didn't want to do it on September 11. I really wanted to do it at night, so I wouldn't be seen. I wasn't trying to get caught. I wanted to get my own video footage. I was going to try and hook onto it. I didn't know exactly what I was going to do with it. Maybe write something on the side. But I wanted to do it at night."

At the end of July, with the help of friends and neighbors, he put the *Acorn* in the water for its first test run. In the wrenching tides of Buttermilk Channel, he quickly realized he would have to concentrate on riding the currents; maneuvering would be minimal. It was also during this test, while off the coast of Red Hook, that the Coast Guard approached him.

"They said, 'What are you doing?'" according to Duke. "I said, 'Oh, I'm just testing my submarine.' And they said, 'Oh, that's fine, but the *Queen Mary 2* is on its way.' And I said, 'Oh, really?' We told them we were filming a movie. They said, 'Fine, as long as you stay out of the shipping lanes.'"

*Some accounts describe the *Turtle* as being made from a giant elm tree, cut in half, cored out, and resealed.

Duke and his friends towed the *Acorn* back in for a few days of repairs and modifications; it was damaged while tied up, the hull bashed by the tides against the riprap at the Red Hook pier. They pulled the craft onto the beach and worked on it at low tide, patching holes. "It took all day and twenty people to move it," he remembered. The night before he planned to meet the *Queen Mary 2*, the tide gave them five hours and fifteen minutes to work on the beach, and as the water rose, Duke, panic-stricken, ran electric blowers and driers out to the sub on extension cords—to dry the fiberglass, to pump out water. "It was dangerous," he said. "The most stressful day, to get this thing out of the water. I made calls to friends, my friend Jesse from Providence, whose last name is actually Bushnell. This was like the total most wrong insane way for me to do everything."

His arms were folded as he spoke, tattoos revealed. He had been shaking his head as he described the panic of the repair day, but at this point he unfolded his arms and motioned to the rocks, decorated by sand, seaweed, and bits of trash. "This is where I launched it, right here on a ramp," he said.

THE GUY FROM U THANT ISLAND

"That was August third," he went on. "If I had done it on the day Bushnell did it, then that would have been ideal. Let me see, he launched the *Turtle* after the Battle of Brooklyn. It was very close to September 11. I think September 9 was maybe when they went to do it in 1776. But that day, on August third, I don't even know if I went to sleep. I think I was working on it, making preparations pretty late. I think I went to bed and it was five-thirty or six, and, yeah, I basically remember taking a catnap at five or six and then drinking a coffee and then drinking a beer and then just kind of kept rolling from the night before. People were helping out. The word in the neighborhood was that I was taking it out. A few supporters started to gather. I think people knew I was gonna do it, the people from the neighborhood who had helped out."

Thus, by eight-thirty the *Acorn* was launched, rowboats towing it out, the craft loaded with large rocks for ballast, lifted hand-over-hand from shore. Duke used the current, rather than Bushnell's hand-cranked propeller. "I had a rudder to steer it, and that worked really well," he said. "I figured I would just get some guys and some dinghies to get me where I wanted to go."

He pointed to a ripple, above a submerged jetty that I recognized from my Washington inaugural boat trip.

"This second time, we were just trying to go around this corner." He pointed again. "So they towed me out there, and I got the current and just got around the corner."

Duke took me around the corner by land, down the Red Hook shoreline, along the path that people in the neighborhood had taken that day while following the progress of the *Acorn*, some cheering him in the water. At the end of Wolcott Street, there was a fence with razor wire blocking access to the shore. We stood in the garbage and reeds, and Duke remembered that his friends, the two guys in the rowboats towing him into Buttermilk Channel, were getting nervous as they approached the *Queen Mary 2*, a huge ship, twenty stories high and eleven football fields long. Newspaper accounts describe people appearing in the streets, reporters quoting some who called Duke crazy. A *Times* reporter wrote that a woman described the *Acorn* as resembling a bomb. Photos of Duke in the sub show him peeking out the top, wearing a drab-green life jacket. Video he took inside the submarine shows water lapping at the portholes, and features a hollow dripping sound, the soft clank of beer cans bobbing in the bottom of the leaky craft.

"My friends were saying, 'You're getting too close to the ship,'" he remembered, "and I was saying, 'Wait a second—*that's the idea!*' But at this point, we had all moved too close." Meanwhile, Duke was gaining in determination. Bystanders cheered from the shoreline, but soon a police boat was on its way. "Apparently what had happened was somebody had spotted me from inside the cruise ship. And it turned out that somebody I knew was actually on the ship, actually on the *Queen Mary 2*," Duke said. "And later on, when I talked to him, he was saying, 'Yeah, that was really fucking scary.' I said, 'Oh, yeah.' And he said, 'No, actually, it was really fucking scary.'"

He told the cops what he called "the dumb story"—that he had gotten caught in the current. "Generally, I'm pretty good at talking to the cops. Then the cops got a call. And then they said, 'Sorry, we're gonna have to follow protocol here 'cause you're on CNN right now. Let's get you out.'" In a flash, there were scuba teams, antiterrorism police, in addition to the police bomb squad and the FBI—a large fleet of law enforcement officials. What amazed Duke was that the police knew the story of the original *Turtle*. "Almost every one of them said, 'Oh, it's the *Turtle!*' They all knew *exactly* what it was!" Duke remembered. "They had remembered it from history class. I mean, they all seemed to me to appreciate it. They knew it was a Revolutionary thing. They took it as a kind of positive thing, a patriotic thing. They were basically into it. The big problem was the FBI. Also, there were a couple of problems with my story."

His story began to spring leaks when the Coast Guard crew recognized the *Acorn* from the sub's test run, and the official with the Department of Homeland Security turned out to be the same Homeland Security official who had detained Duke for videotaping on the East River, along the FDR Drive, a short time before.

"When they figured out that I was the guy from U Thant Island," he said, "it was over."

WATERMELONS

We reconsider the past continually, of course, judging it from different vantage points, with time increasing, with experiences building. We remember our forefathers differently as we step into their shoes. First, the Delaware was crossed, then remembered, then revered. By contrast, the Battle of Brooklyn seems in its early stages, just recently remembered. And yet, in Brooklyn itself, the summer sings of the battle that was, at least to me. And when it does, I think of it as a tumultuous opening salvo of the full-fledged war, as part of the prism through which a soldier in Pennsylvania a few months later might have seen the imminent Delaware Crossing. After a summer of fort building, after hot months of trench digging and citadel constructing, the port of New York was suddenly lost, an all-new army trounced. Surely, the Revolution's veterans—those displaced from the city and returned, or those who stayed and spied, or those who stayed put because life offered few alternatives—would look to the west early on summer evenings, when the red sun lay down behind the Watchungs. Surely, the general who took the oath of office as first president of the United States in New York strolled along a New York shore and looked across to the village of Brooklyn and thought back to a summer past, in 1776, when the city and the wannabe nation stepped at last into full-scale war.

In that heat-crazed summer of historic hot temperatures that occurred not too long ago, I kept a high level of battle awareness as the August anniversary of the Battle of Brooklyn approached. I sought out citizens who, like me, watched the alignment of dates. I searched out a street artist, working under the name General Howe, who was semi-covertly placing toy soldiers at key points in the battle: at the British landing site under the Verrazano-Narrows Bridge, he fashioned a landing barge from a discarded pizza box, for instance. I managed to catch up with the faux general, surprising him near the point of Washington's evacuation—he had just posted a replica of General Howe's original broadsheet to the rebel New Yorkers, asking them to turn themselves in: "On delivering themselves up at the head quarters of the army, they will be received as faithful subjects; have permits to return peaceably to their respective Dwellings, and meet with full protection for their persons and property." I called a filmmaker who had once used kids on bikes to reenact Battle of Brooklyn skirmishes: he was busy with an interview on local-access TV, describing the battle, its ramifications, its resonances. I went to Green-Wood Cemetery, observing the tree-covered hills, topographical remnants of the battle site. And at some point I remembered that the Battle of Brooklyn itself began on a hot summer evening in August 1776, over watermelons.

The British soldiers, overwhelmed by the abundance of food in farm-rich Brooklyn, began to eat the watermelons in a Brooklyn watermelon patch. According to the historian John Gallagher, the watermelon patch had been planted near the Red Lion Inn. Tourists stopped at the inn when visiting a rock formation known as the Devil's Hoofprint. The watermelons added to the attraction. At ten in the evening, on August 26, the British took some watermelons. A Pennsylvania regiment fired. The Battle of Brooklyn commenced. The incident at the watermelon patch in Brooklyn was like the wrong turn that Archduke Franz Ferdinand's driver made in Sarajevo that ended in the shot that began World War I—a spark in the woods near a giant rock that Brooklynites liked to go look at that would eventually involve the French, Spanish, and Dutch, as well as numerous Native American tribes.

In the waning days of August, I visited my local farmers market. It's in a park that has a large rock, dug up by a utilities crew during street construction—in New York, people still love giant rocks; residents sometimes fight over the right to get them sited in their neighborhood parks. At the farmers market, the tomatoes tasted like all the summer's sun, the corn sweet as the cool mornings: What more need we praise? I spotted some watermelons. The farmer believed it to be a type native to the New York area.

"When are these watermelons in season?" I asked the farmer.

"They come in at the very end of August," the farmer said.

THE KING'S HIGHWAY

In modern times, interest in the Battle of Brooklyn remains low for two reasons: (1) it happened two centuries ago; and (2) the Americans, outnumbered by about five to one (approximately four thousand Americans facing twenty thousand British), lost, big time. What happened is complicated; you could read a book about it.* But one way to summarize is

---

*A book I would recommend is *The Battle of Brooklyn*, by John Gallagher. I didn't know Gallagher very well, but my son and I bought his book from him when my son was about ten. Gallagher signed our copy. We went home and read about how a Major Benjamin Tallmadge saw the last Continental soldier leave Brooklyn during the evacuation, a dramatic touch: "Major Tallmadge, in one of the final boats, wrote of seeing a very tall man, in a cloak and boots, coming down the steps to be helped board a skiff by one of the men from Marblehead," Gallagher wrote. "It was Washington, who left with the last of his troops." I recall seeing Gallagher in Prospect Park at a reenactment of the Battle of Brooklyn in August 2001, on the 225th anniversary. Normally, a small reenactment takes place in Green-Wood Cemetery, but for this year it was moved to Prospect Park. Signs had been posted on telephone poles all over Park Slope the week before, saying, "Between the hours of 1 p.m. and 3 p.m. there will be loud noise (cannon fire and muskets firing) coming from Prospect Park." Though this was probably one of the few times in the history of New York that gunshots were announced before a shooting, the cops stationed alongside the battlefield jumped when shooting commenced. When the reenactment began, a small group of soldiers marched out of a grove of trees near the park's Third Street entrance—identified over loudspeakers as General George Washington's guard and portrayed by the members of Alpha Company, a real infantry unit of the United States Army, dressed up as an old one. Alpha Company looked sharp, as opposed to the rest of the Continental forces,

to say that the rebels planned on the British coming at them from the harbor. They spent a lot of time building lookouts and forts and battlements facing the East River, with a British approach by harbor in mind, when what happened instead was that on the hottest days at the end of the summer the British faked them out. The British came at them from behind—i.e., from the depths of Brooklyn, better known, at the time, as Long Island (Brooklyn was just a village). Thus, the Battle of Brooklyn was originally known as the Battle of Long Island. In the final hours, in fact, with the British coming at them from the east and south, along old Brooklyn roads, through passes in the Brooklyn hills, the Americans, in their first formal post–Declaration of Independence appearance, were suddenly trapped by the water they had, hours before, hoped would protect them.

How did the British manage this? They landed in Brooklyn, along the narrows, and, early on a summer morning, quietly marched in behind the Continental forces, down the old King's Highway. Then they made a left into the hills of Gowanus, into the neighborhood that is today in and around Prospect Park.

---

who looked reenactorish, no offense. The British came down from the woods at the north end of the park, marching around a man in a tie-dyed shirt, who was sitting on a blanket with children also in tie-dyes—he apparently felt the Redcoats had no right to make him get out of the way. The British quickly advanced toward the American line, then stopped in front of a row of port-a-johns. Flintlock rifles discharged, men shouted, drums drummed; puffs of smoke rose slowly from the lawn and drifted over the trees. Americans began falling, amid shouts of simulated terror. The master of ceremonies announced, "These incredible foolhardy men, with great courage, with great love for their country, are holding on!" Moments later, the foolhardy men retreated, with first the Redcoats and then the spectators in hot pursuit. Everyone headed five blocks down Third Street, toward the Gowanus Canal, past families sitting on the stoops of their brownstones, past people selling stuff on their stoops, past a man begging some police officers to let him pull out of a parking spot so that he could get his family to the airport. At the Old Stone House, the reconstructed version of the Dutch farmhouse that was there in 1776, the Continental forces seemed to vanish mysteriously. I remember facing the Old Stone House and seeing John Gallagher, mustached and towering over the crowd, with a small party of reenactment organizers. Gallagher would die within the year, and he would be buried in Green-Wood Cemetery, on Battle Hill, near the statue of Minerva that looks out toward the Statue of Liberty. But I mostly remember that Gallagher was the very last person I saw step into the bar on the corner on that day, a very tall man.

It is easy to rewalk a surprise British troop maneuver in a city—unlike a Civil War battlefield covered over by a strip mall, city roads survive. Thus, I walked along the King's Highway, as it is still known, through neighborhoods called Gravesend, Midwood, Bensonhurst, the Flatlands, and Flatbush, entering Prospect Park from the south. I was with a philosopher, as it happened, a friend with a day job as an art mover; we had to get to the American lines in time for him to get to work. Near where the British commenced marching, we stopped briefly for bagels and coffee. We walked past shops opening up, an elevated subway, and felt a warm wind blow through the oak trees at a triangle named for Joyce Kilmer, a .001-acre park. A teenager ran for the bus, but the door closed, just missed. We crossed beneath an elevated subway line, which I recognized from the excellent car chase scene in the 1971 film *The French Connection*, as well as from early scenes in the 1977 film *Saturday Night Fever*, which, incidentally, opens with an overhead shot of the area in the East River that is where the American army eventually evacuated from Brooklyn.

When I looked north through a summer haze, up Coney Island Avenue, I saw that the bottom fifty floors of the Empire State Building were blocked by a flank of green tree-covered hill, still known on maps as Mount Prospect, marking the battle site in what is today called Prospect Park. From there we passed a monument to Greek American veterans outside the Three Hierarchs Greek Orthodox Church, a poster in Russian for math tutoring, and a poster for a missing pit bull, Gabby. As Kings Highway widened out, we passed a memorial to a Brooklyn marine who died in Iraq in 1991: "A field of broken rock, a battlefield . . ." And then, nearby, we saw a small square named in honor of a policeman, a veteran of World War I, who was killed during a holdup, in 1934. He was off duty and had captured two men, after being shot, and later dictated the police report to his wife, who had come to the scene and was at his side as he died. Mayor Fiorello La Guardia awarded him a posthumous medal of bravery. His name was John J. Fraser, and the city recently filled the square with tulip trees, eastern redbuds, brave pines.

WISDOM SITS IN PLACES

It is not difficult to discern that *something* had happened at the inter-section of Flatbush Avenue and Kings Highway, the site where some of the British army kept going straight and some of the army turned—you can tell it is an old junction, even standing in a gas station that sells plants and eggs, a gas station with a vaguely tropical feel. The philosopher I was with talked about the idea of places having about them a kind of wisdom, mentioning in particular Nietzsche, who saw a relationship between a physical view and a philosophic one. "I draw circles and sacred boundaries about me; fewer and fewer climb with me up higher and higher mountains," Nietzsche wrote. The philosopher talked about how Nietzsche maintains, too, that the body senses a place: "The *body* is spirited—let us leave the 'soul' out of play." And the philosopher recommended a book to me, *Wisdom Sits in Places*, which includes these words: "When places are actively sensed, the physical landscape becomes wedded to the landscape of the mind, to the roving imagination, and where the mind may lead is anybody's guess."

The philosopher was in his late twenties and Irish, as were many Revolutionary War soldiers. He had just come back to Brooklyn from Ireland, where his father had passed away. He talked about his father's farm, and the land there, describing it not as rich but as usable, with work, for grazing.

I was thinking about his father's passing, and then, of course, of my own father, who had lived in Brooklyn as a child before moving to what was then farmland in Queens, and, most recently, during this particular summer, to Connecticut, the land of his father. I was thinking about father-to-son communications, and at some point I asked the philosopher when he felt his father had come to understand what it was that the philosopher wanted to do with his life—be a philosopher, in other words. "I think when I wrote a book," he said. "I think that's when my father probably understood. It's when he said, 'Oh, I see! This is what you want to do.' I think the book really did it for him."

Near Brooklyn College, we split up. The philosopher had to get to his day job, a project that had to do with Gordon Matta-Clark, the artist who, among other things, coined the term "Anarchitecture"; I kept going up Flatbush Avenue. I picked up the pace in the area where, in 1776, the British trusted an innkeeper to help them find a path in the dark through the wooded Brooklyn hills. The area is now a Haitian neighborhood. As I stopped to take notes, a man coming out of a Haitian bakery mistook me for some kind of inspector.

"*Bonjour!*" he said to a woman going into the bakery. He looked at me. "You're insurance?"

"No."

"I saw the news this morning—last night, they had a big fire."

I told him I was retracing the path of the British army at the start of the Battle of Brooklyn. He implored me to tell him more, and I wanted to, of course, but I had some stuff to do later that morning and was racing now. Additionally, he would not believe there had been a giant Revolutionary War battle in Brooklyn.

"*You are kidding me!*" he said in a Haitian accent. I was suddenly thinking of Toussaint L'Ouverture, the leader of the Haitian revolution, in 1791: "I was born a slave, but nature gave me the soul of a free man."

Not being familiar with this Brooklyn neighborhood, I asked the man at the bakery how far I was from Prospect Park.

"You're close," he said.

PASS

On the anniversary of the Battle of Brooklyn, I signed up for an evening walk through battle sites with an archaeologist, and while I was prepared for one kind of a battle walk, being a veteran of park battle tours, I ended up with another kind entirely. The archaeologist, William J. Parry, a professor at Hunter College, gave us maps that described old routes, forests, swamps, hills, traces of which still survived in Prospect Park's 585 acres. He told us about a tremendous thunderstorm a few days before the 1776 attack. He walked us down a hill, against oncoming angry bikers and joggers: he either didn't notice their shouts and taunts or was fearless, or some combination. Down he went, through a split of rock into a wooded glen. He informed us that the Flatbush Avenue outside the park was an impostor; that the interior route was

the authentic Flatbush Avenue. Frederick Law Olmsted, when designing the park, had shifted soils and filled in swamps, and reconfigured
most everything, but this pass was one of the still intact places wherein
the Americans had been surprised by the British, and where General
John Sullivan had been captured. We walked up through the cut as if
we were attacking invisible Hessians. Myself, having walked through
the pass on a weekly and sometimes daily basis, I was not prepared for
any great revelation, that's for sure. I was feeling ready to be unfazed.

There are three historic markers at that location, each of which I
can just about recite by heart, each describing what is called Battle Pass
and noting the always-noted cutting of the Dongan Oak. The Dongan
Oak was a landmark chosen by Governor Thomas Dongan, an Irish
parliamentarian who was administrator of the colony of New York
from 1684 to 1688, to demark the boundary between the villages of
Flatbush and Brooklyn. In the hours prior to the Battle of Brooklyn,
the tree was cut by the rebels, to block a road with dense woods on one
side and a swamp on the other. After exploring the cut, the archaeologist took us up off the main park road to view Battle Pass from the adjacent overlook, only about twenty feet away from where I have walked
in the park maybe thousands of times. We looked down on the bikers
and runners, and I suddenly saw the route very differently: from this
new vantage, it was transformed from a ho-hum rise on a park road
into the perfect spot from which I could imagine firing a cannon down
on oncoming Hessian soldiers and having some success, before eventually being overrun. I could also imagine a large fallen tree being a
complete hassle for anyone oncoming, especially if they were carrying
heavy guns.

I wondered if other people on the tour had had a version of this
before-and-after reaction, and I looked around and saw that one couple had wandered off into the woods to be alone, and that a few other
people smiled at me as I smiled at them, though I couldn't tell if it was
because of a shared hill realization or because they, too, seemed to have
noticed the couple, who were by now making out.

We all traced the route of evacuation, enjoying the mercifully cool
dusk—it was a quiet, anonymous reenactment—and came at last to the
Old Stone House. The Old Stone House was a Dutch farmhouse that
was partially buried by road construction in the nineteenth century,
after reportedly being demolished in a Gatling gun demonstration. The

stones of the house were rediscovered by ditch diggers in 1933, and in 1934 it was reconstructed, using the original stones. The archaeologist gave us a short talk about the Old Stone House, and told the story about the regiment of Maryland soldiers who died defending the house. The Maryland regiment managed to hold back the British long enough for the rest of the Continental Army—ragged and ailing after their first official appearance as an army—to escape to Brooklyn Heights. The story goes like this: the British charged, the Marylanders fought, the Marylanders dispersed, the British charged, the Marylanders were decimated but stuck around, and in the end the British killed nearly all the Marylanders, as the retreating Americans got safely away, crossing the swamp in and around the Gowanus Creek, then holing up in the heights of Brooklyn. The archaeologist talked about the Marylanders being buried in an unmarked grave somewhere in the neighborhood.

Now it was dark and late, the long summer day of the battle over, a breeze hinting of summer's end, and the archaeologist led us inside for light refreshments, including beer, one of which I discharged. I wanted to ask the archaeologist a lot of questions about the battle, but I held back, because I quickly realized that everyone was trying to ask him a lot of questions. He was besieged. He looked around the room, his eyes darting, a little desperate. He looked at me, and I could see clearly the whites of his eyes.

"Where's the beer?" he asked.

THE EVACUATION

The Continental Army's evacuation of Brooklyn is in some ways an opposite of the crossing of the Delaware. When remembered, it is not as the beginning of a reversal of fortune so much as a capstone of the devastating American loss. It is a mad dash from the failed battle to another month of nearly game-ending defeats, and it is not the subject of an iconic painting but of a forgotten and fairly unremarkable stamp.[*]

---

[*]The evacuation is not recalled in the hearts of schoolchildren everywhere, either, though certainly it was impressive in some ways, gamely orchestrated, historians tell us, by the same crew of men from Marblehead, Massachusetts, who managed the logistics of the Delaware Crossing, which would occur four months after the Brooklyn

Yet if you spend a hot summer or a few years, or even a lifetime looking at the harbor, or if you go out in a kayak or a motorboat or a canoe, it becomes clear that the harbor does not afford a Delaware-like river crossing, not the least because the East River is technically not a river but a tidal strait. Despite historic markers that indicate the contrary, despite accounts that indicate a specific point of embarkation—"The ferry landing still exists today next to the elegant River Café at the base

---

evacuation. In the stories, there is a rebel-hiding fog, as well as rag-wrapped oarlocks. In the accounts, the winds first make things difficult, then help, blowing from Brooklyn toward Manhattan. At dawn, the British troops are shocked, then impressed, though not *that* impressed, given that they tortured their prisoners in America, as well as in their subsequent wars with colonial subordinates, such as in Ireland, where they were notoriously brutal, in 1798, against participants in the Irish uprising against colonial rule. Edmund Burke wrote: "Those who were best acquainted with the difficulty, embarrassment, noise and tumult, which attend even by day, and no enemy at hand, a movement of this nature with several thousand men, will be the first to acknowledge, that this retreat should hold a high place among military transactions." At they retreated, the weather calmed, the violent storms, still common to late summer in New York, backed off. From a memoir describing the Brooklyn evacuation: "Unluckily, too, about nine o'clock the adverse wind and tide and pouring rain began to make the navigation of the river difficult. . . . However, at eleven o'clock there was another and a favorable change in the weather. The north-east wind died away, and soon after a gentle breeze set in from the south-west, of which the sailors took quick advantage, and the passage was now direct, easy, and expeditious. The troops were pushed across as fast as possible in every variety of craft—row-boats, flat-boats, whale-boats, pettiaugers, sloops, and sail-boats—some of which were loaded to within three Inches of the water, which was 'as smooth as glass.'" It was then, as now, a time of year for violent storms. "Lightning strikes Gen. McDougall's Camp, 'near the Bull's Head in the Bowry,' and instantly kills Capt. Van Wyck and his two lieutenants, Versereau and Depyster," reported the *Connecticut Gazette* at the time of the Battle of Brooklyn. The last time a tornado came to Brooklyn in a late summer storm, in 2010—with hail and eighty-mile-an-hour, tree-destroying winds, and torrential rain that linked the streets and subway tunnels to the old creeks and buried streams—I noticed that the tornado followed paths identical to those of the British and American armies during the Battle of Brooklyn, the strategic routes along the slopes of a neighborhood now known as Park Slope. There were tremendous winds coming off the harbor, rattling our windows—I thought they would break—and the next day, after the car-denting hail, when I walked up to the park (a.k.a. the former battlefield), I saw huge old oaks and sycamores down, getting chainsawed. People walked mournfully among the ruins of the groves, a great sadness in the air. It really did feel like a war zone.

of the Brooklyn Bridge," a recent New York history notes, and a plaque marks the spot—there is no logic to this often-made historical point. In crossing the river they weren't following a line from here to there, but entering into the chaos of the harbor, putting their trust in pools and eddies rather than challenging a one-way stream. Like history itself, the evacuation was a mess, a semi-organized chaos.

I had this idea confirmed for me late one summer when I was poking around along the edge of the Hudson and, on Pier 40, walked into the Village Community Boathouse. There was a lot of boatbuilding going on in the boathouse—people working on large rowboats, twenty-seven-foot-long plywood-and-epoxy replicas of nineteenth-century Whitehalls—and I began asking questions about the evacuation of Brooklyn, happy to find someone who had thought about it.

"It wouldn't have been straight across," said Rob Buchanan, who marched to a nautical chart of the harbor, using it to illustrate his point. "It would have been more like this . . ." He proceeded to draw many lines across the tidal straight from Brooklyn, and I was able to imagine large boats rowing across and smaller boats floating across, many semi-aimlessly, going up the tidal strait and landing perhaps in the Manhattan swamp named for Gerardus Beekman, a merchant who arrived in New Amsterdam in 1647. And as the tide went out I could see a boat ending up near Wall Street. I could even imagine, if the rivers and tides were so inclined, men in boats or without them being swept around the tip of Manhattan and off toward the swamps of Jersey.

"I mean, they would have used everything that floated," Rob said.

I recalled a remembrance by an officer under Washington, Colonel John Lamb, that included a litany of East River points: "Col. Hughes received by Joseph Trumbull, the Commissary General, a verbal order from Gen. Washington, to impress every kind of water craft from Hellgate on the Sound, to Speyghten Duyvel Creek, that could be kept afloat, and that had either sails or oars, and have them all in the east harbor of the city by dark."

Rob began to walk across the boathouse. "I also don't think there was any one point of embarkation," he said. "And the books say they wrapped their oars," he went on. "Well, what does that mean? So look . . ."

He took apart the metal oarlock on a Whitehall gig, a descendant of the boats that General John Glover of Marblehead would have pulled together for the evacuation. Wrapped, the oarlock was silent when engaged. Rob also handed me a notepad-sized piece of plastic with a spinning disk in the middle, a wheel that calculated the tides of the harbor. It was a New York Harbor Tide Wheel. On its back, I found the following:

> In most places in the world, tidal currents flood (come in) until high tide and then ebb (go out) until low tide. Not so in New York Harbor. Depending on the location, the average tidal current lag—the gap between high or low water and the beginning of the flood or ebb—can be as much as two hours and 45 minutes.

The Tide Wheel is the invention of a boatbuilder named Don Betts, who, with a naval architect named Mike McEvoy and a boater named Mike Davis, founded Floating the Apple, a boating group based at Pier 84 on the Hudson River. Davis was a general in the fight to reestablish, for people who live in and around the harbor, what he referred to, over and over until his death in 2008, as "universal public access."

When Mike Davis died, Rob explained his legacy in a note to a kayaking group. "One of the greatest—and, occasionally, most maddening—things about Mike was how stubbornly he pursued his agenda," he wrote. He continued:

> His belief that there could be no compromise when it came to the right of the public to the waterways and the foreshore was a huge inspiration to many of us, and key to the development of recreational boating in the harbor. It also sometimes made him difficult to work with, to put it mildly. But the fact remains that without his clear vision and unwavering advocacy, there's just no way we'd be where we are today.

THE PEOPLE'S RIVER

It was only by leaving America and returning that Mike Davis realized that New York Harbor was off-limits. Born in Baltimore, the son of a Coast Guard captain, Davis studied archaeology in Oklahoma, later working for years with University of Chicago archaeological teams in Turkey. In Istanbul, he became enamored with the small boats he saw sailing on Bosphorus. He convinced mosque guards and fishermen to loan him their rowing boats so he could row across to Asia. "Anyone can rent a boat and row on the Bosporus," Davis would say after moving to New York. "That's the way it should be on the Hudson." He used to tell people that as late as 1933 there were forty-one boathouses in Manhattan. "While now there is just one." Also, there are—or were—no boats. In 1994, Davis founded Floating the Apple, in hopes of seeding other community boating groups. Floating the Apple decided they needed a Whitehall, a species of old boat native to the harbor. Because the only available Whitehall was for sale in England, for twenty-two thousand dollars, they decided to build one. They worked with school groups in donated space just off Times Square. Kids from well-to-do private schools built one, as did kids from schools in tough neighborhoods, as did kids with mental health issues. People off the street volunteered to work on the gigs, as well as foreign tourists and homeless men.

"Being as this island of Manhattan is surrounded by water," recalled Lewis Norris, a boatbuilder who worked with Davis, "it was a shame that the local residents, the kids in particular, didn't have any access to it. So we *made* access."

They had their first boat on the water within a few months, and the fleet grew, rowers volunteering, rowers enticed by seeing other rowers enjoying the water. Next came the Village Community Boathouse, where I had stopped in, as well as the East River Crew, on East Ninety-sixth Street in Manhattan, and WeeRow, across the Hudson, in Weehawken, New Jersey. A Davis apprentice helped start a community group called Rocking the Boat, based in the South Bronx. Over the course of a few years, the harbor went from being a place no one went to a place that Floating the Apple reminded people was New York City's largest public space.

"Mike had this idea that if you really want to get in touch with what's happening, then get in touch with the river," Rob said.

They put the first Whitehall on wheels and carted it across town. By the end of the 1990s, boats were no longer an anomaly in the harbor—a quiet sea change, as well as a return, in a way, to an older time, it was a transformation of the harbor that was as radical as it was unnoticed. "People don't ask us, 'Isn't the water polluted? Isn't it dangerous? Aren't there sea monsters out there?'" Davis told a reporter in 1998. "We just don't get those sorts of questions anymore."*

Something that I eventually learned about Mike Davis when I visited one of the community boathouses was that most years he would get a bunch of people in a Whitehall and stage his own personal reenactment of the evacuation of Brooklyn.

I asked Rob Buchanan if he would consider reenacting one of Mike Davis's evacuations—there had not been a Floating the Apple reenactment of the evacuation of Brooklyn since Davis's death. Rob was interested. Coincidentally, the people who organize the regular reenactment of the Battle of Brooklyn at Green-Wood Cemetery had called Rob to ask if his group might help organize a reenactment of the retreat from Brooklyn by water—normally the Green-Wood Cemetery reenactors eschew the water portion of the defeat. Checking the calendar and the tide charts, Rob saw an opportunity, a Sunday that was the actual anniversary of the actual evacuation on which everything aligned, from the Village Community Boathouse permit to offer public boating on that day

---

*A triumph for harbor craft was the September 2001 evacuation of the World Trade Center area by small boat. It has been described as the largest sea evacuation since Dunkirk; between three hundred thousand and a million people are estimated to have been carried to safety. The fleet of ships was a collection of tugboats, ferries, excursion boats, buoy tenders, fireboats, patrol boats, and yachts. Researchers from the University of North Texas and the University of Delaware called it an "unorganized evacuation." It was begun when the Coast Guard requested that anyone with a vessel in the area head to the shore of lower Manhattan, issuing no further directive. "By any criteria, the evacuation, one of the largest ever in American history, was an extremely successful endeavor," the researchers wrote. "There appear to have been no fatalities or casualties in the operation; no vessel was involved in any accident. In the course of about six–seven hours, according to the Coast Guard, perhaps up to 500,000 persons were moved." The researchers noted that previous studies of evacuations during disasters and other crises have shown that "much of the organized behavior is emergent rather than traditional." The report continues: "In addition, it is of a very decentralized nature, with the dominance of pluralistic decision making, and the appearance of imaginative and innovative new attempts to cope with the contingencies that typically appear in major disasters. Fortunately on 9/11 no attempts were made to impose a command and control model . . . on the evacuation by water transport from lower Manhattan."

to good tidal conditions. He agreed. Then the reenactors called back to ask if the reenactment of the crossing could happen on another day. The new date did not align with the tides, which was frustrating to Rob, to say the least. "They don't get it," he said. "You can't change the river."

For our own Mike Davis memorial reenactment, we made a plan that consisted of Rob getting a boat and some of the people who had previously evacuated with Mike, and then giving me a call. A couple of days before we evacuated Brooklyn, Rob sent me an e-mail to say that crossing from shore to shore was a murky legal issue.

"There is a real political undercurrent here because the politics of it is we're not supposed to land on the Manhattan side," he said. "I mean, they want us to get a permit to land—and that would require us getting some white-shoe lawyer that we really can't get. So this is really part of a larger thing—something revolutionary—and it's about people's rights to the people's river."

A GOOD LEADER

"For this to be a Mike Davis evacuation," Rob Buchanan said, "you need to have a ranger on this side saying, 'Don't do this—you can't do this!' And then you need to have cops on the other side saying, 'If you try to land, your trip will be terminated.'"

I asked Rob about the last time that happened.

"Mike said a few things to the cops—but then he urged the rest of us to stand down, which we did."

It was a perfect day for a reenactment of a Mike Davis reenactment, a clear and noble sky, a flood tide beginning to slack—ideal for evacuation. Aside from being the anniversary of the evacuation by the Continental Army, the Brooklyn-based contingent of the Village Community Boathouse (VCB) was winding up its free kayaking session on the beach beneath the Brooklyn Bridge. People who looked as if they had never been on the water before were paddling, happy, buffeted by the chop, laughing as the small oncoming waves slapped them playfully. We were standing on the shore, in a little cove between the Brooklyn and Manhattan Bridges. It was a sandy beach, though Rob informed me that it had been relandscaped, and so, in some sense, it was not the original sandy beach. Rob collects information on beaches in New

York City. A sandy beach is defined by Rob as an original beach, a beach that has never been paved or covered with concrete, or made into a cement pier—an original shore. A sandy beach might also be a beach that has naturally accreted. "Largely unknown to the public, and frequently uncharted, these beaches are tangible reminders of the thriving estuary and public space that the harbor used to be—and could be again," Rob has written.

The Manhattan beach we planned on landing at—as Mike Davis had done previously—is considered the only natural sandy beach near the foot of the Brooklyn Bridge, right about where an old swamp would have been in the time of the Revolution. Everything else on the shore is bulkhead or pier.

Suddenly, a high-speed ferry raced by, too close to the cove. A wake hit the shore, the boaters more thrilled than concerned. Rob frowned. "What is that guy thinking?" Rob said.

A Hasidic family, a mother with three children, approached Rob; they were carrying a small inflatable canoe.

"Excuse me, where could we put our boat in?" the mother asked. "We are used to floating down the Delaware."

"I wouldn't advise you to put in here," Rob said. He recommended they try instead Valentino Pier in Red Hook, a relatively gentle spot. The mother borrowed my pen to write down directions.

As the paddlers left, a small crew of us got into the beautiful banana-shaped Whitehall—its exterior was painted black, gunwales a varnished black, and at the stern a small American flag.

Emily was the coxswain. Emily is a teacher and a former crew member of the *Pioneer*, an 1855 schooner that has sailed for years out of the South Street Seaport Museum. "She's kind of piratical," Rob said. Nadia, a student of Rob's who had heard Mike Davis speak at a lecture in Rob's class, was along for the ride. A Frenchman named Étienne was assisting with photographs, and he had a nice camera, a Canon.

I had invited Duke Riley to come along, having cleared the invitation with Rob. Duke had e-mailed me. "Definitely count me in," he said.

"Duke is always welcome on board any VCB vessel!" Rob e-mailed me. As we boarded, Rob said, "Duke totally understands where we are coming from."

Sally, a longtime Floating the Apple member, was rowing, along with Duke, a guy named René, and me. Rob took control of the yoke-lines, to steer.

We pushed off. As Emily called the strokes, the boat cut easily through the waves. We quickly left the cove and were out in the open harbor in seconds—away from Brooklyn—*evacuated!* We were beneath bridges and in between islands of New York, in, from my perspective, a turbulent blue paroxysm of ocean and river forces, though entirely navigable, thanks to the current-slicing abilities of the replica Whitehall. Indeed, the Whitehall seemed oblivious to water rushing out of the East River, which, in turn, seemed oblivious to us. The cove had one kind of current, a slight counterclockwise swirl, and then out in the open water the tide was heading out of the harbor as fast as it could. Away to Liberty Island! Off to Governors Island, called Noten Eylant (meaning Island of Nuts) by the seventeenth-century Dutch sailor Adrien Block. "You can see the tide's still moving pretty hard," Rob said.

Looking out across the water, into the open bay, I could just discern a soft enveloping haze, a white but nearly invisible mist, as opposed to the fog the history books recalled. It served to heighten the details and refract the harbor's sparkling, so that I felt as if I were inside a luminist painting.

"This is cool," said Duke.

At one point, a small powerboat began to circle our craft. The powerboat was crewed by bare-chested men and bikini-clad women, all armed with drinks in cans, protected by can-covering thermal insulation devices. With a wide, boring arc, the boat drew a ring of white around us, but we rowed on. At another point, Étienne's camera was knocked out of the boat, so that we realized we had lost a Canon. Other than that, we proceeded without incident, and we eventually pulled up safe on the beach in Manhattan—no police or Coast Guard boats stopped us. Upon landing, the water was clear; you could easily see a submerged shopping cart. People leaned over the fence at the level of South Street to chat with us as we dragged the boat up. As we looked back on the harbor, there was a shared feeling of reenactment triumph.

Standing on the sandy beach in Manhattan, Sally recalled a

reenactment with Mike Davis that ended up at this spot, in a foul version of this same water. "I mean, we were on the beach," she remembered, "and we were going to go swimming, but the water was really nasty, like a rancid oil. And, I mean, I don't hesitate to go in the water around here. My little grandson goes in all the time." She went on about Mike, the water lapping at her ankles. "He had this air of boyish enthusiasm," she said. "He could get people excited about whatever he was excited about. His joy was infectious—like Tom Sawyer and the fence. He could always get a team together."

I could see that René wanted to tell me about Mike, too. I couldn't figure out how René fit in; he wasn't talking a lot, and he didn't socialize with the others in the same way. I got the feeling that he was a guy who liked to hang out at the boathouse, another person who just showed up. Now he was standing close to me, seeming anxious, until I realized he wanted to talk about Mike Davis. "I heard about him," René said finally. "I wasn't there. But I was at the boathouse the day he died. There was a poster. It said, 'Dear Mike, We miss you. Bye.'"

AUTUMN

❧ ❧

THE SEASONS add their perspective to the Revolution, and as summer inevitably turns to fall, autumn offers a view of what came after the battles, after the retreats and evacuations, after the soldiers who survived the war returned home—after histories were published, over and over again, remembering and eventually forgetting. Of course, what happened after the battles was that men died, some on the battlefield, though mostly as prisoners, while sitting on ships in the harbor. A part of the harbor that was, as a result, considered a Revolutionary War graveyard long after the war is an inlet in the East River, on the Brooklyn side, called Wallabout Bay. It is a deep, marsh-edged cove fed by a stream that is today a large sewer pipe.

It is estimated that as many as 8,000 American soldiers died in battle over the course of the entire Revolutionary War and that as many as 11,500 prisoners died on what came to be known as the "prison ships." The conditions were described as barbarous. Prisoners who survived recalled meals served from a large green-encrusted copper pot: worm-filled bread, sour oatmeal, and beef that came apart in strings described by one prisoner as "a rope-like yarn." One prisoner held aboard a ship called the *Huntress* recalled eating "the heads of sheep . . . the horns and wool thereon." Some prisoners cooked food with firewood smuggled aboard; women came to bring food to the ships. Officers sold their clothes to pay for fruit; sailors were covered in "rags and filth." When their British captors threw a bag of apples in the hold, inmates fought over it. Prisoners ate vermin and died of camp fever, dysentery, yellow fever, and smallpox. People living in Brooklyn during the war remembered the prison ships' stench wafting toward them, dead prisoners stacked on the deck. When enough bodies collected, they were carried to shore, often buried in trenches the Americans had dug for defensive purposes, sometimes buried on the beach. "They dragged them out of their prisons by one leg or by one arm," wrote a witness.

A few of the prisoners got off—officers, mostly. Most of those who did subsequently died, emaciated skeletons, happy, by most accounts, not to be buried in a mass grave in Brooklyn, a great fear. The poet Philip Freneau escaped and wrote a poem:

> Shut from the blessings of the evening air
> Pensive we lay with mingled corpses there,
> Meagre and wan, and scorch'd with heat, below,
> We look'd like ghosts, ere death had made us so—

The prisoners included foreign sailors, privateers, and civilians; there were French prisoners, and possibly Spanish and Dutch sailors. In the winter of 1779, an escaped prisoner ran across the frozen river but died from exposure before he reached the shore. George Washington and Congress protested the treatment of the soldiers, to no avail.

PRISON SHIP MARTYRS

After the war, the prisoners were referred to as "the prison ship dead" or "the prison ship martyrs." The largest prison ship was the *Jersey*, a retired sixty-four-gun man-of-war in which seven thousand people may have died. Sometimes the bones that surfaced on the shore, bleached white in the sun, were referred to as "the *Jersey* dead." The *Jersey* was left to decay, sunk eventually by the borings of small sea creatures. In the 1780s and '90s, people continued to note the presence of bones. In 1785, Congress asked Henry Knox, the secretary of war, to see that the bones of "those virtuous citizens . . . be buried together in the nearest public burial ground." Nothing happened. Brooklyn was still remote in relationship to Manhattan, and the bones remained untouched, a macabre decoration on a distant shore, often spotted by passengers on the ferries to and from Brooklyn. A plan in 1792 to reinter the bones on the shoreline of Wallabout Bay was denied by the property owner, John Jackson. In 1794, in lieu of reinterment, the anonymous author of an essay (he signed himself "A Lover to His Country") suggested that a monument be erected "to stand as a memorial which those heroes rendered their country; and transmit to posterity a sense of the virtue and merits of their ancestors, that thus they may know the value of liberty, and view with abhorrence, the schemes of tyranny and arbitrary power."

In 1800, a merchant in Providence, Rhode Island, gave a speech that was reprinted around the country, praising the "defenceless prisoners" buried in "the unconsecrated bank." He proposed that their remains be collected in a "vast ossory," or ossuary. In New York, the Tammany Society took up the case. The Tammany Society had been started in the 1780s as a group of artisans, shopkeepers, and merchants, Republicans and Federalists. The thirteen sachems, or lodge leaders, met in their Grand Wigwam, dressed like Native Americans, in honor of Tammany, a Lenni-Lenape chief of the Delaware Valley. It was a democratic club; at the time, dressing like Native Americans meant that social ranks temporarily disappeared. Washington, as president, condemned democratic societies, and the Federalists withdrew from Tammany, turning it into a Republicans-only association.

Thus, the fortune of the nameless prison dead became a political issue at a time when the United States was on the verge of another war with England. In terms of politics, it was the Federalist Anglophiles versus the Republican Francophiles; in terms of Founding Fathers, it was Alexander Hamilton versus Thomas Jefferson; in terms of the election, it was John Adams versus Thomas Jefferson; and in terms of war memorials, it was wealthy New Yorkers who paid one hundred dollars a person to finance a statue of George Washington that eventually ended up on Wall Street versus the artisans and small shopkeepers who argued that it was disgraceful to erect a statue of Washington and forget the prison ship martyrs. "To erect a monument to their chief, before they have a common grave, you would deservedly draw on yourselves a reproach never to be wiped away," said a writer in the *American Citizen.*

---

*Like the bones of the prisoners, Evacuation Day—a holiday that for decades was celebrated every November 25, to remember the day in 1783 when the British left New

In 1801, when John Jackson sold part of his property to the U.S. government for the purpose of building what would become the

---

York—took on different meanings for different New Yorkers. In 1783, Washington
marched down Broadway to the Cape Tavern, where toasting began, and continued,
liberty poles going up throughout the city, while numerous thirteen-gun salutes were
fired off. Newspapers marveled at New York's orderliness, with a British officer
quoted in the *New York Packet*: "These Americans . . . are a curious people. They
know how to govern themselves, but nobody else can govern them." Initially, New
Yorkers used the term "evacuation" in reference to the occasion when the Continental
Army escaped from Brooklyn to Manhattan in 1776; indeed, this new November
Evacuation Day was not called anything. But over time, people were satisfied that the
war was over, and they forgot the first evacuation. The first celebrations following 1783
were dinners for the elite, which the *New-York Journal* likened to "the old British
conviviality," an embarrassment, the *Journal* said, for a republic. In 1787, the Federalists used Evacuation Day as part of their campaign to ratify the Constitution and root
for a strong federal government; the celebration included troop maneuvers and parades, in addition to the invitation-only balls. The organizers were, ironically, at pains
to pad the federal troops, the army consisting of only 672 men at the time—they
brought in about 1,300 men from local militias. In 1791, Republicans began counter-
celebrations, ridiculing standing armies, privilege, monarchy, and governmental oppression. By 1801, the day had become merely a big celebration, with parades, family
dinners, and popular entertainments—e.g., cycloramas and illuminated transparen-
cies depicting Revolutionary War battle scenes. People who had lived through the
war were rapidly passing away in the 1820s. The holiday lost spirit, though the parade
remained, and a relative of John Van Arsdale—a sailor who had climbed a flagpole on
the Battery in 1783 (after the British greased it) to raise an American flag—repeated
the flag raising through the 1950s. The evacuation's one hundredth anniversary was
called "one of the great civic events of the Nineteenth Century in New York City," and,
in the early 1900s, New York's large number of Irish immigrants supported Evacuation Day enthusiastically, as it evoked their own resentment against the British. But
by the 1920s, after the United States had teamed up with Britain during World War I,
just a few patrician groups in New York remembered. Slowly, the day had transformed into another parade-oriented holiday, partly because President Washington,
while living in New York, had made Evacuation Day a day of national prayer, or
Thanksgiving. "A variant of Thanksgiving became a haven for working-class New
Yorkers repelled by Evacuation Day's nativism and elitism," wrote the historian Clifton Hood in a discussion of Evacuation Day in the *Journal of Social History*. Hood
cites a radical strain of Thanksgiving practices that existed before the New England
Pilgrims' Thanksgiving took over Thanksgiving celebrations around the nation. This
proto-Thanksgiving came out of Protestant and Catholic churches, and, Hood writes,
"critiqued American capitalism by reinterpreting its themes of a bountiful harvest
and gift exchange as an argument for the redistributing of wealth and power."

Brooklyn Navy Yard, more bones were uncovered—"skulls and feets, armes and legs, sticking out of the crumbling bank in the wildest disorder." The Tammany Society petitioned Congress for a monument, as Congress debated monuments to Revolutionary War generals. The petition was denied, while storms continued to wash up still more bones, but public opinion was shifting, especially since, after the British evacuated, Revolutionary War soldiers were viewed skeptically, their pensions frequently denied. But Tammany's efforts to memorialize the martyrs were mostly a political maneuver. The society began to take up the cause of sailors in an effort to inflame anti-British and anti-Federalist sentiment. Thus, Tammany took it upon itself to memorialize the prison ship martyrs. Benjamin Aycrigg, a Tammany member, got hold of twenty hogsheads of skeletal remains collected by the Navy Yard.

On April, 13, 1808, two thousand sailors and workers marched to a makeshift interment site on John Jackson's land. On May 26, after a rain delay, a Tammany procession began at City Hall Park in Manhattan, processing down Broadway and Wall Street, to the thirteen ferry boats that took the marchers to Brooklyn, carrying thirteen coffins filled with bones. They processed to the edge of Wallabout Bay, on the hill. They carried a flag said to have been flown in 1783, on the day the British evacuated New York. They carried banners. "Americans! Remember the British!" said one. "Sires of Columbia! Transmit to prosperity the cruelties practiced on board the British prison ships." Another said: "Tyrants dread the gathering storm." There were prayers and eulogies, one speaker demanding that the *Jersey* dead warranted a tomb just as any wealthy person did. "Here shall the brave sufferers in the British Prison Ships receive the just tribute of everlasting fame to their memory," he said.

After this burst of attention to the martyrs, however, they began to fade away again. After the War of 1812, anti-British sentiments declined; the alliance between Tammany and dead sailors weakened. By the mid-1800s, the neighborhood where the dead were interred became crowded with new residents—homeowners who regarded the bones as "undesirable neighbours." The vaults were blamed for impure air, for the miasmas that were thought to spread disease. In 1873, the remains were moved to the old Fort Greene, the Revolutionary War stronghold once called Fort Putnam. Writing in the *Brooklyn Daily Eagle*, Walt Whitman editorialized for a memorial. "The writer of these lines has been told by old citizens that nothing was more common in their early days than to see thereabout plenty of the skulls and other bones of these dead—and that thoughtless boys would kick them about in play," he lamented. "Many of the martyrs were so insecurely buried that the sand, being blown *off* by the wind, exposed their bleached skeletons in great numbers."

Finally, in 1908, President-elect William Howard Taft dedicated the Martyrs Monument. People stood in a cold autumn rain, looking up at a 198-foot-tall tower designed by the eminent architect Stanford White. A descendant of a prison ship martyr carried a banner from the 1808 Tammany procession. Shortly after World War II, the monument again fell into neglect.

WHAT IS HAPPENING?

For the past couple of decades, the prison ship dead have been remembered at an annual ceremony on top of the hill that is Brooklyn's Fort Greene Park. It is generally small and sparsely attended. I showed up at one not too long ago. As I approached, I could see the Martyrs Monument from almost a mile away, towering over downtown Brooklyn and the East River, a column on a hill. I was a little late, and I raced up the marble stairs, out of breath at the top, near the stone eagles that guard the monument. It was a clear day; through the trees I could see lower Manhattan. The master of ceremonies was Mark Spinner, the president of a car wash equipment manufacturing company founded by his father. Spinner wore a suit and tie and a Yankees cap. He stood at the base of the memorial column, a small group of speakers alongside the podium. Spinner had recently taken over the emcee position, since his father had passed away a few years before. "Your father would be proud," several older people said to him that day. As was his father, Spinner is an officer of the Society of Old Brooklynites, which sponsored the ceremony, and he used much of his time at the podium to encourage people to become members of the society. "I appreciate your presence here," he said. "Join. We have wonderful meetings."

To start the memorial, a brother from nearby St. Francis College offered a benediction—"a moment of graceful retreat"—and a woman sang the national anthem. Spinner then turned to his prepared text, saying, "Last year I don't think I had to wear these glasses." The cere-mony included local politicians and historians. Spinner addressed the martyrs as well, and their dead commanders, as if they were all pres-ent. "We ask that any commanders who are holding prisoners realize that they deserve a little sunshine as we are having today," Spinner said, for instance. The centerpiece of the service came when a boat-swain's whistle was used to muster the prison dead to the decks of the prison ships. For many years, the whistling was done by a former chief boatswain in the Merchant Marine, Bernie Flado, who piped out the signals. Since Flado, too, had recently died, Spinner played a recording of a boatswain's whistle. After the whistle, Spinner addressed the as-sembled prison ship martyrs; if you had just arrived, and had never been to the ceremony before, you might have wondered who Spinner was talking to. "We know the hardships," he said to the martyrs. "As I call the names of the ship, I want you to muster," he said. "Since you are all assembled, I will ask you to rise to attention." At that point, a recording of a trumpet playing taps. The dozen people in attendance stood quietly.

A state representative got up. "Although the battle between America and Britain seems faint, the battle resounds," he said. He made a point about the inhumane treatment of prisoners. "We still have the privi-lege of living in the greatest city in the greatest state in the greatest country in the world," he said in closing.

Spinner returned to the podium, taking the politician's point about the forgotten aspect of the Battle of Brooklyn. "He's right," Spinner said. "It's not in the history books. I never learned about it in school. That's probably because we lost." As he introduced the next speaker, he made another pitch for new members. "Join," he said. "Our next meet-ing is the first of the month in Surrogate Court, and it's a ten-dollar donation. Sherman? What's our yearly dues now?"

Sherman shouted something.

"Yeah, ten dollars," Spinner said. The next speaker was Wilhelmina Rhodes Kelly, a Brooklyn historian. "I have to confess, I haven't read your book—I'm gonna look for it," Spinner said as she came to the podium.

"It's hard to picture the landscape," Rhodes Kelly started out by saying. She described the hills in the area, and gave their position in the contemporary panorama. She described American troops on flat-boats, and recounted eyewitness reports of the men and armaments

in the harbor "glittering in the sunlight." She described the British putting their boats in Newtown Creek, as well as a British presence in
Queens, evidence that she herself had only recently stumbled on, after
fifteen years in the borough. "I had passed it so many times and had not
realized that the British were in Queens," she said. "It was mandatory
to tip your hat to British soldiers and stand with eyes lowered when
talking," she said.

"Evidence of committed remembrance by the general public seems
to be waning," she went on. She offered as an example an old road called
Red Hook Lane, the route thought to have been taken by the Continental Army to escape from the battle into Brooklyn Heights. "It now only
exists as a one-block fragment off the roadway," she said. "The road has
been demapped." It was a sharp, passionate speech. "What is happening?" she asked.

SPEAKING ON BEHALF

Spinner returned to the microphone. "Very informative," he said. "It's
interesting that everywhere there are countless little shrines that people don't know about—spread the word!"

The congressman representing the Fort Greene neighborhood,
Edolphus Towns, got up. He had just returned from a visit to Afghanistan with a congressional delegation. "I came today to say thank you."
He quoted Martin Luther King, Jr.: "I cannot be what I ought to be
until the world is what it should be." He continued, "Thank you, Society
of Old Brooklynites, for helping us be what we should be." There was
applause as he waved and left the stage, at which point Spinner stopped
him. "Are you a member of the Old Brooklynites?

"I will be Monday," the congressman said.

Following a brief interpretive dance, a few more speakers made remarks, including a member of the Fort Greene Park Conservancy, who
said that while growing up in Ohio he had never heard of the Battle of
Brooklyn. When the World Trade Center towers were destroyed, people who lived near Fort Greene came to the martyrs' memorial to watch
the buildings burn. "On 9/11 it all started to snow on you, with ash and
paper," he said.

Ron Schweiger, Brooklyn's official historian, talked about how he never imagined he would be Brooklyn's official historian, given that he was a high school science teacher who merely jotted down dates from history on the blackboard.

During these speeches, a slight breeze came up, and leaves from the nearby London plane trees began to fall.

While these speakers were at the podium, a woman who appeared to be a member of the Daughters of the American Revolution—she was adjusting the DAR flag and wearing DAR paraphernalia—was moving around and talking to Spinner, as well as to an older man who needed assistance walking and who appeared to be a Korean War veteran.

When Spinner came back to the microphone, he did not mention any other speakers. "I have an announcement to make," he said. "Congressman Towns did become a member of the Society of Old Brooklynites. There was a brief transaction, and he had to go."

It appeared as if the ceremony was over. Spinner seemed to be making his closing remarks and final appeals for new members. But the woman from the DAR was now working frantically to bring the veteran to the microphone, helping him to stand. It seemed to be a whether-Spinner-wanted-it-or-not situation, a usurpation of the agenda; there were no other speakers noted on the program. The veteran was introduced as Ed Carter. I later learned that Carter, seventy-three, was a longtime community activist in the neighborhood. After returning from military service in Korea, he founded and cofounded many organizations for senior citizens, young people, and veterans, and he was a member of the Black Cowboys. Carter would die the winter after the memorial service I attended, and Letitia James, the city councilwoman representing Fort Greene, would write a remembrance: "He was a social justice legend, royalty throughout Brooklyn, and could be a royal pain sometimes—another reason why he's so dearly loved."

Carter began his remarks tentatively. "We know little things about George Washington," he said. "George Washington slept here or there." He did not appear to be reading from prepared remarks. "My mentor was Willie Jones, and did they die in vain in Vietnam?"

Carter paused and looked around. The woman with the DAR was nearby, smiling, as he spoke haltingly, with great emotion.

"The eleven thousand, five hundred bodies buried here are people," he went on. "I was on the Brooklyn Bicentennial Committee. We were the ones that fought at the time to bring back this park. We were the ones who brought the eagles back. They had ended up as a hat rack in some commissioner's office."

He gestured toward the four eagles on the edges of the hilltop pavilion. "People didn't come into this park then," he said. "Winos knew more about this park than anybody. Little is told about the other bones that are floating around. We know the history. All of the bones that they threw over the sides of the boats that are still showing up."

There was some commotion among Spinner and the panelists; the woman in the DAR uniform was involved. Carter started up again, undaunted.

"They're only gonna give me five minutes," he said. "They gave all these other people time, and they gonna give me five minutes, like I'm a preacher. I'm not a preacher. I'm an organizer. Willie Jones and me—we felt blacks were going to be written out of the history . . ."

He was urged to continue. "Well, Americans who fought in the Revolution were black," he said. "We want to get this out to the kids, to let 'em know we are all Americans—and that we are all working for the betterment of humanity." He looked around the park, as if he were remembering things. "The winos, the junkies, the people—they said, 'Yeah man, many people gave their lives.'"

There was more commotion on the dais.

"Okay, they are cutting me off now," Carter said. "But the little people—they need to know. I'm speaking on behalf of many of the veterans who died in Vietnam or Korea. Bones are still washing up on the shores of Wallabout Bay, and in the Navy Yard. Spike Lee—they should have him make a movie about the soldier who was a spy with a black girlfriend. She was a spy for him, and they captured her. They put her on a ship, the *Jersey*, and two ladies took her baby, two black ladies. Two women who were feeding the Hessians and the prisoners, they took the child, raised the child . . ." He was given another signal. "Okay," he said, "that's all."

REESTABLISH

Of the forts erected during the Revolutionary War, some were quickly destroyed, some survived, reactivated for the War of 1812. When they were built, they were often diamond-shaped works, circled by pikes, prominent on the horizon. Forts dotted lower Manhattan, as did barricades, sometimes made with precious mahogany logs taken from the cargoes of the British West India Company, then laid across streets and at ferry landings. There were forts named for hills (Bayard's Hill Redoubt), for colonies (Jersey Barrier), and even for reefs, such as the Oyster Battery, in lower Manhattan. In Brooklyn, Fort Greene was the last at the end of a long line of forts that stretched from the high ground over Wallabout Creek to the marshes at Red Hook. In terms of nineteenth-century landmarks, it belonged to a line that comprised, according to a historian, "a chain of works thrown up across the neck from Wallabout Bay to the Gowanus Marsh." In terms of contemporary landmarks, the chain ran along a line from the giant electric power plant in what is today called Vinegar Hill to the IKEA store in what is still called Red Hook. There was Fort Box in the neighborhood today called Boerum Hill and Fort Sterling in Brooklyn Heights, looking over the East River to Manhattan. There was a fort that was once referred to as Fort Swift; in 1885, the *Brooklyn Daily Eagle* reported that bones had been discovered there, and that it was also the site of an old stable owned by Ephrain Snedeker, which was adjacent to a bar that the *Eagle* described as "the rendezvous of many old Brooklynites with sporting proclivities." (It was along what is today called Smith Street.)

"The place," the *Eagle* said, "did not enjoy the best of reputations among the respectable people of the vicinity."

Cobble Hill Fort was built on a cone-shaped hill, on a prominence overlooking the harbor and New Jersey, today the intersection of Atlantic Avenue and Court Street. Like the others, Cobble Hill Fort was stocked with freshwater and food from the local Dutch farms. Because of the commanding view of the British fleet to the southwest, Cobble Hill was a signal point, the fort from which two shots were to be fired to indicate that the British troops had landed. Cobble Hill was taken down by the British immediately following the Battle of Brooklyn. They used Hessian troops, as well as American prisoners, to excavate the hills. In 1878, Henry P. Johnston published a history of the Revolution in New

York bearing the long title *The Campaign of 1776 Around New York and Brooklyn: Including a New and Circumstantial Account of the Battle of Long Island and the Loss of New York, with a Review of Events to the Close of the Year: Containing Maps, Portraits, and Original Documents.* Johnston retraced the location of the old forts, using previous accounts as well as a map drawn by Ezra Stiles, a Revolutionary War soldier who would eventually become president of Yale.

"Although the British obliterated all marks of the Brooklyn defenses of 1776," Johnston wrote, "we thus find nature and the records enabling us to re-establish them today."

Using nature and the records, I often seek to reestablish the old forts for myself—easy to do at the memorial to the prison ship martyrs, with a Stanford White–designed monument and park rangers and maps and guides to assist as you stand atop the big hill; more difficult, however, from Fort Sterling, which is sometimes said to have stood roughly on the site where the author Norman Mailer lived, on Columbia Heights, overlooking the harbor and Wall Street, but sometimes closer to the flagpole that marks the site of the Four Chimneys, a house wherein Washington and his generals held the council of war that determined to retreat from Brooklyn—or, as historians sensitive to the taint of words like "retreat" sometimes put it, "to withdraw the American Army from Long Island." These points both stand on the Brooklyn Heights Promenade, a scenic walkway built above the Brooklyn–Queens Expressway, which was a scenic spot even before the walkway was put there. Upon visiting the site, Abraham Lincoln said: "There may be finer views than this in the world, but I don't believe it." (Lincoln, it should be noted, was looking for votes.)

Reestablishing Cobble Hill Fort is complicated by the fact that one is not merely reestablishing the position of the fort but reestablishing its view. A large plaque on the side of a building at the intersection of Court Street and Atlantic Avenue commemorates the site for what was once seen from inside the lost fort on the taken-away hill:

NEAR THIS PLACE DURING THE REVOLUTIONARY WAR
STOOD THE PONKIESBERG FORTIFICATION FROM WHICH
GENERAL GEORGE WASHINGTON

IS SAID TO HAVE OBSERVED THE FIGHTING AT GOWANUS
DURING THE BATTLE OF LONG ISLAND AUGUST 27 1776
ERECTED IN 1926 BY THE SOUTH BROOKLYN SAVINGS INSTITUTION

HUMAN NATURE

Of all the many plaques and markers, modern and ancient, that I pass and notice or do not notice every day, this is my favorite, not just because it is large, or because its lettering is in a gorgeous style that is somewhere between art deco and arts and crafts and done in what I think of as the Golden Era of Letter-making in the United States, or because it had been there half a century by the time I first walked by, about twenty-five years ago, admiring the hilltop setting of Washington and his horse.

I note Cobble Hill for many reasons:

- because its position on a bank wall nicely frames a time in the twentieth century when banks commissioned Revolutionary War murals and built buildings that harkened back to classical Greek and Roman themes that Washington himself might have admired;
- because the chief executive officer of the South Brooklyn Savings Institution at the time, David Mead, an amateur historian and the son of George Washington Mead, also a banker, was said to be interested in promoting more equitable housing in Brooklyn, and proved it by sponsoring apartments that were small enough for first-generation immigrants to afford but not as small as the overcrowded tenements that housing reformers were hoping to improve upon;
- because on the day that the plaque was unveiled—when the son of the bank president pulled aside a curtain to reveal it—four thousand people were assembled in the company of marching bands and several detachments of soldiers, sailors, and marines, centered at this intersection that was once a hill and a Revolutionary War fort.

On the day of the plaque's unveiling—after the U.S. Navy Band played the national anthem and before lunch at a club nearby and before more ceremonies in Prospect Park, near the battle site—Rear Admiral Charles P. Plunkett, a veteran of the Spanish-American War and World War I and the commandant of the Brooklyn Navy Yard, told the assembled that war would not stop as long as human nature did not change; that people fought because they desired other people's property, a desire, he said, that was as strong in 1926 as it ever was. He said that the Battle of Brooklyn, which was still called the Battle of Long Island in 1926, could very well be refought, an enemy swooping into the Hudson Valley, destroying the United States. The general praised the value of history, declaring, according to a reporter, "that past events were most important for what the present generation could learn from them." Sometimes I think I can feel Plunkett's service in World War I like a dark cloud over the crowd.

"If the American people lack a proper appreciation of their historic ideals, it is because American history books do not tell the truth," the admiral said. "See to it that your histories contain all the facts. There is nothing in American history that any good American is ashamed of. Suppose the people of this city suddenly found out that the English navy was anchored in our rivers, what could we do? Go home and think about that, and remember that no amount of treaties and agreements can change human nature."

He called the defeat of the army in Brooklyn "an apt illustration of our ineffectiveness at a critical time."

Yes, some of the hill on which Cobble Hill Fort sat is still there; the British did not take it all away using prisoners of war. I can look down the slope of Atlantic Avenue, toward the phallus-shaped Williamsburg Savings Bank building, once filled with dental offices and now with condos offering unintentionally commanding views of Brooklyn's forgotten battlefields. I can see south down Court Street toward Red Hook and just make out a rise in the ground that was Bergen Hill, a hill taken down over the course of several years in the late 1800s, Irish diggers dying as rock and earth collapsed on top of them. I can see north toward downtown Brooklyn. And when I look west, I look down what's left of Cobble Hill—out into the harbor, past the clumps of buildings that are Jersey City, and then Newark—I can see the low blue band of hills that I know as the Watchungs, that I myself crossed in full pack, in a manner not dissimilar to that of a Continental Army soldier about to be injured in the back.

On the spot, at the site of this particular historic marker, the original bank was replaced by another bank named Independence, which was subsequently replaced by a discount specialty food store, workers wearing Hawaiian shirts, imported goods sold cheaply.*

*Though the American colonist is today often thought of as a self-sufficient craft-oriented individual, the colonies were, after the French and Indian War, huge importers from England—"numberless useful and useless things" is how an American described what his fellow citizens were inclined to purchase. "A Friend of This Colony" reported in a newspaper that "since the floods of English goods have been poured in upon us . . . family œconomy is at an end." British visitors to rural America were disappointed to see so many cheap imported housewares. Glass-fronted corner cupboards were invented to better show off consumers' collections of things. Americans made some cloth, but it was thought inferior to British imports. "It was in the Interest of Great-Britain to encourage our dissipation and extravagance, for the two-fold purpose of *increasing the sale of her manufactures* and of *perpetuating our subordination*," a South Carolina physician wrote. In the years leading up to the war, consumption became a political issue, and having British goods began to take on a tone of moral impropriety. Commissions were formed in which members pledged to abstain from British goods. T. H. Breen, in his book *The Marketplace of Revolution*, argues that these importation commissions led to the political associations that resulted in the Continental Congress. People shunned the "Baubles of Britain." Tea, at the time of the Boston Tea Party (and other similar tea protests in New York and throughout the colonies), had gone from being a luxury to being common—a cheap, easy-to-find-and-buy import. To drink tea became a kind of public sin. "In the present case the use of tea is considered as a *public* not as a *private* evil," a writer calling herself "Woman" wrote in a Massachusetts journal. Ben Franklin testified before Parliament in 1766: "Q: What used to be the pride of the Americans? A: To indulge in the fashions and manufactures of Great Britain. Q: What is now their pride? A: To wear their old clothes over again, till they can make new ones." I mention this in part because when the last bank left the old South Brooklyn Savings building on which the Washington plaque is mounted, it was replaced by a store called Trader Joe's, which sells inexpensive goods imported from all over the nation and the world: sun-dried tomatoes from California and alstroemeria flowers imported from Colombia, as well as Gouda cheese from Minnesota, to name a few. In 1979, Trader Joe's was sold by its founder, Joe Coulombe, to a family trust owned by Theo Albrecht, who had served in Erwin Rommel's Afrika Korps, in Tunisia, until he was captured by the U.S. Army in 1945. After the war, he took over his mother's dry goods store with his brother, discounting goods steeply, eschewing displays. Until he died, in 2010, he was known for cutting costs. When he was kidnapped in 1971, he was asked for ID by his abductors, the kidnappers not believing one of the world's richest men would be wearing an old suit. Then Albrecht reportedly negotiated a lower ransom.

But even now, the plaque still commands. And the plaque—at least for me—memorializes not something Washington did, but a viewpoint of Washington's, a place from which he observed, noted, pictured, or so it is alleged. It is a place where, if you believe the story of the Maryland regiment, as it has been passed down, Washington realized that there was nothing he could do, that in order for the army to go on, the Marylanders would die. It is a place, I like to think, where he might have imagined what was happening at a faraway but perceivable distance, in a little valley surrounding the Gowanus Marsh. Appearing on horseback in the plaque, holding hat and reins in one hand, Washington points with his free hand, like a surveyor or a tour guide, or maybe a painter, or the stout Cortés on seeing the Pacific. *Look!* his pointed hand seems to say.

What Washington is said to have been looking at from the top of the hill on my corner was the regiment of soldiers from Maryland, holding back the British as the Americans escaped to Brooklyn Heights, most of the about four hundred Marylanders dying. "My God, what brave men I must this day lose!" the accounts tell us Washington said. And each year, when the earth revolves back to fall, I think of a man who tried to prove exactly how brave these men were, who in the autumn of 1957 began preparing for the arrival of a team of archaeologists, in hope of discovering the grave site of the Maryland regiment. The man I think of is James Kelly.

OUR HERODOTUS

Can a person's time on earth be viewed through the lens of a single event? Do the Fates weave a life for us in which one moment, one battle, or one about-to-be-failed confrontation becomes our Delaware Crossing, our overnight retreat from Brooklyn, our Waterloo? Can one year of all our years work like a cataract on a river, like the Great Falls of the Passaic River on their way to New York Harbor and the sea? Sometimes I think that James Kelly was born to fight for the Maryland regiment and lose.

Though he was, like many of Washington's staff and troops, born in Ireland—in his case, on a farm in County Longford—Kelly grew up in the area that would have been Washington's view from Cobble Hill. He arrived in New York in 1885, at the age of seven, with his mother, a widow; he grew up on the edge of the Gowanus Canal and worked with one of the neighborhood pushcart peddlers, Thomas Daley, a Civil War veteran. "I helped him, generally on vegetable days," Kelly said of his pushcart work, and by "helped" he meant, in part, read stories of Jesse James to the peddler from three-cent books.

In many ways, Kelly had the upbringing of a typical Brooklyn youth in the late 1800s: he bought ice in the spring from ice boats in Red Hook that had sailed down the Hudson, and, after Buffalo Bill's Wild West Show, he watched the Indians on their break walking down Third Avenue. But his underground credentials are spectacular, atypical, exceptional, even from an everyman's archaeological point of view. Kelly was a distinguished veteran of finding the past in the muck, while digging ditches, tunnels, and holes. He was a decorated veteran of recovering things lost to time.

I speak not just of his early finds, at the dawn of the 1900s, for it is true that while excavating the Collect Pond—colonial New York's source of drinking water, now covered by courthouses and parts of Chinatown—Kelly discovered deer antlers and a Scotch curling stone that may well have fallen through eighteenth-century ice. I speak of his most monumental moment, the accidental archaeological find that made his name. In 1916, while working as foreman of an Interborough Rapid Transit subway construction gang, Kelly's crew dug up the *Tijger*, a Dutch ship thought to have burned in 1614. When he came upon the *Tijger*, Kelly photographed it, filmed it, had the keel and the prow dug out, and, to preserve the wood, found a place for it in the city aquarium, at that time on the Battery, in lower Manhattan. The wood was stored in the seal tank.

The find brought him international fame, even if people quickly forgot about what it was he found. Kelly traveled the world with a vaudeville company, billed as "Jamie Kelly, the Tunnel Foreman" or "The Tunnel Harp." He sang and told stories of digging up things in the subway, toured the United States, Canada, and Australia. Then he fought in World War I, in France, and, while there, wrote songs—"When the Boys Come Marching Home," "If Knighthood Were in Flower Again," "If They Only Moved Ireland over Here," "They're Going to Build a Subway to Ireland," and "Now and Then." He was an amateur boxer and, back in New York, flirted with politics. In 1926, he wrote a song for Jimmy

Walker, then mayor of New York City, entitled "If You Knew Jimmy." That same year Walker appointed him Kings County clerk, with an office in downtown Brooklyn and control of the historical record. "I was not unfriendly with the powers that be," Kelly said later on.

"They hit it off right away, did Jamie and the past," wrote the *Brooklyn World-Telegraph*.

He became known to Brooklynites as "our Herodotus."

As clerk, Kelly took it upon himself to investigate Brooklyn's history while furiously promoting it. He had less of the refinment of, say, I. N. Phelps Stokes, and less of the focus of Thomas DeVoe, the historian of markets. He was the street historian, a Bowery Boy of archival investigations, with chutzpah in lieu of a Ph.D. He officially established that Giovanni da Verrazzano sailed into New York Harbor before Henry Hudson, and got a bridge named for him. He proved, using old census records, that Winston Churchill's mother, Jennie Jerome, was born in Brooklyn—"thus demolishing a rival claim of Rochester, N.Y., as her birthplace," a New York newspaper noted. A plaque was affixed to the house, on Henry Street, in 1952, and Churchill eventually visited the home in 1953. When the plaque was unveiled, school was closed across the street and the Department of Sanitation band played, though later it was discovered that Jennie Jerome's house was a few blocks away, on Amity Street, where today a local building superintendent points it out to people with British accents who ask about the unmarked address. Kelly collected old Dutch deeds and nineteenth-century civil service documents. He managed to officially change the name Battle of Long Island to Battle of Brooklyn.

Kelly was a wiry, bright-eyed guy, answering the phone in the clerk's office, pointing out the painting behind him to visitors. "See this painting?" he said once. "I found it. It was out of frame, hidden behind a radiator. The museum tells me it was done by Gilbert Stuart. Stuart only did the head, though. That was his practice. He used to call these paintings his one hundred dollar bills—that's what he used to charge per head."

STAMP ISSUE

The endeavor to honor the Maryland regiment was the glorious war in which Kelly went down in defeat, but the opening battle was a victory: after years of epistolary assaults, he convinced a reluctant Congress to print a stamp honoring the Battle of Brooklyn. "I feel Brooklyn has long been neglected in the matter of having a stamp named particularly for it and feel that this occasion merits the issuance of such a stamp," he wrote in 1946. "This occasion" was the 171st anniversary of the Battle of Brooklyn.

"It appears the Post Office is amenable to an issue of famous battles only when they are centennial, sesquicentennials and bi-centennial," the Brooklyn postmaster, an ally, warned him.

Kelly waged his battle throughout the years of World War II. "For some unaccountable chance of circumstances, Brooklyn seems to fail to receive recognition from the post office department even though Brooklyners go to war," Kelly wrote. He enlisted congressmen and senators, as well as the press. He sent newspapers articles regarding the battle to Washington, D.C. "It is a story the whole world should know," he wrote. "Certainly it is a story that should be familiar to everyone who lives in Brooklyn." A bill was introduced by a congressman, Abraham J. Multer, but a stamp was refused. A headline in the *Brooklyn Eagle* read: "Boro Defeat." At last, Kelly submitted his own stamp, a drawing by a cartoonist for the *Brooklyn Eagle*. As if envisioning something could make it happen, the stamp was accepted, in 1951.

Kelly planned a giant post–Stamp War victory bash at the Brooklyn Museum, with radio broadcasts by WNYC and the police department's glee club. Kelly kept the RSVPs, pasted them in a scrapbook, and if you page through the aging sheets, you see that the people who accepted included Ernest A. Kohr, the stamp news editor for the *New York Herald-Tribune* (he dated his letter "MCMLI"); William A. Dawkins, the County Commander of the Kings County Spanish Civil War Veterans; John Reidel, the city's chief engineer; F. J. Doyle, a representative of the Internal Revenue Service's Alcohol and Tax Unit; Brooklyn's postmaster; and a deputy U.S. postmaster. People who sent regrets included Vincent Impellitteri, the mayor of New York at the time, as well as the governors of Massachusetts, Rhode Island, and Maryland. The police commissioner of New York could not attend, and Eleanor Roosevelt said she would have if she had not been in Paris with the United Nations. General Willis D. Crittenberger, the commander general of the U.S. Army who had led the forces that liberated Rome during World War II, said he would be at the stamp celebration, "trusting that unforeseen military commitments will not dictate otherwise." And then the governor of Maryland wrote again to say he would show up, a change of heart that I can only imagine greatly pleased Jamie Kelly.

On the first day of issue, the first stamp was purchased by a retired Brooklyn schoolteacher named Edith Shaw, the great-granddaughter of Massachusetts Representative Henry Shaw, the first person to buy a stamp printed by the U.S. government, in 1847 (prior to 1847, letters were embossed or marked). "Brooklyn Wins a 6 Year Fight," the *Brooklyn Record* announced. The *Eagle* ran an advertisement featuring a large reproduction of the stamp that the *Eagle* cartoonist had designed: "But for George's genius . . . the Dodgers might have been a cricket team." The stamp portrayed Washington, on horseback on a Brooklyn hilltop, his army preparing to evacuate, Washington pointing, presumably to Manhattan. A person who went to the event sent a handwritten note to Kelly afterward. "I shall never forget this day," it said.

Kelly's greatest battle lay ahead, however—the fight to memorialize the mass grave of the Maryland 400, who were buried, Kelly believed, on Brooklyn's Third Avenue, in what is today called the Gowanus neighborhood.

"I hope a monument will be erected," Kelly said. He described the site as more sacred than the Tomb of the Unknown Soldier at Arlington National Cemetery, arguing that the Tomb of the Unknown Soldier would not exist if it were not for the Maryland 400.

"No place is more sacred in America," he wrote.

DODGERS

A few years ago, I was walking along Third Avenue in Brooklyn, in an area I know fairly well, having lived in the vicinity off and on for a couple of decades, and I noticed that an old garage was being torn down. I had a vague recollection that we were in the area of the alleged burial site of the Maryland 400. There is a historical marker nearby, hanging from an American Legion hall, and in some distant corner of my memory I can

see the historian John Gallagher, shortly before he died, leading a group of other historians around, pondering abandoned lots that should be scanned with sonar, or some sophisticated underground imaging technology, searching for the graves of the Maryland 400, though I don't know that I actually saw that happen. I returned to the site a short while later and noticed that construction crews were digging a hole. Immediately, my heart raced. I paced back and forth before the blue plywood fence that made it difficult to look in and blocked me from talking to the workers. I went to the library to investigate. Sure enough, I discovered that the old garage was precisely where Jamie Kelly believed the Maryland 400 to be buried, where tradition says the men were laid in a long row of graves, on a hill at the edge of the Gowanus Marsh.

The hole was huge, building-sized. When the wooden fence opened, I looked in and stared at the dirt and tried not to get wounded by backhoes entering the site. I compared notes with Jamie Kelly: "At least 256 Marylanders died and were buried by the British in fifteen long trenches. The site today extends from Seventh to Eighth Street, and from Third Avenue to a line 120 feet to the eastward." The preciseness of the matchup was slightly exhilarating, as well as terrifying. I felt as if I had stumbled onto an archaeological emergency, a trapdoor to the past that was soon going to shut. I called the official Brooklyn historian Ron Schweiger. He was not as concerned as I was. "Can you believe I was a science teacher?" he asked me.

Schweiger wanted mostly to talk about the Brooklyn Dodgers; one-third of his basement is reportedly filled with Dodgers paraphernalia. He told me a story about how as a kid he met Jackie Robinson by waiting near where the players parked their cars. I think that's what he said, anyway. I was focused on the buried soldiers, and I felt as if there was no time to lose; there was an urgency that I could not communicate, and he was making me a little crazy, ignoring the Marylanders in favor of baseball talk.

I spoke to a few more archaeologists, and ended up getting the phone number of one who had worked in Brooklyn, at Revolutionary War–related sites. She was having her kitchen renovated—her house was a construction site, she said—and we missed each other for a couple of days, playing phone tag; when we did speak, she seemed to think the site had already been checked and was not terribly significant.

This was when I set out to dig up Jamie Kelly's own records of h
archaeological investigations of the Marylanders' burial site.

REWIND

As I searched for Kelly's papers—which were difficult to dig up, in fact,
having been dispersed to several libraries—I simultaneously pursued a
third avenue of mental archaeological investigation by imagining the
neighborhood backward. What I mean is, I went down to the Gowanus
Canal and, in my head, began picturing the de-evolution of the Gowanus Valley, watching it move along a route that took it from present-
day toxic waste site to active industrial site to rural landscape of marsh
flowers and salt hay and mollusks and birds, a place known for the size
of its oysters (an early export to Europe), the place through which fleeing
American soldiers raced, hearts probably pounding, the place where the
Marylanders died.

Working in reverse, I attended a recent public hearing on the Gowanus Canal remediation, heard questions pertaining to the removal of
heavy metals, the Gowanus being a toxic waste site under the auspices
of the federal Superfund program. The previous spring, I stood on the
bridge as two contractors from a biological services company used a
bucket-sized scoop to dip into the greenish-brown water and, causing
sulfurous bubbles to surface and burst, draw out a glop of creamy gray
sludge, subsequently placing the mayonnaise-like substance in a small
car that was to drive to a lab in the Boston area. I recalled years of star-
ing into the milk-chocolate circles of raw sewage that appeared in the
canal after rains, seeing a pair of fish-eating cormorants living on an
oil boom, and I remembered, in 2007, spotting a minke whale in Gowanus Bay a day before it repeatedly bashed itself against the Hess Oil
dock, in a fatal attempt to beach itself where there was no beach. I recalled a city block–sized portion of the canal that, in the 1990s, disappeared, illegally filled in. I remembered when people began taking
tours by boat, while a guy with the gas company that keeps an oil tank
on its banks rolled his eyes, saying, "They're in love with the Gowanus.
I don't know what it is—it's a cesspool."

In my mind's eye, I imagined the Gowanus in the early seventies,
before the Clean Water Act went into effect, when chlorine was poured

into it in an attempt to kill bacteria such as cholera and gonorrhea. I saw it in the sixties, after the underground flushing tunnel connecting its head to open waters broke down, when gas-manufacturing plants that made gas from coal dumped tar by-products into the canal. I saw the dye factories in the fifties, dumping colored dyes into the water—purple, pink, red, and green. In 1952, a harbor cop called the Gowanus a "region of the dead," comparing it to the mythical River Styx. According to an old report, the cop recalled collecting "a couple of thousand bodies" from the canal over the course of his career. In the forties, tugboats and barges used megaphones that I could picture ("Ahoy there, skipper!" shouted Bill Van Pely, a dispatcher).

Further on in my mental dig, the squatters' colonies of the 1930s reappeared—squatters named Ben Schwusky and Adolph Werner, for instance, living in neat little shacks decorated with bushes and vines, drinking water carried in with buckets. In 1911, Miss Gowanus threw flower petals off a barge. By 1899, a rural Gowanus was a memory, as indicated in a song by Michael Shay, the Gas Drip Bard:

> *Way down in old Gowanus, Slab City and Darby's Patch,*
> *Where squatters lived in years gone by, all jumbled in a batch,*
> *The frisky goat he roamed at will and chewed the verdant grass.*
> *But 'tis years since any flowers grew, down where they make the gas.*

The remembered valley, I could see, was full of junkmen, longshoremen, and day laborers, living cheap, combing the dumps for "all kinds of treasure for those of archaeological or antiquarian proclivities." In 1883, the cops had cleared the area near the Gowanus known as Darby's Patch, part of Park Slope now: "A year and a half ago they got notice to leave their places, and when they did not go Deputy Sheriff Hardy and a posse of men went down and threw their furniture out upon the road," the *Brooklyn Daily Eagle* reported. "Some of the ladies and gentlemen of the patch objected to these summary proceedings and there was an exciting discussion and much strong language was used."

I was farther and farther back in Gowanus history, watching an old man with a small flock of geese in the mid-1800s patrolling the low, soft hills, not yet covered with garbage. I saw a creek surrounded by fields at the beginning of the War of 1812, and in the 1700s the tidewater mill called Denton's was up and running, permission to dredge the canal having been requested of Peter Stuyvesant by a Dutch farmer in 1664.

NOT UNIQUE

My fingers all but trembled when, after a long search through archives around New York City, I arrived at the Brooklyn College Archives, in the basement of the Brooklyn College Library, to dig through boxes of Jamie Kelly's papers. I was in Flatbush, the neighborhood where my father was born. I sat near that glass-case-enclosed chair that President Bill Clinton had used when speaking at Brooklyn College and very close to a display of the home plate from Ebbets Field, home of the Brooklyn Dodgers baseball team. In the boxes were films of Jamie Kelly finding the *Tijger*; books of deeds and records from the founding of the original villages that made up Brooklyn; copies of old wills; examples of forgeries ("It is unclear," says the archivist's note, "if Kelly planned on doing anything with this material besides preserving it"); and clippings about a murder story in the old Brooklyn village called Gravesend. "The loud report of a pistol rang out in the stillness of the evening and Dagiero fell forward mortally wounded," one story said. "His wife ran down, threw her arms around his neck, and held him up, but he died in her arms, on the street, before anybody could reach him."

I also found the program and menu for a dinner marking Jamie Kelly Day, January 31, 1966.

Finally, in the bottom of a box, I discovered the document that I can only assume was heartbreaking for Jamie Kelly to read—a report to the U.S. Congress, dated May 21, 1957, entitled "The Maryland 400 at the Cortleyou House, Brooklyn: The Action and Burial Site."

The report was written by a team of archaeologists and historians who had come to Brooklyn under the auspices of Congress and the National Parks Service. They dug for several days in the area of what they had calculated to have been the old Van Brunt farm. They used picks and shovels to dig through the floor of the old Red Devil Paint Factory. Their goal: the long row of trenches that tradition said once paralleled the avenue, keeping in mind that the avenue had since been elevated.

The team had read the accounts. Thomas Field, in 1867, thought perhaps the bodies had been moved from the site. John Van Brunt, who had bought the farm from Field, denied that the bones had been mixed in with the bones of slaves, whom the Van Brunts referred to as "the servile sons of Africa." Van Brunt said his father, Cornelius Van Brunt, and his dead brother, Adriance, had "held that island sacred and never suffered the plough or the axe, not anything else to desecrate the ground." A coal dealer named Henry Wildhack recalled burial trenches that he said were still just visible in 1907, fifteen of them, each a hundred feet long. Wildhack's son remembered playing on the mounds as a boy.

Kelly was at the dig, and I imagine him acting like an expectant father, or like George Washington looking out from the fort at Cobble Hill, or perhaps like one of the thousands of nervous soldiers waiting to be evacuated from Brooklyn in 1776. "The burial trenches were still visible in 1905, when Henry Wildhack paved over them to make a coal yard," Kelly told onlookers. "And Peter Bacenet, who lives at 427 Third Avenue, told me he had found some bones and part of a gravestone in his backyard two years ago, but threw them away."

The dig did not go well, from Kelly's standpoint. The report was harsh, from my perspective. I quickly paged through it—maps, photographs, pages and pages of annotated notes—and went right to the findings, which first discussed the actions of the Marylanders themselves:

> The action of the "Maryland 400" was a dramatic and gallant incident in the best tradition of American military heroism, very probably the most noteworthy field action in the Battle of Brooklyn, but it was not unique as such among all the battle actions of the Revolution.

Then it got worse, the authors firing off a list of "not"s: the soldiers were *not* "a unique example of heroic military gallantry"; their action was *not* of national significance, compared to actions at the Battle of Saratoga or at the Siege of Yorktown, or even, the authors argued, compared to the signing of the Declaration of Independence at Independence Hall. The report said the Marylanders had *not* saved the lives of enough people, that they had saved only men under the command of William Alexander, who called himself Lord Sterling, claiming the title Earl of Sterling, which the British disputed, though General Washington did not, just calling him Lord.

"Significantly," it said, "no responsible historian has been found who attributes to the Marylanders' action anything more meaningful than the saving of the balance of Lord Sterling's own command."

The Marylanders had waited too long, the report decided. Their action had come at the end of the battle, when the day had already been lost for the Americans, and, as such, their fight was a gesture that did not change the greater course of the war. The suicidal action of the Marylanders was, in other words, a kind of military moot point that "accomplished no more than the saving of some 650–750 men."

The final blow was a sort of countercharge. The authors claimed that the Marylanders were not selfless heroes but just self-serving. "With the battle already a defeat, this 'saving' was no more than the snatching of brief glory from the jaws of imminent disaster," the report said.

"The burial site," the commission concluded, "cannot be recommended for establishment as a national monument."

And then, regarding the site itself, they buried any remaining hope Kelly might have had for congressional recognition: "Despite hearsay and traditional evidence, the burial site of these Marylanders killed (more may have been captured) in this action cannot be conclusively authenticated, either by historical or archaeological means."

Though I cannot know a person in the past, though old letters and yellowing accounts offer only glimpses of a life that is gone, I cannot but think that Jamie Kelly was deeply affected by these words, wounded, perhaps—especially regarding the site itself, which he was certain was significant. Sitting there in the archives, it almost hurt to read these sentences. I thought the archivists were looking my way as, repeatedly, I winced.

I continued to return to the construction site as the building went up, as the giant hole became a garage in the bottom of the building, and I thought occasionally of the troops that survived the Battle of Brooklyn and eventually went on to cross the Delaware. The defeat, Washington wrote to Congress, "dispirited [too] great a proportion of our troops and filled their minds with apprehension and despair." These days, now that the building is up, I tend to avoid the place entirely.

WINTER

꿈ꁉ꩜ꤜ

IN THE CRISP CLARITY OF WINTER, I return, invariably, to the Revolution; not to the beginning but to the very middle, or thereabouts. I look at the sky above the harbor—to see the belt of Orion or the seven stars of Pleiades as they appeared over the resting heads of eighteenth-century men and women concerned about money and family, as well as the future and, probably, peace—and I invariably think back to the coldest nights in the course of the war. The coldest nights occurred long after the Delaware was crossed, a decade before George Washington would return to the city in his inaugural spring; the coldest nights occurred when prisoners were still huddled in the prison ships, which were not yet sunk. When each new New York City winter arrives, I think of the coldest remembered winter in the history of New York, in December 1779, when Washington was camped about twenty-five miles away, in Morristown, New Jersey, in the Watchung Mountains.

Twenty-eight separate snowstorms hit Morristown, beginning in November 1779 and ending on April 1, 1780, those months sometimes referred to as the Hard Winter. Washington's winter in Valley Forge, Pennsylvania, from 1777 to 1778, is more often remembered as being the most severe winter of the Revolutionary War, if Morristown is remembered at all, a situation some historians find frustrating. "All evidence indicates that the winter of 1779–80 at Morristown," wrote the Washington biographer Douglas Southall Freeman, "was far worse than the corresponding months at Valley Forge. Yet one wonders why every schoolchild in America knows of the gloomy camp on the Schuylkill yet so few know of the camp at Morristown." New Jersey historians in particular take offense. "Why, as Freeman so bluntly states, should ignorance of this vital story be so prevalent?" one echoed just a few years ago.

In and around the area of New York City, cold winters prior to the Hard Winter date back to 1641, when a journal entry noted: "The frost was so great and continual this winter, that all the bay was frozen over, so much and so long, as the like, by the Indian's relation, has not been these 40 years. . . . It was frozen also to the sea so far as one could well discern." In 1697, the Earl of Bellemont spoke of experiencing "the terriblest winter in New York." There were ferocious winter storms in the winter of 1719–20, and newspapers tell us that in the winter of 1732–33 the harbor froze—in the journals you can just about feel the wind. "A very severe night we have passed through, by God's mercies," a farmer wrote in 1733, "and now this morning which is bright without clouds, and silvered by the icicles every where shining and the trees glistening. But it is still cold. As the day gets up, the wind rises. 'Tis as much as we can do to take care of ourselves and the children, provide for and tend the fires, and the cattle."

But the Hard Winter is thought to have been worse than all of those winters. And it wasn't just bad in New York Harbor; it was the only winter in the recorded history of America during which all the inlets, sounds, and harbors on the Atlantic coastal plain—from North Carolina to what was not yet called Maine—were frozen, closed to boats for what is estimated to have been a month or more. Many people wondered if they would survive the Hard Winter, and when I recall it today, the coldest winter seems to freeze time, to work like a fermata in the middle of the long, murky conflict—neither side winning, a landscape frozen in fear and loss, amid propaganda skirmishes and civilian casualties, a time of low temperatures and low military morale. Nathanael Greene, who was based in New Jersey, called the Hard Winter "the most terrible winter that I ever saw.

"Almost all the wild beasts of the fields and the birds of the air have perished with the cold," he said.

A SHAME

Colonial folklore held that winds blowing from the north, on December 21, the solstice, foretold a bad winter, and in 1779 winds had been blowing from the north for weeks. In New York City, by December, there were no trees remaining to be cut—wood had to be carted in from Long Island. Snowstorms began in November, and by December they were occurring in rapid succession. There was a two-day blizzard that began on December 1 and another that began on December 5. By December 14, two feet of snow stood on the ground. Further blizzards occurred on December 15, 16, and 18. A German soldier who had come to America with the Marquis de Lafayette in 1777, and had wintered at Middlebrook (New Jersey), and again at Valley Forge, went to write in his journal and found his ink frozen. When it thawed, he wrote: "Those who have only been to Valley Forge or Middlebrook during the last two winters but have not tasted the cruelties of this one know not what it is to suffer." As December turned to January, there occurred three successive storms that the weatherwise David Ludlum described as ranking among "the greatest such combinations in our meteorological history."

In Morristown, on January 2 and 3, a local doctor described the storms as deadly. "No man could endure it many minutes without danger of his life," he said. The snow was now four to six feet deep. At the time, the soldiers were trying to build huts, as wood was plentiful in the area—Washington had picked the spot for its supply of trees as well as for its protective terrain. The men slept on straw, a fire at their feet, huddled together for warmth in groups of five or six. On January 6, there was another two-day storm. Troops of men packed down the snow with their feet to keep the road open for supplies, but none came. "We were absolutely, literally starved," wrote Joseph Martin. "I do solemnly declare that I did not put a single morsel of victuals into my mouth for four days and as many nights, except a little black birch bark which I gnawed off a stick of wood, if that can be called victuals. I saw several of the men roast their old shoes and eat them, and I was afterwards informed by one of the officers' waiters, that some of the officers killed and ate a favorite little dog that belonged to one of them." The men stole supplies from nearby farms and homes.

John Cunningham is a New Jersey historian who laments the

forgotten hardness of the Hard Winter. Cunningham graduated from Morristown High School in 1932, the bicentennial of Washington's birth, then served in World War II, and subsequently spent a long career writing about the history of New Jersey, both for the *Newark Star-Ledger* and in numerous books. "John Cunningham and history are synonymous in our state," the director of the Newark Public Library once said. Cunningham cites two reasons for Morristown's Hard Winter having been forgotten. First, Valley Forge was closer to Philadelphia, where the nation celebrated the one hundreth anniversary of the Declaration of Independence in 1876. With visitors from all over the nation, Philadelphia was able to use its Centennial Exposition to successfully promote Valley Forge's less-hard winter as the number one winter deprivation spot in the American historical consciousness.

By contrast, the national historical park at Morristown was only created in 1933, when the former Ford Mansion, Washington's headquarters at Morristown, was donated to the federal government by four men who had bought it in a dilapidated condition. The men first tried to convince the state to take the property; the state didn't want it. The four men eventually founded the Washington Association, forever fighting against apathy in their own state, in their own local community.

"The answer to Freeman's question about why Valley Forge far surpasses Morristown in national attention mostly lies in a simple answer," Cunningham wrote in his book *The Uncertain Revolution: Washington and the Continental Army at Morristown*. "Morristown doesn't seem to care, any more than town fathers cared when the Ford Mansion was up for auction in 1873." *The Uncertain Revolution* ends with sadness, with tough observations about the state of historical education in New Jersey and beyond. Cunningham notes that teachers don't come to the seminars offered by Morristown National Historical Park, that high school history classes don't visit, that children in Morristown grow up thinking that the winter in Valley Forge was worse. He ends his book with these words: "What a shame."

Cunningham presented a paper to the Washington Association in 1979, during the bicentennial celebrations, two hundred years after the Morristown winter began. It was entitled "Morristown: Worse Than Valley Forge." Toward the end he considers the soldiers living in the cold:

Those winter soldiers died often—slowly, agonizingly, despairingly. Far more died in winter camps than in summer battles. The wonder is that mutiny did not come sooner, that desertions from the ranks were not greater at Jockey Hollow. The selfish, grasping quest for power in Congress should have discouraged even the toughest of armies. . . . Why did they keep the faith? I don't know. I often ask myself this. Was it patriotism, an innate quest for freedom, a passion for independence—all of these? I don't know. I just don't know. No one ever will know.

FROZEN

The City of New York was frozen at the beginning of 1780, locked in by the iced-over harbor, the coves of the Hudson solid by the first week in November. On January 30, a Hessian soldier, Johann Conrad Döhla, reported that the Hudson and East Rivers were frozen solid, ships imprisoned in ice up to eighteen feet thick. Then the Arthur Kill, the tidal strait between Staten Island and New Jersey, froze. Then the rivers of New Jersey—the Passaic, the Hackensack, the Raritan, the Pequannock—turned solid, reportedly to their bottoms. Where the ice made water travel impossible, it opened up new roads; horse-drawn sleds traveled the Delaware from Trenton to Philadelphia, and people walked across the sound from Long Island to Stamford, Connecticut, like the Israelites on the floor of the Red Sea. Due to the lack of wood, newspapers were published infrequently. The *New York Journal* was printed at two-thirds its normal size. Döhla wrote that ships were destroyed in the crush of ice, or, in open water, carried off in tremendous winds, despite two or three anchors. "An astonishing wind arose, accompanied by rain, which was almost like an earthquake and lasted 24 hours," Döhla wrote. Old houses in the city collapsed, while the newer houses suffered "notable damage." "The inhabitants of New York remembered no such storms," Döhla said, "and it was believed that the world and the city were sinking and that it would be the day of final judgment."

William Smith was a lawyer whom the rebels called "the Weathercock," due to the fact that it was difficult to tell which side he was on, though he eventually ended up on the side of the British. He chronicled everything in British-occupied New York, including the snow, though on January 7 the ink in his pen kept freezing, despite his resting his inkstand on the grate of the fireplace. "God have mercy on the Poor," he wrote one night when the ink thawed. "Many reputable People lay abed in these Days for Want of Food." There was no wood left to be cut anywhere in Manhattan; the hills in the northern, more rural portions of the city had been razed before the war and now were bare: picture a treeless horizon. Firewood for the troops and the populace had to be shipped in from Long Island. Three thousand cords sat on landings opposite Manhattan's shores, unshippable. Meanwhile, people took wood anywhere they could find it. An order went out from the British command to desist from cutting "Fruit or Ornamental Trees round Gentlemen's Houses," while ships frozen into the ferry slips were broken up for wood. A board from a house could be bought for eight pence.

A week later, William Smith said the weather had been "intemperate to an Extreme." "The ice is this morning fixed from Side to Side tho' the Sky is clear," he wrote. "Every Day People have been interlocked by the floating Cakes & many have perished." He added: "We often Hear of the Deaths of the Poor frozen in their Houses." There was a dance on January 18, to celebrate the birthday of the Queen—"a most splendid ball," said the *New York Mercury*. Baroness Charlotte Riedesel, a German officer's wife, represented the queen. Afterward, the baroness wrote that she was greeted by trumpets and drums and stayed until two in the morning. Smith observed that the money would have "been better laid out in Fuel for the Poor."

By January 20 the cold still had not relented. Rebels deserted the American cause via the ice; a deserting Hessian had his frozen feet amputated. The *Royal Gazette* reported that three men walked across Long Island Sound from Saybrook, Connecticut, to Oyster Pond Point, on Long Island, twenty miles, at the beginning of February. On the evening of February 13, a wildcat was reported to have come across the ice from New Jersey, to terrorize a henhouse on the shore of the Hudson, a mile north of the city. "The first Instance of such Game on this Island I ever heard of and perhaps in 100 years," wrote Smith. "The oldest man in this Country does not remember such a long continuance of very severe cold—since yesterday afternoon it has been intensely so."

William Smith himself rode in a sleigh along the Hudson, three hundred yards from shore. He got out out of his sleigh and walked on the river near Dey Street, crossing water that would be filled in as land two hundred years later, becoming Battery Park City and the World Trade Center; he might have used the pier alongside, from which I would one day see a ship's carcass buried in World Trade Center muck. When I think of this moment, I picture the Weathercock looking down to the ice at his feet, amazed, and a little startled.

SURPRISE ON EVERY SIDE

I think of the city itself in its coldest winter as something akin to a work of art; with the water frozen in and around New York, the city was metamorphosed from view-rich and green-fringed archipelago to a series of bare hills surrounded by slippery, snow-dusted plains. Naturally, the freeze had great strategic implications. Both the British and the Americans worried about the other side taking advantage of waterways that had suddenly become land routes. George Washington fretted that the British would use sleds to go north, up the Hudson, to outmaneuver him. The British were worried that Washington would stage raids from New Jersey. "If the Ice grows stronger & a Snow Storm rises Washington may find us open to Surprise on every Side," wrote a Tory. At what is now Jersey City, a British garrison felt vulnerable, and the soldiers there worried that if the post was taken over, the rebels would fire cannons on the brittle city, which was tinder, only a few hundred yards away. Washington, in Morristown, asked Lord Sterling to devise a plan for an ice excursion. "I cannot relinquish the idea of attempting it," Washington wrote.

Eventually Colonel Moses Hazen was assigned by Washington to stage an attack on Staten Island with one thousand men. General Greene convinced farmers to donate three hundred sleds and accompanying horses; the soldiers were given mittens the night before. The sleds set out, the farmers following. The troops carried a large gun but had no ammunition for it. They carried two thousand board feet of planking, to slide the sleds down the banks of the Arthur Kill. American historians have worked hard to stress that Washington insisted the soldiers not plunder the predominantly loyalist Staten Islanders, but a militia leader made a speech before they set out, vowing to "remove all Staten Island, bag and baggage, to Morristown." Washington also hoped the attack might remain secret, but as the contingent traveled, it picked up more soldiers and farmers who decided to come along for the ride. They spent the night of January 15 on the New Jersey side of the Arthur Kill, with large fires raging, a growing crowd of citizens joining them. The *New York Gazette*, a loyalist paper, published the secret. "Whispers that the Rebels meditate an Attack in Staten Island. Still very Cold. Very Severe indeed."

The next day, the rebel contingent set up camp on Staten Island, on top of a hill, building another roaring fire, this time noted by diarists in Manhattan—even today, from the top of that hill there is a glorious view of Manhattan. An American soldier wrote: "We took up our abode for the night on a bare, bleak hill, in full rake of the northwest wind, with no other covering or shelter than the canopy of the heavens and no fuel but some old rotten rails that we dug up through the snow, which was about two to three feet deep. The weather was cold enough to cut a man in half."

The British evacuated soldiers and men from Staten Island, pulled them back into their forts, while the Americans seem to have cruised the area, plundering the citizenry and ending up with severe frostbite. Five hundred rebels suffered from the cold in one way or another, six killed by a British light horse regiment that attacked the American rear guard as they began to retreat. When they got back to New Jersey, a minister, the Reverend James Caldwell, was ordered by Washington to return the loot taken from citizens, an estimated ten thousand dollars' worth.*

A few days later, the British counterattacked, soldiers crossing the

---

*Washington could be severe when he considered it important to be so: he regularly hanged Continental soldiers for insubordination, and in cases of mutiny, when Americans were being shot, the firing squad was instructed to shoot from a close range, blood splattering on the executioners as a visceral warning. He was, however, insistent on British prisoners being treated well. He also severely punished soldiers who took from the populace, the war also being a public relations battle for the skeptical colonists. The British were not as good at this kind of public relations, even if they were not always as bad at it as the rebel press might indicate; they were used to being colonial masters. After the Staten Island raid, Washington wrote: "From the vast majority who greedily rushed to plunder, our country has received such a disgrace as will not easily, I may say possibly, be wiped off."

ice from Staten Island to Elizabethtown, to loot, burn, and kill. From Manhattan, five hundred British soldiers crossed the frozen Meadow-lands, entering Newark, posting guards on street corners, taking over the town, as homes and barns were burned. The British described the ice attack on Staten Island as "villainous barbarity." Rivington's *Loyal Gazette* reported that the Americans shot a "very little boy" who had been playing on the shore of Staten Island, after which the soldiers cheered. And then, in the return volley, a rebel paper described the British hanging a citizen who had been stripped naked. "An officer of distinction in the American Army" described "the particulars of the horrid depredations"—houses burned, people left in the cold without blankets or clothes, rapes.

There were reports on the American side that one winter night in Elizabethtown, after the British destroyed a church by fire, the sky over New Jersey was glowing red, evident to Washington's scouts on the peaks, I would imagine. Even today, when, say, the reeds in the Mead-owlands burn, you can see the fire late at night over the swamps from tall buildings in Manhattan, or from certain points on the shore.

HIGH HILLS

In the winter, the possibility of the old peaks becomes clear. The old sight lines return as leaves fall away, and, if you notice the hills, they begin to call, to shout out from the horizon so that, if you are me, you want to put them to strategic use. I saw them from the coast of Brook-lyn over the years, as I walked my kids to school, as they surprised me in the view from lower Manhattan. I saw them when I drove out to see my parents before my parents moved away from Morristown. I saw them from the top of the Empire State Building, though before I began to think about the Watchung Mountains, I didn't really notice them from the Empire State Building at all. At some point, one winter a few years ago, I felt as if the long line of the Watchungs was watching me everywhere I went—as if I were the British and the Watchungs were the Continental Army, Washington with a spyglass, a cold soldier watching for fires in the view of a winter night, all eyes on a war that seemed to never end. Hills that I had hardly noticed for most of my life were suddenly the most obvious hills in the world.

You who make your home in the Rockies, or have lived among or hiked upon the Pacific Northwest's mighty Cascades, those of you who call the Adirondacks, or even the Catskills, home—you may scoff at the very notion of hills in or near New York City; you might hesitate to use the word "mountains" in referring to the Watchungs. The highest peak, after all, is a mere 879 feet, the height of a smallish skyscraper. That would be High Mountain, in the northernmost reaches of the range, just above the Passaic Falls. And yet the peaks of the Watchungs have their faraway-seeming secrets. High Mountain is home to numerous plants endangered in New Jersey, not to mention plants endangered around the globe. Torrey's mountain mint, for example, is a plant from another time still thriving in the Watchungs.

The Watchungs are indeed mountains, volcanic in origin—igneous rock extruded, then cooled, forming a mineral-dotted traprock, a leak in a volcano that became these crystal-injected hills.* At some point, I learned the names of the different ranges that make up the Watchungs— the name itself is said to be derived from the Lenni-Lenape name and means "high hills." There are hills named Pill, Lees, and Goffle, and mountains named Hook, Campgaw, Orange, and Preakness. In studying the hills, I looked at maps from around the time of the Revolution and noticed the fishhook-shaped uprisings that Washington may have seen—a geologic gate that held back the British, that offered views to New York—and I saw the stream-carved routes to Princeton and Philadelphia in the south, a hill-protected route north through Connecticut to Boston. War, like human settlement, is a function of geology.

I have some history in these hills, and I can recall my first car, a little Yugoslavian number, the factory that made it bombed by NATO

---

*I feel compelled to mention again that the artist Robert Smithson spent a lot of time in the Watchungs, in the old quarries—if only to note a piece he wrote for *Harper's Bazaar* in 1966. He took a trip to the hills with his wife, the artist Nancy Holt, as well as with the artist Donald Judd and his wife, Julie. They went to Upper Montclair quarry, which Smithson said was "also known as Osborne and Marsellis quarry or McDowell's quarry." "For about an hour Don and I chopped incessantly at the lump with hammer and chisel, while Nancy and Julie wandered aimlessly around the quarry picking up sticks, leaves and odd stones," he wrote. "From the top of the quarry cliffs, one could see the New Jersey suburbs bordered by the New York City skyline." In another piece, he chastised artists who "would rather *retreat* to scenic beauty spots than try to make a concrete dialectic between nature and people."

troops during a war in the Balkans, breathing heavily as it toured the Watchungs. See me driving through these hills in my youth, while working as a newspaper reporter, reading about Revolutionary-era iron forges in the north, places where munitions were said to be made. See me reading about battles I could not imagine in the southern portions of the range. In terms of the growth of New York and its suburbs in the time since I was a kid, see the Watchungs as they thwart the advance of housing developments, as the sprawl of the city attempts to march west to New Jersey and Pennsylvania.

I was beginning to feel qualified to try to signal from the hills, or at least I thought I knew some old hilltop roads that could take me to some signal points. Indeed, I got a little crazy to re-create a signal from New York City to New Jersey, to re-see what Washington and his comrades saw. I mapped the hills, took photographs, studied the horizon for landmarks. It sounds easy, even now, as I remember those early stages of signal work—all I had to do was find the perfect signal point. It was a struggle, however, that took me a few months, from the end of winter into the beginning of spring, at which time I knew I would be thwarted by green leaves limiting my view. It was a race with the earth's orbit around the sun, in other words, and on several occasions I gave up.

FINE

In a small pamphlet that I found in the New York Public Library, I read about an old map of the Continental Army's signal points in the Watchungs—a map that might be found, so far as I could figure, only in the library of a town near my parents' home in New Jersey. On several occasions over the course of a number of years, I would set out to visit my parents, a few blocks from Washington's Morristown headquarters, with plans to see them and, on the way home, stop into the nearby library to look for that old map. Invariably, I would lose track of time and miss my chance to find the map. In fact, in all the time that my parents lived in Morristown, I only walked over to Washington's Headquarters twice, the first time with my son, who was a little boy then and is now an adult—who knows where the time goes? On both occasions it was closed.

Toward the end of the winter when my parents were getting ready to move—away from Morristown, as it worked out, to Connecticut, where my father's father happens to be buried, a geographic coincidence that I wondered if my father had given any thought to (I had not asked)—I went over to see them, thinking once again that I would check out that map on my way home. This time my father, who has endured a chronic ailment for many years, had just come home from a long stay at a rehabilitation unit; he was relieved to be home at last. So was my mother; it occurred to me at that moment that dealing with a long-term illness is like a siege, a war of attrition in which all parties suffer. My mother went out to get some groceries, and I stuck around, hoping to leave in time to stop at the library to see the signal map. My father was chatting with me, trying to relax during his homecoming, when, all of a sudden, he had a horrible look on his face, and then a distant look; then he gasped, his head fell forward, and he slumped in his chair. At first he seemed to mumble, but then he slowly stopped mumbling, his head slumping forward further. As I tried to rouse him, he was not making any sound.

I felt for his pulse. It was gone. His breathing had stopped. I remember the moment clearly. It was as if he had left the room; his body was lifeless. I called an ambulance and unlocked the front door, and I was starting an attempt at CPR when he suddenly gasped and began breathing again. He was confused and didn't seem to know what had happened, and as he was getting his bearings, the paramedic crew came in the front door—reinforcements, to my great relief. My father was asking what was going on as they approached him, and then it seemed to dawn on him that they were there for him—to take him back to the hospital—and he began to put up a fight.

"Nah, I'm fine," my father said matter-of-factly, though his face was pale as a sheet. He seemed to be working very hard to appear relaxed. "Really, I'm fine," he said.

"You don't *look* fine," the paramedic said.

In fact, his color was improving from a few moments before, when it had left him completely. Naturally, I felt horrible, sending him on a return trip to the hospital. A couple of days later, he would call to say thanks, and I would subsequently spend some time wondering how I would feel in the same situation—reenacted—and how my children would feel, and so on. But at that moment, as my father looked over at me, I thought he was going to kill me.

A POET

One winter day, out on an edge of New York, in Sheepshead Bay, Brooklyn, when the winds were whipping up the water and a chill was ripping through my jacket, I gazed out at the open jaws of New York Harbor and over toward Sandy Hook and the Atlantic Highlands, and I thought of Philip Freneau, who died, as it happened, just beyond the Highlands, in the snow. Freneau is often called the Poet of the American Revolution, a title that has more to do with him being a poet than with his poems, which are not very good, if you ask me, or if you ask most people, in fact. In 1941, the critic Herbert Gorman wrote of Freneau: "His poetic aspirations were beyond his actual capabilities, although he appears to have been unaware of this lack." For me, he is the last Revolutionary War figure in my Revolutionary almanac, a time straddler himself, and I tend to bypass his poems, per se, focusing mostly on their titles, which, when taken together, give me a sense of his time and place—the time being that of a poet who began writing before the Declaration of Independence and died in 1832, having seen almost all the Founding Fathers pass away; the place being New York, New Jersey, and the harbor.

For example, leading up to the Revolution, he wrote "A Poem, On the Rising Glory of America." After being captured at sea and held on a prison ship in Wallabout Bay, Freneau wrote "The British Prison-Ship." "On the Removal of Congress from New York to Philadelphia" was written on September 11, 1790, when the government left New York. In 1791, he published "Lines Written Some Years Ago on the Death of a Fiddler." Other titles I think of occasionally are "Reflections on the General Debased Conditions of Mankind" and "Advice to Ladies Not to Neglect the Dentist." And then there is Freneau's funeral train of poems written as the onetime rebels, now elder statesmen, depart the national stage: "Stanzas Occasioned by the Death of General George Washington," "Lines Addressed to Mr. Jefferson, On His Approaching Retirement from the Presidency of the United States," and "Stanzas on the Decease of Thomas Paine."

As Freneau gets older, he becomes a relic, or seems like one, anyway, even though he tries to keep up with fashions: in 1810 he wrote "Lines of an Old Dotard, Who Had Cut Away the Blossoms of Sixty-Eight, and Upwards, to Put on a Fashionable Tye-Wig." It seems to me that in the years just before he died he wrote poems that took either a wider view—often from the vantage of a hilltop—or a smaller one, as with a poem about a particular aspect of his natural surroundings, the difference between presenting a wide sweep and presenting one small note, a point of light. Examples include "Ode Written on a Remote Perspective View of Princeton College (or Nassau Hall) from a Remarkably Woody Eminence in Monmouth, Commonly Called Pine Hill" and "On Observing a Large Red-Streak Apple Hanging on the Tree in January."

It was during a blizzard in January, as a matter of fact, that he died, in a frozen swamp in Freehold, New Jersey.

PURSUITS MOST CONGENIAL

Freneau was not from New Jersey. He was born in New York City, on Frankfurt Street, the son of Pierre Fresneau, in 1752, during a week remembered for the appearance of the aurora borealis. It was also a year in which the harbor froze, as well as the year Benjamin Franklin first attempted his kite-flying experiment—a kite in an electrical storm collecting energy from the sky being a little like writing a poem, in my opinion. Freneau's father was a merchant who, due to debts, switched from a cosmopolitan life in New York to a rural one in the Raritan Valley of New Jersey. When Fresneau the father died, Freneau the son, age fifteen, wrote a line in the back of the father's letter book: "Here ends a Book of Vexation, disappointments, Loss and plagues, that sunk the Author to his grave short of 50 years."

At the College of New Jersey, which would one day become Princeton University, Freneau was friends with James Madison and Hugh Brackenridge, with whom he wrote his first poems, fired up by youth and the turbulent political times. "I burn, I hasten to engage / to vent my poison with a serpent's rage," he wrote. He graduated and went off to work as a teacher in the village of Flatbush, in Brooklyn, though he lasted there just thirteen days. To Madison, he wrote: "Long Island I have bid adieu, with all its brutish brainless crew!" He returned to Princeton, where, a biographer says, he attempted to "devote himself to those pursuits most congenial to a young poet." When the war began, his work was reprinted in colonial newspapers, poems such as "A Poem, On the

Rising Glory of America," which he cowrote with Brackenridge—and it was just the kind of poem that people enthused with the cause of colonial rights wanted to hear:

> *Americans! at freedoms fane* adore!*
> *But trust to Britain, and her flag, no more;*
> *The generous genius of their isle has fled,*
> *And left a mere impostor in his stead.*

He joined the New Jersey militia for a short time, and then, after signing up for duty on a frigate bound for the Caribbean island of St. Eustatius, was captured by the British; he was identified as a rebel by a Tory on board and put in a prison ship on the East River in New York. When released, he returned to New Jersey, where friends described him as "a perfect skeleton." A quarter century later, he went back to the site of the prison ships and wrote "On Walking over the Ground of Long Island, Near New-York, Where Many Americans Were Interred from the Prison Ships, During the War with Great Britain. Written in July 1802."

After the war, he lived in Jamaica, returning to the United States when George Washington was inaugurated; he watched the first president arrive in the harbor from the deck of the schooner *Columbia*— "dressed and decorated in the most superb manner," he reported. Freneau commemorated the scene in verse: "Verses Occasioned by General Washington's Arrival." He tried to run a newspaper in New York and failed. "My attempt to establish a Newspaper in New-York was the wrongest step I could possibly have taken," he later wrote.

RASCAL

In 1791, James Madison and Thomas Jefferson persuaded Freneau to take on the editorship of the *National Gazette*. It was a time when Whigs like Madison and Jefferson were concerned that Federalists like Hamilton were trying to hand the country, with Washington's support, over to the bankers and stockbrokers, people who were generally

*A shrine or temple.

in cahoots with the old enemy, England; Jefferson saw himself as battling to restore the republican values that people had fought the Revolution for. Jefferson and Madison used Freneau like an attack dog against Washington, deploying so-so rhymes instead of teeth. Jefferson appointed Freneau, whose father was French, the official United States French translator, a no-show job that allowed the poet, an idealist's idealist, to rail against the president in editorials and satiric couplets. In his biography of George Washington, Washington Irving called Freneau a "barking cur."*

Freneau just kept going, like a radio talk-show host on a tear. Jefferson claimed that Freneau "saved our constitution which was galloping fast into monarchy." Notoriously, Freneau supported and encouraged "Citizen Genet," a French citizen who came to the United States in 1793 to win support for the French Revolution. Washington wrote an

---

*Washington Irving, who was named for George Washington, was a baby in a carriage in 1789 when, according to Irving family legend, his nurse stopped the president, then in residence in New York City, to point out his namesake, the president reportedly patting him on the head. Irving's first book, a tongue-in-cheek study entitled *A History of New York from the Beginning of the World to the End of the Dutch Dynasty*, was a hit in New York. (Before it was released, Irving anonymously published ads in the papers seeking the whereabouts of Diedrich Knickerbocker, a fictional character whom Irving referred to as the author of the book.) Irving would famously go on to write a biography of Columbus, and then, as Irving was dying, a five-volume biography of George Washington, for many years the most popular book in America—it still washes up en masse at estate sales. Washington Irving is also a founding father of American literature, the first American with an international reputation. The British called him "the first literate American," according to Van Wyck Brooks. Even today, Irving is cast as the genial poet, the happy-go-lucky American. In fact, the man was a nervous wreck, his family's business having collapsed as he began writing, the young republic in a deep recession; he had watched his prospective wife die of tuberculosis. "He had to write amusingly while feeling funereal," wrote the literary biographer Richard Ellmann. "The truth is that the famous collection of sketches, essays, and stories, which lifted American literature out from the cultural backwater and into the mainstream, was conceived and produced in a time of great anxiety for its author," writes Jeffrey Rubin-Dorsky in his essay "Washington Irving: Sketches of Anxiety." In other words, Irving's first international success, *The Sketch-Book of Geoffrey Crayon, Gent.*, was not a genial collection of unconnected tales. "*The Sketch Book*'s very harmony derives from the working out of this anxiety—the process of recreation, examination, and release that takes place in the interstices of its tranquil, and therefore more easily recognizable, emotions."

eight-thousand-word letter about why the United States could not assist Genet at that time. Genet decided to appeal directly to the people. He eventually captured ships for French use and proceeded to attack the Spanish in North American waters, which made Washington anxious, from the standpoint of international relations, and angry, from the standpoint of Washington's oft-noted hot temper and intolerance for dissension. Yet when even Jefferson abandoned Genet (as had just about all the other Republicans), Freneau stood by him—Freneau thought of himself as loyal to Revolutionary ideals at all costs. Washington tried to appear to be above politics, though he wasn't by any means, and Freneau was an early political rabble-rouser. On the rare occasions Freneau is mentioned in history books, it is usually to quote George Washington calling him "that rascal Freneau."

After the partisan squabbling, Freneau tried to get a publishing business going in Patagonia, worked off and on in the West Indian shipping business, and at some point got himself shipwrecked in South America. He was reportedly offered a position in the New Jersey legislature. "This was rather better than being sent to Jail for editing Newspapers," he said. But he definitely failed at farming, not able to slaughter his animals and not proving himself a capable manager. His wife was said to have become angry with him when he commented on her hoeing in verse: "Ho, ho, Missie Freneau, if that's the way you hoe, the corn'll never grow." It is not clear which was more upsetting to her, his criticism or the quality of the verse.

"No wonder the farm doesn't pay when even the slaves talk in rhymes," she replied.

"Fortune had not been kind to the poet in his efforts to make a living," wrote Lewis Leary, in 1971, in *That Rascal Freneau: A Study in Literary Failure*. "Literature had failed him, the sea had been a stern master, and journalism had brought him almost to the gates of a debtor's prison." Freneau's literary failure was such that in his own time he was thought of as already gone. In 1829, in *Specimens of American Poetry, with Critical and Biographical Notices*, one editor wrote: "We had always been accustomed to hear this gentleman spoken of as deceased. . . . But on making inquiries . . . we learned that he was still living."

Unable to make a living as a poet, or a newspaper editor, or a farmer, or anything, really, Freneau mostly didn't make a living. He eventually sold off his land and moved to Freehold, New Jersey, where he lived on a relative's farm. In his seventies, he repaired public roads to pay his taxes; according to local tradition, he went from home to home repairing clocks, a tinker. People of means in Monmouth eyed him warily. His last poem, "Winter," describes the happiness he took from wintry days, a view of spring through the sharp crispness of ice: "These to mind a thousand pleasures bring / And give to winter's frosts the smiles of spring."

In the summer of 1832, he was still in debt.* He went to court to ask for a pension, thirty-five dollars a year, as a veteran of the Revolutionary War. On December 18, 1832, he stayed late in the village of Freehold. Some reports say he was at a tavern, others at a library. He began

---

*One way history repeats itself is that Americans think of the colonists living at the time of the Revolution—a group you might call the Founding Children—as being of like minds, when the opposite was true. In Philadelphia, at the time of Pennsylvania's referendum on independence, supporters of independence included landowners like George Washington, as well as the political descendants of the Levelers, people who wanted government relief from landlords and credit difficulties. Washington's Virginia colleagues were not interested in the landless being allowed to vote, but many Pennsylvanians were landless, and they eventually were allowed to vote, even if women and slaves were not. Thomas Young, a young, idealistic doctor from the Hudson River valley, had worked to create communities in the western settlements that were out of reach of city-based landlords, utopian settlements where small farmers were free of the burdens of rent. (The historian Pauline Maier called Young "as much a loser as any Loyalist even though he opted for the winning side.") Also voting for independence were millennialists, charged by the Great Awakening, as well as evangelicals, those who thought that Christ might prefer property more evenly distributed. And on the western edge of Pennsylvania, in the land where Washington first worked as a land surveyor, there were settlers who thought government meant one thing: armed protection, mainly from the Native Americans and French, but also, after the Declaration of Independence, from the British. Washington started the war as a critic of the debt-based government spending that created the eighteenth-century British military. The Walpole government had invented a kind of permanent surplus spending predicated on an economic machination known as a sinking fund, which paid off debt through bond issues, which in turn encouraged speculation. At the war's end, Washington, in contrast to his fellow Virginians, had changed his tune on government debt and Walpole's sinking fund; he had decided against a loose confederation of locally run states, which was bad for sovereignty and thus, he seems to have been persuaded, bad for business. The Whiskey Rebellion was a citizens' uprising that

the two-mile walk to the farmhouse he was living in, crossing through a bog meadow. A blizzard blew in quickly from the Navesink Highlands, coming off New York Harbor. The next morning he was found lying in the field, off the path. An obituary in the *New York Mirror* called him "a warm patriot." A prediction made in another New York paper turned out not to be true: "Many of his productions will live when much of the fashionable, new-fangled, mawkish verse of modern poets will have sunk into endless oblivion."

---

popular histories perennially gloss over, as if it were merely the rabble acting up. Alexander Hamilton, Washington's brilliant aide during the war, managed to design and implement the strong federal treasury that Washington pined for, by subsuming the states' debts within a federal debt structure. (The fatherless Hamilton egged the sonless Washington on.) To finance that debt, Hamilton encouraged speculation, as per the British model. This backfired politically; Hamilton's Wall Street friends tried to corner the market on government bonds and were caught red-handed. "These extravagant sallies of speculation do injury to the government and to the whole system of public credit by disgusting all sober citizens and giving a wild air to everything," Hamilton complained. Echoing both conservative and liberal populists of the early twenty-first century, Jefferson called speculation "destructive of morality" and asserted that it "introduced its poison into the government itself." On the western frontier, where many debt-laden veterans had gone to try to work the land, there was rebellion. Hamilton looked for revenues from the citizens in the west—what would now be the Appalachian Mountains region that today frequently makes up the swing vote in American presidential elections. Hamilton imposed an excise tax on whiskey. Farmers converted excess grain to whiskey and hauled it over the mountains to the east; they were dependent on this income, and a tax on it hurt them in eastern markets, where, not coincidentally, the absentee landlords who owned the land they rented charged them rents they considered exorbitant. In 1794, in the very field where the young Washington had been ambushed while fighting alongside the British in the French and Indian War, seven thousand farmers and tenants burned effigies, put up liberty poles, talked of independence, got violent—a Revolution redux. Alexander Hamilton, the trusted treasury secretary, called out the army, and Washington led them, in perhaps the only instance of an American president leading troops in combat—"to check," as Washington put it, "so daring and unwarrantable a spirit." The troops herded locals (including congressmen from the area who were Hamilton's political enemies) out of their homes and through the woods, imprisoned them without charge, and interrogated them for evidence of treason. Destruction of property while rioting against taxes still seems uncivil. However, using twenty thousand federal troops to terrorize low-income communities is by no means a warrantable spirit. Washington and Hamilton were using the army as a thug, and today you have to wonder how it would have gone if the farmers had had Internet access. Washington

JAWS

In the middle of the winter, I put my search for a signal point on hold as snow covered the Watchung Mountains and the suburban valleys, as well as the ice-ravaged city. I waited as it snowed again and again, the city hit with blizzards, roofs caving in across the Northeast, cars and buses stranded, people dying because they were inaccessible to emergency personnel on streets that were under four feet of snow. Storm after storm piled new snow on layers of old frozen, street-gray slush, with a hard Christmas Night blizzard underneath the new year's landscape. On the night of the blizzard, I went out to help some guests home, a couple in their seventies: my in-laws. They insisted on walking, but as soon as we got outside I realized walking was a bad idea, the snowdrifts disabling, the wind fierce, sleet and ice unfaceable—a punishment, no joke. Cabs stood stranded everywhere, the sound of spinning wheels drowned out only by the wind's howl. Miraculously, a subway carried us the mile's distance, and then I walked that mile home, the wind at my back. On my street, I looked down an alley of soft, white curves. The low, racing clouds overhead made the street a dark, rumbling cave. In the light of a streetlamp I saw wind-blown spirals of snow, a punishing design.

The city was crippled for several days; I couldn't get out. But after the next storm came and went, I drove out to New Jersey, to Freehold, to try to find the bog swamp where Philip Freneau died.

---

turned back halfway, letting Hamilton take the army to the finish line, where farmers were brought back to Philadelphia jails and soon released, with only two trumped-up convictions. In recent years, newly labeled "activist conservatives" have been talking about the federal government as a powerful tool in "national-greatness conservatism," a phrase coined by David Brooks (a *New York Times* columnist) and David Kristol in a 1997 *Wall Street Journal* piece. Hamilton, via Washington, has become the architect of modern financial markets, the seat of national greatness, it would seem. Washington, via Hamilton, becomes the too-big-to-fail president. William Hogeland, the author of a penetrating history of the Whiskey Rebellion, wrote recently in *Inventing American History*: "Neo-Hamiltonians of every kind are blotting out a defining feature of his thoughts, one that Hamilton himself insisted on throughout his turbulent career: the essential relationship between the concentration of national wealth and the obstruction of democracy through military force."

My friend Brian, a college professor who teaches film and lives in my neighborhood, offered to drive me, and we used snow shovels to dig out the car. In a few minutes we were across the Verrazano-Narrows Bridge, crossing Staten Island and the not-frozen Arthur Kill, and safely in New Jersey. Soon, on a road into Monmouth County, we were passing some old-looking homes and many recently built strip malls. In Freehold, we drove up and down the main drag, Brian on the phone with his wife, who was at home on a computer, the two of them debating whether we ought to eat at the Tex-Mex place or the falafel restaurant. We decided on falafel, and when we were inside, Brian realized that the people running the store were related to the family that runs a falafel place he loves back in Greenwich Village. The falafel was delicious—a lunch victory! We walked down the street to the library, and I hung out in the local-history section for a while, reading about the Battle of Monmouth, which occurred in extreme summer heat, soldiers passing out, horses dying.

Brian went straight to the library's computer and somehow elicited the ire of the staff, apparently not having followed a computer sign-up rule, although that blew over pretty quickly. As relations warmed up, I was permitted to use the copying machine, and soon we were all chatting happily, so that I thought it was a good idea to ask where the last home of the Poet of the Revolution was. Nobody knew. I had a pretty good idea of my own, but Brian encouraged me to ask at the Monmouth County Department of Economic Development and Tourism, located on Main Street in Freehold. In a few seconds we were sitting in the office of Jeanne DeYoung, the director of tourism, who gave us a book about Monmouth County–related Revolutionary War events, ferry schedules, some brochures about bike routes, and a book on the Revolutionary War in Monmouth.

Though she did not know where Freneau had last lived, she knew his grave was in Matawan, a few towns north. Generally speaking, she seemed happy we had stopped in, and as we chatted about the history of the area, she recalled burying a time capsule with a troop of Girl Scouts she had led, and she also remembered that her own kids had been fascinated with the bullet holes in a colonial house on Matawan Creek, where British soldiers chased a rebel out a window. "They loved it," she said.

I looked over at Brian, who seemed a little bored at that point, but then just about jumped out of his chair when she told us that the creek was the place where a shark had been killed, a story that was the basis for the film *Jaws*. *"Jaws!"* he said. "You're kidding me!"

We took directions to the battlefield for later, and then set out to calculate the path that Freneau would have walked from the tavern late that snowy night, even though, accounts say, people in the tavern told him to take the long way, rather than walk through the swamp, a detail that sounds like guilt management to me—the tavern drinkers feeling bad that they had let the old guy go out and freeze to death (just my theory).

SPIRAL

As is the case for a lot of old towns, the road map of Freehold resembles a wheel with spokes, the hub being the center of town, meaning the place has been there a while, or at least since before the invention of modern streamlined highways, before straight lines ruled the day.* We

---

*Circles offered amusement, too, in pre-interstate times, as in the case of something called the Shepherd's Labyrinth, a spiral maze that appears to have been witnessed by the English ancestors of George Washington. This maze is mentioned in *The Washingtons: A Tale of a Country Parish in the Seventeenth Century Based on Authentic Documents*, published in 1860 and described in a spiral-bound notebook kept by the artist Robert Smithson. Other spirals that Smithson took notes on include the spiral drawing by Constantin Brancusi that is a portrait of James Joyce ("Well, Jim hasn't changed much," Joyce's father said when he saw it); a quote from a book entitled *The Novels of Flaubert*: "One of his most symptomatic literary projects is that of *La Spirale*, which was to describe the state of permanent somnambulism of a hallucinated madman"; and a quote from Samuel Beckett's *The Unnamable*: "It must have got embroiled in a kind of inverting spiral, I mean one of the coils of which, instead of widening more and more, grew narrower and narrower, and finally, given the kind of space in which I was supposed to evolve, would come to an end for lack of room." According to an essay by Thomas Crow written for the catalog of a Robert Smithson show at the Whitney Museum of American Art in 2005, Smithson underlined this passage in his copy of the Beckett novel. You see the spiral show up early on in Smithson's work, in the crooks of the limbs of trees he draws as humans, and in quasi-religious paintings featuring spirals that are stigmata-like. Eventually, it seems to me, spirals became a life-affirming symbol in Smithson's work, but in the beginning they speak to me of death.

drove down an old street toward Freneau's former farm—I had gotten the approximate location of Freneau's last home from a man who lived in a house that Freneau had once lived in, in Matawan. I calculated what I thought was the oldest route to the site of the farm. I had imagined I would walk it, but then we took a lot of time at the falafel place, and I felt bad keeping Brian from things he had to do that afternoon. So we drove the two miles, and to my amazement ended up in a housing development called Poet's Corner.

We entered on Freneau Boulevard, passing Poe Court and Thoreau Drive. Ahead were courts named for Henry Wadsworth Longfellow, Edna St. Vincent Millay, and Walt Whitman, as well as Twain, Cooper, and Irving. Cummings Court intersected Bryant Drive, and Frost Court was a cul-de-sac, a road that circled back to where you started, as if you hadn't taken it. To get to the street named for Joyce Kilmer, you took Lazarus Drive, a long uninspiring loop road. There were signs everywhere on the carless streets about unauthorized parking, little haikus to anxiety. I guessed that the place where Frost Court intersected Freneau Drive was probably where a farmhouse would have been—just off a little hill, and looking down into some remnant wetland, as well as fields that are now a park. I walked around a little.

We got back in the car and parked on the side of the road, roughly equidistant between the house that wasn't there and the tavern that no longer existed. I entered the park near some old streams that seemed to me to have once been swampy, close to a sewage treatment plant, a hint.

The sky was bright and clear, no sign of the storm from the night before, and I took up Freneau's last path in the empty, snow-filled field, the snow a foot deep, maybe a couple in the creamy drifts. I began to trudge my way across the field, which was difficult through the thick snow. It occurred to me that when a person is lost, he tends to walk in circles, unintentionally, especially in woods, especially when it is dark, especially when his feet drag, especially when he is in the midst of a blizzard.

In the big, open field, I began to walk in a large, left-turning circle the size of a baseball infield, and then, coming back around, walked in a slightly smaller version of the same. I repeated the circle, so that I was spiraling in, making a slow, narrowing circumference. Brian was waiting for me by the car, which seemed faraway. I picked up speed, circling faster and faster. The snow being deep, it was slow going, as I have noted, and I was quickly tired, beginning to breathe heavily. Then I started to run, and as I continued, I suddenly began to feel terrible for Freneau, the failed poet. I felt a heaviness, a visceral dread, and I thought I was going to cry.

No one was around except Brian, leaning against the car, waiting, looking away, and I was now running in a tightening circle, finding it, in fact, harder to breathe. As I ran, I tightened the circle still further, and, running faster, I felt my heart pounding more, with a strangely consoling intensity. I stopped at last at the very center of the circle, and when I finished, my head was spinning, my heart pounding. I was perspiring, and I was stooped over, and then just kneeling in the snow, finding my breath again.

BATTLEFIELD ORCHARD

As we started the drive home, Brian and I were talking about how difficult it seems to be to understand war if you have never been in the military, a topic that gradually brought us to our respective fathers, both of whom had served. I recalled my father, who served in the Korean War, telling me about how he was once ordered to accompany a train to Alabama, escorting the remains of a soldier who had been missing in Korea, whose body was then recovered and sent home. I remembered, too, that my father had learned that his own father was going to die on the day he went off to the army. "I guess I won't see you again," my grandfather told my father. Sure enough, the next time my father came home was for his father's wake. At least, that's how I remember the story.

Brian reminisced about his father, who was an army captain in World War II. Brian had been watching a documentary about the war on television, years after his father had died, and the documentary happened to mention his father's army unit, a unit that had liberated a concentration camp in Germany. As Brian sat in a kind of shock, the documentary proceeded to report that his father, who was a doctor, had ordered a German officer at the camp to get water for a liberated camp victim who had been too weak to retrieve it on his own. Brian was startled to hear this story, and, of course, he listened with extreme interest. The program's narrator then reported that after the officer severely disparaged the victim and refused Brian's father's order, Brian's father shot the German officer, killing him. "He never told me that," Brian said.

Before we got on the road, we debated stopping at a farm stand—there were orchards on and around the old Revolutionary War battlefield, peach and apple trees. Brian was not convinced it was a good idea to stop; he thought the farm-stand food would be of poor quality. But I was hungry, and he relented. When we went inside the shop at Battlefield Orchards, we were both immediately in heaven, as they made their doughnuts on the premises—we both love doughnuts.

"Were these doughnuts made today?" Brian asked excitedly.

"Yes," a woman answered. I bought a coffee and some doughnuts and began to eat the doughnuts. They were delicious.

Brian had more questions. "How many minutes ago?" Brian wanted to be close to the birth of the doughnut.

The woman looked at him. "I don't know how many minutes," she said.

As we pulled out of the parking lot, we could see a long row of apple trees across the street, the trees craggy and leafless, the tips of their longest branches reaching up and standing out against the fresh white snow, fine-fingered tips of deep red.

PART FOUR

A

SIGNAL

I WILL LONG REMEMBER the day I finally signaled back to New York City from the mountains. I felt as if I had spent a lifetime working on signaling, even though it was a relatively short period of time, just a few months. It was at the end of winter, and I remember racing the green buds of spring, thinking that my view would soon be blocked by leaves, that by April, when the leaves came out again, my chance would be gone. In this way, the coming of spring seemed to me to be particularly personal. At this point in the earth's yearly revolution around the sun, I felt invested, as if this were my revolution, my one beautiful chance.

I began my signaling attempt thinking about using some kind of artificial light. The troops had used fires, calling them "signal beacons." The plans for the first beacons were drawn up by General William Alexander, a.k.a. Lord Sterling, who happened to live in the Watchung Mountains. He made the sketch reproduced on the following page.

They were wooden structures, sixteen feet square at the base, rising like pyramids, stuffed with dry twigs and brush, ready to be ignited. In 1778 and 1779, six of them were placed along the Watchung peaks that protected the Continental Army. There were beacons farther up, in the Hudson Valley, and there was a beacon outside Princeton on the peak called Remarkable Hill. The beacons stretched north and south, though by the time of the Hard Winter at Morristown, they were likely neglected, fallen into disrepair. "I have requested Mr. Caldwell to have them re-established and proper persons appointed to give the alarm

in case of necessity," General Arthur St. Clair wrote to Washington, "but I am not certain but this may interfere with some regulation of the state, which some time ago put the matter into the care of the militia general, and it has gone into the hands of the subordinate officers in gradation until it is nobody's business." In the city called Summit, there was a beacon spot remembered with a marker on a boulder. The historian John Cunningham suggests that no physical evidence of the beacons remains because they were burned for joy at the conclusion of the war.

Since, for sundry reasons, I did not want to attempt to light a giant bonfire along hilltops, I thought about using electric lights of some kind, and using them at night seemed as if it would be most effective. I researched businesses that sold the powerful search lights used on ranches and for construction purposes. I became briefly conversant in lumens, the measurement of light emitted per second in flashlights and spotlight beams. Things got pricey fast, though, and I abandoned the light idea when I realized that I might be able to use a mirror. Mirrors had a part in the history of long-distance communications, after all, as a type of upgraded semaphore. Mirrors were used by the French during the time of Napoléon, signaling from one military installation to the next, and surely some nation or tribe that I do not know about signaled to a place far away with something reflective during the time of the Greeks and the Romans, who extolled the virtues of large fires. Virgil in his *Georgics* writes: "Cattle graze on clover, the towering forest yields pine boards, wood is tossed on nighttime fires, and they blaze up with light. How can men hesitate to sow and give their care? Why pursue a greater theme?"

The first successful long-distance signaling in the United States occurred in 1801, in Massachusetts, where, for six winters, a chain of men on hills used spyglasses to note the position of moveable arms attached to a tower as a means of relaying information about incoming ships from Martha's Vineyard across Cape Cod, and over the low peaks to Telegraph Street in South Boston. In New York in 1812, the inventor Christopher Colles set up a signal chain from Manhattan to Sandy Hook. Colles used a system of black and white balls suspended from poles, a semaphore.*

---

*In a book-length essay entitled *Circles and Lines*, the historian John Demos argues that the Revolution marked a shift in colonial society, roughly put, from circles to lines. In other words, prior to the Revolution, colonial life was arranged according to circular or, more specifically, cyclical markers—tides, lunar cycles, seasons, and the movement of the sun. People farmed, traveled, conceived children, and, according to Demos's research, died according to these cycles. Atmospheric disturbances were just that: disturbances, interruptions of the cycle, and thus omens. A comet that appeared at the time of the Boston Massacre was widely considered a good omen, for instance, a sign of colonial fortunes improving, and quickly became associated with revolution. This so-called Lexell comet could be seen by the naked eye in America, coming within 1.4 million miles of the earth, the closest comet ever; in a sense, the Lexell comet is the father of the American flag's stars, arranged as a "new constellation." The *Boston Post-Boy* first mentioned a star and a flag in 1770: "The American Ensign now sparkles a star." A conception of life as linear came after the war, as devices such as the clock and the time card more and more replaced the sun, as the railroad set the country to schedules, as telegraphs ran along lines, literally, to bring news at any time of day. While reading the journals of people alive before and after the Revolution, looking for signs of a shift from circle to line (and watching especially for mentions of schedules or moons), I read about Mary Fish, who lived from 1736 to 1818. She survived three husbands, and for her a good marriage seemed to be a combination of circle and line, a sine curve that went through deaths and sad illnesses and through, in her words, "thankfulness while I had it." In March 1805, Fish saw a loved one off on a boat to England, and shortly after the ship left, word arrived that another ship coming from England had sailed into a field of icebergs and sunk. Two months later a letter came saying that the England-bound ship had made it safely across: the same field of icebergs had been successfully navigated under a full moon. "What do you cry for?" a man asked Mary Fish when the letter arrived. "For joy, sir," she said.

In January 1813, British war vessels were spotted, and the signal
back to New York City meant that furnaces were started up, to heat
cannon balls in preparation for battle. A similar signal chain was used
in the 1830s from Sandy Hook, across Staten Island, and over to the
roof of the United States Hotel at the South Street Seaport, and, in the
race to get information to the city (mostly stock reports), carrier pigeons were sent ahead from the incoming boats to the signal stations.
Sometimes surveyors used lamps to mark locations at night. With the
invention of a device called the heliotrope, which used mirrors to aim
sunlight across distances, the sun could be reflected during the day,
targeted from point to point as a beacon. When Thomas Jefferson commissioned the first coastal survey, the triangulation involved was begun in New York Harbor. The very first survey point was just south of
Paterson, New Jersey, about a mile from the Passaic Falls, on a peak in
the Watchung Range called Garrett Mountain. The survey point itself
was called Weasel Point, and in 1934 a U.S. Geologic Survey search team
determined that the marker had been buried in a part of the mountain
that had been blown off, most likely for use as traprock.

To aid in my signaling, I studied maps of the first coastal surveys by
the federal government, and I found the sketches that surveyors made
on top of a hill in Staten Island, looking out at Manhattan and Brooklyn, the Palisades and the Watchungs in New Jersey on the far left.

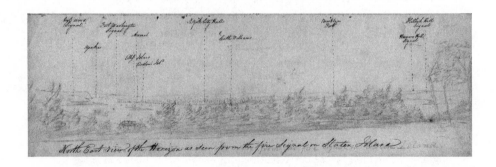

I took out my compass and maps and went around my neighborhood, looking for views to the old beacon sites—in a little park, for
example, overlooking the Brooklyn–Queens Expressway, and even
standing in a crosswalk of the very busy Atlantic Avenue.

I thought about the quality of the air that I would be signaling through. Was the air worse than in the time of the Revolution? Would the atmosphere thus limit my view? It was certainly better than when I was a kid. People got sick, passed out, and even died from pollution in the 1950s in New York, when factory emissions and other pollutants combined to choke people—an estimated two hundred persons died when atmospheric conditions locked in air pollution over New York on November 12–21 in 1953, what public health officials called a "toxic smokeshade." (The Clean Air Act was passed in 1963, the year I was born.)

During my signal-point search, I went out to a neighborhood in Queens, near where I had lived as a kid, to look at one of the oldest tulip trees in the city, in the woods in Alley Pond Park. In the city, large old trees are like important sentries, repositories of time. On the walk there I saw lichen on all the street trees, a bright yellowish dust in the midst of a drab January. I asked a naturalist how I had missed all the lichen as a child, and he said I hadn't. "You wouldn't have seen it," he said, "because it wasn't there. It couldn't survive because of the air quality back then."

I plotted from our apartment, on the top floor of an old brownstone, from where I could just see the top of the Watchungs. In particular, I could make out some sort of tank and a radio tower. If I could only determine where the tank was, I reasoned, I could find a point near it and signal back from that point to my home, enlisting a member of my family, who might spot me. GPS would have to be outside of my strategic arsenal, and likewise, for instance, a pair of high-powered binoculars. I used only maps and sight lines, and regular-strength binoculars. Recognizing the top of a wind turbine from a site just across the harbor, on the waterfront in Jersey City, I connected the dots and determined that the tank was in East Orange, next to the radio tower belonging to WFMU, a college station—a point just shy of twenty miles away, as the crow flies. One cold, clear Saturday morning at the beginning of February, I rented a car for a few hours and headed out there.

I had only a couple of hours—my wife was working on Saturday mornings in February, and my daughter had to go to a chorus rehearsal around lunchtime. (My son was off at college.) Also, the sun was best early, rising in the east, blaring at the Watchungs, where I hoped to bounce it back to New York before it began its still-wintertime fade. I looked out our open window with my daughter, who was fourteen at the time, and attempted to point out the place in the hills where I thought I would be, though I was not absolutely certain, since I didn't know what exactly I would find when I got there. I gave her a rough idea, anyway. Then I got the car, raced through the Holland Tunnel, into the bright openness of the Meadowlands, and, where the interstate highway cuts through the Watchungs, I exited, driving just a few hundred yards southwest along the hilltop road, aptly named Prospect Avenue. I looked for the widest possible prospect.*

Impatient motorists deterred me as I drove near the water tank and the radio tower. I found a hilltop housing development nearby, but circled the parking lot to turn around quickly when I realized it was an Alzheimer's care facility, private property. I drove down a steep hill a few yards on a busy road, Mount Pleasant Avenue, though it was not pleasant in terms of the chances of being hit while signaling. Nevertheless, the view of the city was almost overwhelming—it was a front-row view of a giant tableau twenty miles away: a splendid, sparkling city. I parked on a side street, scrambled to the shoulder of Mount Pleasant Avenue, and, as a guy unloading big bags of cat food from his car watched me curiously, used an official Boy Scout pocket mirror, a gift from my wife, and called my daughter on my cell phone, all while trying not to get run over.

What the guy lugging cat food might have heard: "Can you see me? . . . Are you looking where I said? . . . I'm still signaling . . . Okay, look now . . . Okay, can you see me? . . . Are you sure? Look now . . . How about now?"

It was in this fashion that the first signal trip ended in disappointment.

I thought it would be a cinch, a one-shot deal, signaling. I tried several more times, repeating the process, always on Saturday mornings, which were of a limited supply. I went to the same general area, gave

---

*A 1789 entry from the journal of President George Washington, after visiting Middletown, Connecticut: "While dinner was getting ready I took a walk round the Town, from the heights of which the prospect is beautiful."

my daughter similar directions. The second time, I stopped at a diner a little farther up the hill and tried signaling from behind a Dumpster in the parking lot, wondering what I looked like from the tables that had the view of the guy with the Boy Scout mirror in the trash area. When I went in to buy a cup of coffee, the waitress said, "The blueberry muffins just came out of the oven." I bought one—it was great—and asked her where the best view of the city was. She directed me to a nearby county park, Eagle Rock.

I called my daughter and signaled again. "I still don't see you," my daughter said repeatedly. "It's freezing," she also said. I had her standing in an open window again.

I consented to a plan whereby she could close the window and step down from the stool she was standing on. Next, I called our landlord, a history buff and outdoorsman who had volunteered his aid the day before. As I waited at Eagle Rock, he climbed to the roof of our building. Surely, roof access would do it, I thought as I waited alone, with only a dog walker in the distance and a man napping in his car at the hilltop overlook. It's a quiet thing, signaling. No sound, and nothing to indicate you are or are not reflecting light toward your signalee; the city does not notice you at all, despite its being so close, the person on-stage who doesn't know you are there. I could see the Empire State Building—I was in *its* view now, an at-this-point invisible speck in the panorama. More important, I could see the hills back in Brooklyn, where my landlord was ascending to the roof. He called to say he was in position. I resumed signaling from Eagle Rock.

"I don't see anything," he said. "Where am I looking, again?" After a while, his eyes were tearing in the cold. "I promised my wife I'd go get groceries," he finally said.

When my wife was able, I enlisted her, this time from a slightly different vantage point, in Brooklyn Heights, a place on the waterfront with a wide view of New York Harbor, a less obstructed view, I thought, of the Watchungs—the view that Abraham Lincoln overpraised: "There may be finer views than this in the world, but I don't believe it." I went to my same places in the Watchungs, in the vicinity of the radio tower. I raced from the Eagle Rock to the street where I had seen the guy with the cat food, who wasn't there this time. My wife was watching with a friend.

"Can you see anything?" I asked.

"No, we can't see you," she said.

Of course I had doubts. Was it a problem with my signaling? Or were my aides looking in the wrong direction? Did they understand the view of the hills? Did they even know what the reflection would look like? Come to think of it, what *would* it look like?

I put the project off for a couple of weeks. I researched the history of the viewpoints. I investigated the Cunard Steamship Company's cemetery in Jersey City, where the graves had a view of the harbor, and thought about trying from a shorter distance. My wife got me a slightly larger mirror, to supplement my Boy Scout pocket reflector. The hills continued to enjoin me.

At one point, I was driving my parents from New Jersey up to Connecticut, where they were now moving, out of the New York area. It was another crisp, cold day; eagles rode the ice floes as we crossed the Hudson River, and I could easily see the Empire State Building, twenty-two miles south of the Tappan Zee Bridge. It was also the winter that a dovekie had washed up alive on the shore of Staten Island. Dovekies live in the Arctic in the summer and winter as far south as New York. They live in huge flocks, floating by the thousands off the coast of New York, but rarely if ever come to shore, unless blown in by storms. (Thousands of dovekies were blown into New York Harbor during a winter storm in 1932, the year of George Washington's bicentennial.)*

---

*I learned about the dovekie from my favorite almanac, the *Hudson River Almanac*, a weekly journal sponsored by the New York State Department of Environmental Conservation. Its stated aim: "The *Hudson River Almanac* is a natural history journal that covers the Hudson from the High Peaks of the Adirondacks to New York Harbor. It seeks to capture the spirit, magic, and science of the river by presenting the observations of many individuals who delight in the diversity of nature in the Hudson Valley." On February 5 of the winter of my signaling, the almanac featured this entry, submitted by a Staten Island resident who identified himself as Dave Taft:

> If this occurred anywhere upstate, no one would have batted an eye, but Ray Matarazzo and I stood in a small park on Staten Island staring at what might be the last patch of wintergreen (Gaultheria sp.) on the island. We counted about 30 plants under and between the heavy oak-leaf litter. Then we carefully selected one leaf and crushed it between our fingers. The unmistakable scent was like cracking open a bottle of fine champagne for Ray and I. Though probably once more abundant on Staten Island, records show it was considered rare in the last botanical survey of 1981. Though the rough location of the record had been passed along

I took this as a sign, a signal to me, a rarely seen bird appearing. I began to feel confident that I would signal successfully—I knew it would work.

One day I was out in Sheepshead Bay, looking across to the Atlantic Highlands, when I saw what looked like an easy signal point. On Mount Mitchell, near Sandy Hook, in New Jersey, a park boasts a direct view of New York. Investigating further, I realized that Sandy Hook had been the site of a Cold War missile base. I soon discovered that the U.S. government built a ring of missile sites around New York in the 1950s, to operate radar and intercept incoming Soviet bombers. "Throughout the Cold War, these sites were manned on a 24-hour per day basis on constant alert, ready to defend the region, the nation and the North American continent," wrote a historian of the missile sites.

The sites are now in parks and alongside farms, and, in the case of New Jersey, along the Watchung Mountains. The locations of many of the bases coincided with Revolutionary signal points, due to shared strategic interests. "Radar cannot see around corners," said a 1955 news account in *The New York Times*, in explanation of the sighting. "This requirement of a clear view greatly restricts the engineers' choice of a site."

More recently, viewpoints in the vicinity of the former missile sites had become hosts to memorials to those who died when the World Trade Center towers collapsed on September 11, 2001. When the towers were on fire, people came to the hills, to the old viewpoints, to look out on the city. I would end up, I felt, in a place where the Revolution, the Cold War, and modern memorials all coincided.

I continued plotting, going to our apartment window all the time. Looking at the hills, I was thinking about a spot between the former Nike Missile Battery known as NY-73, in Summit, New Jersey, the site of stables now, and a radar base in Livingston, at what is now an art park. On the Brooklyn side, I scoped out a parking structure at the

---

verbally to a few Staten Island naturalists, none were located in several searches from the mid-1980's on, and the plants were finally considered lost. How nice to reclaim them for the flora of Staten Island, if not all of New York City. Earlier in the afternoon, we found two small plants of rattlesnake plantain (Goodyera pubescens), another great rarity within New York City limits.

bottom of Atlantic Avenue. It was tall enough to have an unobstructed view of Watchungs; though it felt like trespassing being there, not a perfect location to send my wife to. I thought a lot about angles, about the curvature of the earth and the refraction of light. I learned about what mariners call looming. In certain situations, when the moisture in the air refracts light and bends it in a particular way, a person on land watching for a boat can spot the boat *before* it comes over the curve of the earth. They can see the boat, in other words, on the other side of the world.

I was, eventually, to rethink my approach to signaling by reading about surveyors and the towers they built, their strategies in the wild, their general perseverance. I got hold of an old formula used by U.S. Geologic Survey teams to deal with the earth's curvature and so forth: "On a 10 mile line, absolute flat terrain, 15 ft. towers at each end, or 58 ft. at one end, would be required for minimum clearance; and for a 20 mile line, same situation, 58 ft. at each end, or 230 ft. at one end." I decided to go higher, and to completely reverse my plan of attack. Instead of worrying about finding a place to signal back from, I would concentrate on the place where the signal would (hopefully) be seen— put myself in the viewer's shoes, in other words.

At the end of a school day, I convinced my daughter to take me into her school, up to the eleventh floor of an old building in Brooklyn Heights, not so far from what Washington would have known as Fort Sterling, and very close to the house called Four Chimneys, where the retreat from Brooklyn was ordered. From a large, westward-facing window, I saw the Watchungs, a dark-blue swath in the afternoon winter sun. Within the Watchungs, I could easily see in one particular spot, a large indent in the ridge that is known as the Springfield Gap, a cut in the hills where the British tried to surprise Washington, but the New Jersey militia saw the British coming, even used a beacon. It was a beacon point, and it was close to the Nike missile bases. It was building-less—a park, I figured out when I got home.

I woke up early—the older I get, the more I enjoy the dawn, the more I believe in it. Out the window, the buds on the trees were opening, the hills turning that joyous spring green, nature's gold. Crepuscular rays melted a hazy morning sky. I made arrangements with my daughter to call her during a morning class period that she had free, at a time when the sun would be right for signaling. This would mean I was taking the project to a larger arena—namely, her school. She was understandably wary, due to my previous failures to signal successfully, but agreed nevertheless. I woke up early the next morning and boarded a train, and got out at Short Hills, and walked toward the hill that marks the northern edge of the Springfield Gap. I asked a man in the commuter parking lot for directions. "Sorry," he said. "I'm visiting my grandparents." I passed a large sycamore, as well as a memorial for the people who died in the World Trade Center attacks, and entered South Mountain Reservation, a large hilltop park. I passed through a picnic area and saw a natural spring, fenced off. The water was bubbling up out of the ground, but a sign attached to the fence said: "Not for Human Consumption."

I followed a path up the steep hill, my old back creaking, and, even though it was a clear March day, bright and breezy, imagined myself climbing the dark shadows of the Springfield Gap as I remembered seeing it in the late-afternoon light, in the large, westward-facing window of my daughter's school, a music room actually—I felt as if I were walking up the hill in a painting. I climbed up above an old reservoir, and had a small panic attack that I would cause some kind of accidental security threat, with my Boy Scout mirror near a reservoir. I made it to the top of the ridge unaccosted and positioned myself for the best view. It was a wide-open vista, but it was not what I had hoped. It was looking south, toward Elizabeth and New Brunswick and Princeton, toward the Revolutionary War encampments of the British. I was trying to look east, toward my daughter.

Time was running out. I was going to miss her, due to her class schedule. Frantically, I got onto a park trail and began to jog north along the ridge, but there were thick trees blocking the view. Eventually, I came upon walkers—two women and a dog. "Is there a good view of New York City anywhere around here?" I asked. They pointed ahead.

"It's very close," one woman said.

I was running and came to a little bench commanding an incredible view, the city sitting in the bottom of the bowl of blue sky, resonating like a thick and gorgeous major chord.

I quickly retrieved my mirrors from my backpack, both the new larger mirror and my smaller Boy Scout one. I called my daughter. There was no answer. I was a few minutes late. I called the main number of the school and asked for the music room, and got no answer. In desperation, I called the school office. I realized it would take a lot of time to explain my mission, but I tried. "I'm in New Jersey," I began by saying.

"Really? I got lost in New Jersey recently," the woman answering the phone said.

I asked her about my daughter and she had just seen her. She kindly offered to track her down. I hung up, waited, paced, took a photo of the panorama. My phone rang. It was my daughter.

"Dad?" she said.

She sounded hesitant, which, sure, I could understand. On the other hand, what could I do really? I needed to signal to her, and she was one of a very small number of people on earth who could understand what I might be up to.

I asked her to go to the window of the music room. I could hear other people in the room, including the woman who had answered the phone and found my daughter in class. Later, my daughter would tell me that she was concerned about the signaling that morning. After all, every single one of our previous attempts had failed, as in failed completely. Looking out the window at a distant hill where your father was signaling from a Revolutionary War vantage point and not seeing the signal is not the kind of thing that wins you respect among your middle school peers. Unfortunately, I was not contemplating the impact of any possible failure at that moment—one of my larger flaws, I have to say. Why can I not remember that what's good for the signaler is not always good for the signalee?—and when I think about that now, it saddens me. Washington learned to retreat, after attacking failed. Why can't I? Incredibly, my daughter went through with the mission.

I had the new mirror that my wife had given me ready. I could see Brooklyn. With binoculars I could sort of make out the neighborhood my daughter was in. I aimed the reflection toward the city, toward her. All of a sudden, I heard screams in the room.

"I can see it!" she shouted.

"Can you see me?" I said.

"No, I can *really* see it." I could hear other people saying they could see it, too, a pleasing commotion.

I tried with my Boy Scout mirror. "Yep, I can see it," she said.

I couldn't believe it. I was ecstatic. I didn't know what to say. Where I stood, there was no one around, a place made more beautiful by its loneliness. The city was sparkling in the morning sun, the harbor glistening. "What does it look like?" I asked her.

"Like a bright white flash."

I thanked her profusely. I took another photo of the city out across the tops of the budding green trees, and hung out a little and called another friend, and then suddenly realized I had to hurry to catch the next train back. I rushed down the hill. The train was coming when I got to the station, and when I shouted ahead to ask which way to the New York–bound platform, two people pointed two different ways. I went left, and just made it through the train's closing door, perspiring.

On the ride back, the train paralleled the hills for a while, then set out across the Meadowlands, across the Passaic and the Hackensack, for the millionth time, and I kept looking back at the Watchungs, having signaled. I was so pleased and exhausted that by the time we were headed back into the tunnel to New York, I was falling asleep.

NOTES ON SOURCES

꒰꒱

PART ONE: THE PANORAMA OF THE REVOLUTION

For an overview of the American Revolution in general, I read Gordon S. Wood's *The American Revolution* (New York: Modern Library, 2002), and for an overview of the war in New York City in particular, I referred over and over to *The Battle for New York* (New York: Penguin, 2002), Barnet Schecter's excellent study of the city during the rebellion. I read Ron Chernow's *Washington: A Life* (New York: Penguin, 2010), as well as what I think of as a companion volume, *The Way of Duty: A Woman and Her Family in Revolutionary America* (New York: W. W. Norton & Co., 1984), by Joy Day Buel and Richard Buel, Jr., a husband-and-wife team. *The Way of Duty* is a portrait of Mary Fish (1736–1818): "After following you with my eyes as far as I could see your [ship], I retired into the house with the consoling thought that you were going where providence calls you, and the way of duty is the way of safety," Fish wrote in her diary in 1805. John Adams's letter about the Revolution was brought to my attention in a lecture given by Joanne Freeman, a professor of history at Yale University ("Freeman's Top Five Tips for Studying the Revolution" can be viewed online), while a signed copy of *Episodes in the History of Griggstown: A Bicentennial Tribute Covering 300 Years* (New York: Albert H. Vela, 1976) was loaned to me by the owners of the former Black Horse Tavern in Griggstown, New Jersey. Richard Brookhiser is the historian who notes that it takes twenty minutes on a shuttle flight to pass over the area in which the war was primarily fought, and I am grateful for a conversation I had with the historian Robert Gross regarding the importance of the Middle Colonies as the original so-called Middle America. I read William Hogeland's *Declaration* (New York: Simon & Schuster, 2010) and was joined by Hogeland at an anniversary reading of the Declaration of Independence at Federal Hall, on Wall Street, in July 2010. (Later, Hogeland wrote in his blog: "And along with being predictably bizarre—passersby completely ignoring the unignorable, giggling tourists getting photographed with reenactors, a guy asking me 'Is this a protest? or a reenactment?' etc.—it was great, because two of the readers really shouted out the list of grievances, and they hit hard. I actually got goosebumps.")

Notes on Washington's teeth come from the National Dental Museum, and I read about Viscount Bolingbroke in several sources, especially *The Invention of George Washington*, by Paul Longmore (Charlottesville: University of Virginia Press, 1999). The 1910 edition of the *Encyclopaedia Britannica* includes an entry on Bolingbroke: "His genius and character were superficial; his abilities were exercised upon ephemeral objects, and not inspired by lasting or universal ideas."

The excerpt from a colonial almanac comes from *The Common People of Colonial America*, by Louis K. Wechsler (New York: Vantage Press, 1978). I found some information regarding the Battle of Pelham on the Village of Pelham's website, in papers authored by a Pelham historian, Blake Bell. Blake argues that Glover's Rock is in the wrong place: "In effect, the place where the battle began today is a rise near about the second tee of the Split Rock Golf Course. The battle then progressed across the remainder of today's Split Rock Golf Course toward today's New England Thruway, crossing that Thruway where the troops proceeded in the areas along today's Split Rock Road in the Village of Pelham Manor, along Wolf's Lane to today's Colonial Avenue where it essentially ended at the grounds of today's Pelham Memorial High School where the British and German troops camped." My guide in Pelham Bay Park was Michael Feller, the chief naturalist for New York City's Department of Parks and Recreation.

The mayor of Morristown was quoted in *The New York Times*, in an April 29, 2007, article entitled "Should Immigration Be a Police Issue?" by Kareem Fahim. There were vigils and demonstrations around Morristown, where people held signs that said, for instance, "We Affirm Human Dignity."

William Carlos Williams's notes on the construction of *Paterson* (a poem that, in the poet's words, "follows the course of the Passaic River") can be found in an edition of that epic poem edited by Christopher MacGowan (New York: New Directions, 1995), and I read about Robert Smithson's birth in *Robert Smithson*, a collection of essays published in 2004 by the Museum of Contemporary Art, Los Angeles, that accompanied an exhibition of Smithson's work. An essay by Eugenie Tsai entitled "Robert Smithson: Plotting a Line from Passaic, New Jersey, to Amarillo, Texas" discusses Smithson's work through his notion of "sites": "One of the most important concepts Smithson advanced was that of the 'site,' a place in the world where art is inseparable from its context."

Smithson's own essay, "The Monuments of Passaic," published in *Artforum* in 1967, begins with a bus trip from the Port Authority bus terminal in downtown Passaic, a trip I have myself taken on countless occasions while working in Passaic as a newspaper reporter in the mid-1980s. I did not know about Smithson's work until I met my wife, in 1987. More recently, I took Smithson's bus trip again, and was startled to see that it follows the path of Washington's 1776 retreat through New Jersey, toward the Delaware River—an intersection of the interests of a Father of Our Country and a father of earth art, I would argue. Smithson, as I note, spent a great deal of time, as a young person and later as an artist, in the Watchung Mountains, which were a central geographic factor in Washington's war strategy. I have not been able to determine where exactly Smithson grew up in Clifton, New Jersey, but I know that when he lived in New York City, he lived on Washington Street in Greenwich Village, one of the oldest surviving thoroughfares in the city.

In Wallington, New Jersey, across the river from the City of Passaic, there is a marker denoting Washington's crossing of the Passaic River, after which he burned the bridge; and across the river in a field between a church and a Burger King, a plaque says: "Under the parent of this tree Washington first took command of the American Army July 3rd 1775." There is no tree near the plaque today. I am grateful to Jill Desimini, assistant professor of landscape architecture at Harvard University's Graduate School of Design, for assistance in retracing the route of the Continental Army through the New Jersey Meadowlands, the so-called Retreat to Victory.

PART TWO: ACROSS THE RIVER AND OVER THE MOUNTAINS

The destruction of Leutze's painting in Germany by British bombers that is described as "a final act of retribution for the American Revolution" came, as did many details of Washington's crossing itself, from *Washington's Crossing*, by David Hackett Fischer (New York: Oxford University Press, 2004). I learned about the Leutze painting and its context in German and American politics from many sources, including " 'Washington Crossing the Delaware': The Political Context," an essay by Barbara S. Groseclose in *American Art Journal* (November 1975). "Curiously, elucidation of *Washington Crossing the Delaware*'s German context does not lessen its force as an American patriotic monument," Groseclose writes. "Leutze's devotion to the cause of democracy, acquired in his youth in America, stimulated his perception of a despotic European political structure and led to his vow to create a 'cycle of freedom,' which he envisioned as arising from Columbus's discovery of the New World and culminating in the American War of Independence. An awareness of the painting's true political nature raises the artist Leutze from a Pollyanna image-maker of Revolutionary War themes to a true proponent of democracy." I also read about Leutze in Henry Theodore Tuckerman's 1867 book *American Artist Life, Comprising Biographical and Critical Sketches of American Artists: Preceded by an Historical Account of the Rise and Progress of Art in America*, as well as in *Appleton's Cyclopaedia of American Biography*.

I learned of the origin of the Indiana stone in Washington Crossing, Pennsylvania, on a website, quarriesandbeyond.org, compiled by Peggy B. Perazzo, a member of the Association for Gravestone Studies and of the Early American Industries Association, Inc.

Henry James's recollection of viewing the Leutze painting comes from *Young Henry James: 1843–1870*, by Robert C. Le Clair (New York: Bookman Associates, 1955). Early reports on the exhibition of the painting came from *The New York Times*, as did reports on the painting's status in 1932, culminating in the January 12, 1932, dispatch, "Museum to Rehang Historic Painting." The *Times* reported that Governor Franklin D. Roosevelt proposed finding a spot for it in a state building. When William

Sloane Coffin died, his family moved to the West Coast, where his son William Jr. first became interested in social justice issues; a noted civil rights campaigner, he later led protests against the Vietnam and Iraq Wars and in support of nuclear disarmament. The death of William Sloane Coffin, Sr., is described in Warren Goldstein's biography of the younger Coffin, entitled *A Holy Impatience* (New Haven: Yale University Press, 2004). In the winter of 2003, shortly before Coffin's death, Ben McGrath visited Coffin at his home in Vermont, just as Coffin published *Credo* (Louisville: Westminster John Knox Press, 2004), a collection of meditations on such topics as justice and grace. In the December 1, 2003, *New Yorker*, McGrath wrote: "His primary aim in publishing 'Credo,' he said, 'was to teach believers how to be proper patriots.'" "As Americans, we should love America, but pledge allegiance to the earth, to the flora and fauna and human rights," Coffin told McGrath.

The Jane Street Gallery is referred to as the first artists' cooperative in New York by Grace Glueck, in a July 4, 2003, review in *The New York Times* of a Jane Street retrospective at the Tibor de Nagy Gallery, where the works proceed from abstraction toward realism, a move that Glueck explains: "As time went on, the group began to lose its fix on abstraction, partly because of a show in New York by the French artist Jean Hélion. Once a vigorous champion of abstraction, Hélion embraced a more representational style after his escape from a Nazi prison camp in the 1940's, and his new work helped ease the progress of the Jane Street group toward realism." Information about Fairfield Porter came from *Fairfield Porter: A Life in Art*, by Justin Spring (New Haven: Yale University Press, 2000), who notes that Porter's name was changed when he was a child: Fairfield was named John until his younger brother was born and his parents decided to call this second son John, renaming his predecessor Fairfield. Peleg Wadsworth was the grandfather of Henry Wadsworth Longfellow, though it is not clear that Rivers knew any of this, given that Porter was reportedly reticent about his patrician roots.

I read Grace Glueck's *New York Times Magazine* profile "Rivers Paints Himself into the Canvas," published February 13, 1966. Rivers described Leutze, according to Frank O'Hara, as "a coarse German nineteenth-century academician who really loved Napoléon more than anyone and thought that crossing a river on a late December afternoon was just another excuse for a general to assume a heroic, slightly tragic pose." After the first version of Rivers's *Washington Crossing* was burned, he painted another version, which is owned by the Whitney Museum; I have seen only the postcard. At the time I spoke with David Joel, Rivers's longtime assitant, there was a controversy surrounding a film Rivers had shot of his family: his children wanted to destroy the film (which included nudity), but Joel, as an archivist, felt duty-bound to preserve the artist's work. I saw the debate as an aspect of the career of an artist who used his own personal life to the extent that he included his family's lives as well, resulting in what sounded like civilian casualties. When I met Joel at the Museum of Modern Art, he said that he had one day shown up for work at Rivers's studio wearing a bandana on his head, to hide the hair loss resulting from his treatment for the first of what would eventually be several bouts with cancer. In Joel's telling of the story, Rivers asked him to take the bandana off. "You look good bald," Rivers said. "Come with me." The artist took him to a chair, that large, green, floral-patterned chair that Joel described as "hideous." "That's your chair, son," Rivers said. "I bought it for you. Any time you want to you can sit in that chair. I don't care if you sit in it all day, I just want you to relax and not worry about work."

"Of course I never sat in the chair," Joel said. "Until the day Larry died; then I walked over and sat down."

I read about Frank O'Hara's poetry in sources including "Semiotic Shepherds: Gary Snyder, Frank O'Hara, and the Embodiment of an Urban Pastoral," by Timothy G. Gray, in *Contemporary Literature* (Winter 1998), as well as in "'To Be at Least as Alive as the Vulgar': Frank O'Hara and the Dialectics of Sincerity," a dissertation by Andrew Michael Gorin (Wesleyan University, 2009). I visited *Painters and Poets*, the Tibor de Nagy Gallery's exhibition during the winter of 2010. In a review of the show for *The New Yorker*, published on January 31, 2011, Peter Schjeldahl, the poet and critic, noted the paintings of Jane Freilicher and Fairfield Porter: "Their reticently poetic realism bespeaks a commitment that is not only aesthetic but ethical, sacrificing formal ambitions to values of authentically experienced nature and domestic life." Michael Davidson, in "Ekphrasis and the Postmodern Painter Poem," published in the *Journal of Aesthetics and Art Criticism* (Autumn 1983), notes John Ashbery's dialectic between "the extreme austerity of an almost empty mind" and "the lush, Rousseau-like foliage of its desire to communicate." "Poetry," Davidson writes, "occurs as a movement between a state of openness and a desire to move beyond a self-enclosed solipsistic universe."

In researching the origin of the reenactment of the crossing of the Delaware, I read through numerous large volumes of news clippings kept in the archives of the Washington Crossing Visitor Center. I saw photographs of St. John Terrell and his Music Circus on a website, lambertville-music-circus.org, which is, according to the site, "dedicated to the summer stock theater phenomenon that blossomed and flourished for over two decades on a hilltop above Lambertville, NJ in the mid 20th Century." Terrell was a founding member of the New Jersey Council on the Arts and a charter trustee of the American Folklife Center at the Library of Congress. His obituary in *The New York Times*, on October 20, 1998, written by Robert McG. Thomas, Jr., discussed Terrell's attempt to correct Shakespeare's portrayal of Richard III "as a hunchbacked, murderous thug who arranged to have his young nephews murdered in the Tower of London": "Although others have shared the view that Richard was not a villain, Mr. Terrell said he took the matter personally because the deed was supposedly carried out on the king's orders by a Terrell ancestor, Sir James Tyrrel."

Existence of the radioactivity that resulted from the Bomac missile explosion came to light in 1987, when officials in Montclair and Glen Ridge sought a place to rebury radioactive fill used in housing developments in the 1920s, and the Department of Defense volunteered the accident site. The fill was said to have come originally from a New Jersey plant that manufactured luminescent paints used in wristwatches, wristwatches having become popular with soldiers during World War I. According to *Radium Girls: Women and Industrial Health Reform, 1910–1935*, by Claudia Clark (Chapel Hill: University of North Carolina Press, 1997), the factory's use of radium to make the glowing paints caused clothes on laundry lines in the area to turn yellow, and women walking home from work after dark found that their clothes and hair glowed. Often, women in the plant pointed their work brushes using their wetted lips, a practice their managers assured them was safe. Women between the ages of fifteen and twenty-four had unusually high mortality rates in the United States at the time, due to factory work, and the Newark area was considered to be a world capital of radium, benzene, and lead poisoning, especially among women.

The Nine Capitals of the United States (York, Pa.: Maple Press, 1948) was written by Robert Burns Fortenbaugh, a longtime Gettysburg College professor. Discussions positing York as the first capital stress that the term "United Colonies" appeared in congressional records in June 1775; that Jefferson appears to have replaced "Colonies" with "States" in July 1776 ("united" is not capitalized in the Declaration of Independence); that Congress used "The United States of North America" only after the Articles of Confederation were adopted, "North" dropping out by July 1778. Congress was based in York from 1777 through 1778.

"The Trees of Princeton," which appeared in the *Princeton Alumni Weekly* on April 19, 1976, notes that pesticide used to prevent Dutch elm disease destroyed the blowfly collection of a biology professor. James Clark, the Scotland-born arborist on campus from 1928 to 1962 planted a dawn redwood in 1948. "He had nurtured it from one of 150 seeds he obtained from the Arnold Arboretum in Cambridge, Massachusetts," the article notes, "which made them available to colleges and universities after a special expedition brought them back from China after World War II. Before 1942, when the dawn redwood was discovered growing halfway up the Yangtse River, this species had been known only from fossil specimens and was thought extinct." The obituary of Princeton's Mercer Oak, titled "Rooted in History, and Leaving a Legacy," appeared in the *Daily Princetonian*, on March 9, 2000.

I learned about the Atlantic Terra Cotta Company, once the largest terra-cotta manufacturer in the world, in Laura P. Terhune's *Episodes in the History of Griggstown* (New York: Albert H. Vela, 1976). Atlantic Terra Cotta decorated structures such as the Woolworth Building and the U.S. Supreme Court Building. Additionally, the statue of George Washington in the center of Perth Amboy, New Jersey, marked "The Father of His Country," was made of Millstone River terra-cotta. If you think about the Millstone Valley being key to Washington's success in leading the Continental Army away from an early loss, then the Washington statue in Perth Amboy is a kind of concrete poem.

In *Episodes* and in *Rock Hill, Kingston and Griggstown*, by Jeanette Muser (Charleston, S.C.: Arcadia, 1998), I learned that many of the canal workers, most of whom had emigrated from Ireland, often to work off shanty boats on the canal in the 1820s, died in a cholera outbreak in 1832; they are buried in a cemetery in Griggstown and referenced in the poem "The Loaf," by Paul Muldoon, whose book *To Ireland, I* (Oxford: Oxford University Press, 2001) I read while typing up the account of my hike from Princeton to Morristown. The men called "ratters" trapped the muskrats that otherwise damaged the walls of the canal; "walkers" were hired to fill the muskrat holes.

Episodes describes a time in the 1930s when a Nazi group, the Amerika-Deutscher Volksbund, moved into a camp in Griggstown; the group believed, writes Terhune, that "the economic problems of America could be blamed directly on the Jews, Catholics, Negroes, Bolsheviks and others." "Local citizens retaliated against the Bund," Terhune adds, "by displaying signs on their car bumpers and other places reading: 'Love America or Leave America.'"

Operation Ludlum, named for its meteorologist, was finally begun in March 1944 and accounted for more than twenty-five hundred tons of bombs being dropped on Cassino, Italy, one of the highest bomb tonnages ever dropped in a single mission in World War II, according to *Time* magazine. That Ludlum was one of the first weathermen in the United States comes from *The Philadelphia Area Weather Book*, by Jon Nese, Glenn Schwartz, and Edward G. Rendell (Philadelphia: Temple University Press, 2002). In the two-volume *Early American Winters*, David Ludlum noted the appearance of arctic sea smoke in 1758, in Ipswich, Massachusetts—ice fog with tiny needles of frozen vapor, a result of arctic air racing down fast into New England. From a December 25, 1758, journal entry cited by Ludlum: "the harbor and all the rivers smoked from the intensiveness of the cold, so that it appeared like fog in the summer."

"In Defense of John Honeyman (and George Washington)" by Kenneth A. Daigler (who also goes by the name P. K. Rose) can be accessed at the CIA's website in the January 2010 issue of *Studies in Intelligence*; Daigler rebuts the piece in the June 2008 issue of *Studies* by Alexander Rose, author of *Washington's Spies* (New York: Bantam, 2006). In *Episodes*, Terhune notes the site of the Honeyman house, which is near the home of George Harsh, whose story fascinates me, due, no doubt, to the impact of the film *The Great Escape* on my childhood, as well as the impact of World War II movies in general, many of which I watched alongside my father as he commented on military service as he understood it from having served. Harsh grew up in a wealthy family in Atlanta; plotted a murder in which he shot and killed a man; was sentenced to death as a young man; saved the life of a prison orderly by taking out his inflamed appendix on the night of a bad storm when no doctor or person with medical training could be found; was pardoned by the governor as a result; joined the Royal Canadian Air Force before the United States entered World War II, reenlisting as a rear gunner, or Tail-End Charlie; was shot down over Germany; was part of the POW team that dug the tunnels that would later inspire the book and then the film *The Great Escape*; moved to Griggstown with his wife and compared marriage to prison; moved to Rocky Hill with two cats, Leopold and Bloom; wrote against war and the death penalty; toward the end of his life wrote an autobiography, *Lonesome Road*. Tim Carroll's book *The Great Escape from Stalag Luft III: The Full Story of How 76 Allied Officers Carried Out World War II's Most Remarkable Mass Escape* (New York: Pocket Books, 2004) notes that Harsh bailed out of a plane over Cologne and was in a hospital during an Allied bombing raid in which everyone evacuated except a nun who stayed behind to hold his hand. Terhune wrote that Harsh was still alive in 1976, in a Canadian nursing home, "partially paralyzed . . . from a stroke and from an attempt to take his own life."

Information about tar and feathering came from Benjamin H. Irvin's essay "Tar, Feathers, and the Enemies of American Liberties, 1768–1776," in the *New England*

Quarterly of June 2003. The scope of violence in the Middle Colonies prior to the Revolution comes from an excellent study by Joseph S. Tiedemann, "A Tumultuous People: The Rage for Liberty and the Ambiance of Violence in the Middle Colonies in the Years Preceding the American Revolution," in *Pennsylvania History: A Journal of Mid-Atlantic Studies* (Autumn 2010).

Details on the flooding caused by Hurricane Floyd, and the comments of Father Ed Murphy, come from a news account published by the World Socialist Web Site: "The WSWS . . . addresses itself to the masses of people who are dissatisfied with the present state of social life, as well as its cynical and reactionary treatment by the establishment media."

PART THREE: THE SEASONS OF THE REVOLUTION

Descriptions of the war in and around New York City came from various sources, including *The Other New York: The American Revolution Beyond New York City, 1763–1787* (Albany: SUNY Press, 2005), a collection of essays edited by Eugene R. Fingerhut and Joseph S. Tiedemann—in particular the chapter by Edwin G. Burrows, "The Ordeal of Kings County." I also relied on *The City of New York in the Year of Washington's Inauguration, 1789*, first published in 1889, and republished by the Chatham Press in 1972. I spoke on the phone with Eric Arctander, an artist who, while living in the seaport area in July 1980, drew a line demarking the colonial shoreline of lower Manhattan. (Lower Manhattan, he noted, changed drastically with the advent of the twenty-four-hour cash machine in the mid-eighties: people began to stick around after work when they had cash.) A good account of the machinations of Washington's presidency in New York may be found in *The Presidency of George Washington* by Forrest McDonald (Lawrence: University Press of Kansas, 1974). For insights into Early American construction techniques I am indebted to Ruth Steiner and Eamon O'Leary, as well as Ned Steves and the writer and actor Colm O'Leary.

Details of the life of I. N. Phelps Stokes come from an essay on Stokes by Francis Marrone in the August 1997 edition of *City Journal*, published by the Manhattan Institute. Marrone says of Stokes's monkeys: "They used to sit on [his mother's] shoulder and warm their clammy little hands by putting them inside the neck of her dress." The Phelps Dodge Corporation, now known as Freeport-McMoRan Copper & Gold Inc., is ranked as one of the world's biggest polluters by the University of Massachusetts's Political Economy Research Unit.

In addition to reading Philip Hone's diaries, I learned about the onetime New York mayor on one of my favorite history blogs, "The Bowery Boys."

Details of the story of the party atop Washington Square Arch come from *Around Washington Square: An Illustrated History of Greenwich Village*, by Luther S. Harris (Baltimore: Johns Hopkins University Press, 2003), as well as from Emily Kies Folpe's *It Happened on Washington Square* (Baltimore: Johns Hopkins University Press, 2002).

Geoffrey T. Hellman and James Thurber's profile of Kenneth M. Murchison, entitled "Alias George Washington," was published in the January 20, 1934, "Talk of the

Town" section of *The New Yorker*, while information on Denys Wortman came from newspaper clippings and a retrospective on Wortman at the Museum of the City of New York, as well as from a book, *Denys Wortman's New York* (Montréal: Drawn & Quarterly, 2010), which includes a drawing of an elderly couple, the gray-haired, tired, and bespectacled man holding the hand of his wife and saying: "We still wouldn't have to apply for relief if I could get a job—even to start at the bottom." A *New York Times* review tells of how the publisher of the Wortman book, the graphic novelist James Sturm (who is also the director of the Center for Cartoon Studies in White River Junction, Vermont), happened upon some old Wortman drawings. "I was blown away," he said. "I was also surprised that I had never heard of somebody so accomplished and prolific. For me he was this missing link between cartooning and early-20th-century fine art." Articles on the 1932 reenactment ("'Washington' Rides Amid Din of Wall St. in Pomp of Old Days" on May 1) and the 1939 reenactment ("'Washington' Here, a Bit Coach-Weary" on April 25) appeared in *The New York Times*. On September 9, 2001, the *Newark Star-Ledger* published a story on the 1789 inauguration by Tom Hester. The *Gazette of the United States*, which I was able to read at the New York Public Library, reported on the original 1789 inauguration, including an ode in its coverage: "Hail thou auspicious day!"

My references to Herodotus come from *The Landmark Herodotus: The Histories*, edited by Robert B. Strassler (New York: Pantheon, 2007). The modern-day fathers who assisted me in my inaugural reenactment were David Diehl, Dy Tran, Manny Howard (on land), and Josh Lomask. My exploration of the Greek concept of ekphrasis was aided by Matthew Sharpe, and assistance with ancient Greek translation was provided by Andrew Siebengartner. Additional translation services were provided by Louise Grace and Sam Sullivan, as well as by Jonathan Galassi, to whom I am grateful for editing this book.

I looked at Thomas Farrington DeVoe's works at the New-York Historical Society, where the staff also kindly assisted me with old maps, as well as the writings of David Ludlum. A biography of DeVoe can be found in the Michigan State University Feeding America Project, an online collection of some of the most important and influential American cookbooks from the late eighteenth through the early twentieth centuries.

I read Stokes's *Iconography* at the Millstein Division of the New York Public Library, and saw that in the days before the Battle of Brooklyn, public alerts were executed thusly: "The following signals are to give an alarm to all the troops, as well regular as Militia, & the inhabitants of the City—that is—in the day time, two cannon fired from the rampart of Fort George, and a flag hoisted on the top of General Washington's Head Quarters. In the night time, two cannon fired as above, from Fort George, & two Lanterns hoisted on the top of Head Quarters, as aforesaid."

On the hot summer days when I had a fever, in 2010, the queen of England visited New York City to memorialize British citizens who had died in the World Trade Center attacks and to speak at the United Nations, where she had last spoken in 1957. (Newspapers printed photos of her speaking as a young queen, and then as a queen fifty-three years older, a before-and-after.) The queen noted that the UN was a "high-minded aspiration" when she was a child and now was "a real force for the common good." "Many of these sweeping advances have come about not because of governments, committee resolutions, or central directives—although these have played a part—but instead because millions of people around the world wanted them," she said. When she had visited the city in 1976, for the bicentennial, the mayor at the time, Ed Koch, gave her a bag of peppercorns, a reference to the rental of the city's oldest park, Bowling Green, for one peppercorn a year, payment on hold since 1776.

I referred to an interview with Duke Riley conducted by Joe Heaps Nelson in the March 2011 *Whitehot* magazine. I interviewed Duke Riley in Red Hook, where he mentioned that not long after the *Acorn* was commandeered, he came across an old Joseph Mitchell story, "The Bottom of the Harbor," included in a collection of the same name, in which a fisherman proposed standing on a sandbar off the entrance to the harbor, in Ambrose Channel, off the coasts of Sandy Hook in New Jersey and Breezy Point in Queens, where he would wave an American flag as the *Queen Mary* approached—a project that struck Riley as similar to his *Acorn* work. "What in the hell would you do that for?" another fisherman asks in the Mitchell story. "I'd just like to," the first fisherman replies. On reading this, "I just remember thinking that everything's been done already," Duke said. U Thant Island (the island that Duke took over during the Republican convention) is, as the angler and writer Peter Kaminsky once noted in his *New York Times* fishing column, a good spot to catch striped bass: "That rocky upthrust in the river bottom is quite dependable. Moreover, there is a pleasing symmetry to the annual assembly of migrating fish occurring at the same time that the General Assembly convenes ashore."

The street artist I followed around during Battle of Brooklyn week was General Howe. I was aided in my research on Governor Dongan by the Reverend Anthony Andreassi, CO, a historian who teaches at Regis High School. The philosopher I walked with on Kings Highway is Aengus Woods.

A Mike Davis obituary written by Rob Buchanan appeared on rockandwater.net, a Listserv for the paddling community in New York City and vicinity. Michael Kauffman wrote an "About New York" column on Davis in *The New York Times* on February 15, 1995.

I am grateful to the staff of the Archives and Special Collections Division of the Brooklyn College Library for allowing me to examine the papers of James Kelly, wherein I read letters and scrapbooks, as well as news clippings. For biographical details, I relied especially on "Jamie Takes a Look Back," by Cindy Hughes, in the June 20, 1964, *Brooklyn World-Telegram*; a profile in the *New York Journal-American* on November 25, 1959; a *New York Daily News* profile on February 3, 1956; and a Talk of the Town piece entitled "Brooklyn Delver," in the February 21, 1953, *New Yorker*. For details on the *Tijger*, I read "The 'Tiger,' an Early Dutch 17th Century Ship, and an Abortive Salvage Attempt," by Ralph S. Solecki, in the *Journal of Field Archaeology* 1, no. 1/2, (1974). *The New York Times* noted that Robert Moses spoke at what was thought to be the home of Winston Churchill's mother, and the report quoted Moses as lamenting the fall of the empire to "lesser breeds." In 1986, Churchill's daughter, Lady Mary

Soames, visited the correct house. "As the 64-year-old Lady Soames, dressed in a wine-red suit and neat black pumps, neared the house, a disheveled woman in a tattered raincoat approached her," the *Times* reported. "The woman, who was pushing a shopping cart filled with possessions, announced that she was the niece of Sir Robert Stephenson Smyth Baden-Powell, the founder of the international Boy Scouts. Dignitaries in the party winced. Not Lady Soames. Without hesitation, she put her arms around the woman. 'Then you and I must be related,' she said gently."

That one-third of Brooklyn borough historian Ron Schweiger's basement is devoted to Dodgers' paraphernalia is mentioned in the *Times*, on their "City Room" blog. In the same post, Kenneth T. Jackson, the editor of the *Encyclopedia of New York City*, said that there were likely hundreds of local historians in New York—with twenty historical societies just in Queens. In an obituary in the *Daily News* in the fall of 2011, the longtime Queens borough historian Stangley Cogan—who was well known for his work to preserve old cemeteries and was thus nicknamed Head Stone—was quoted as saying he hoped his gravestone would read: "Here lies the Head Stone."

Some information on the reburial of the prison ship martyrs came from *Digging Up the Dead: A History of Notable American Reburials*, by Michael Kammen (Chicago: University of Chicago Press, 2010), as well as from "Commemorating the Prison Ship Dead: Revolutionary Memory and the Politics of Sepulture in the Early Republic, 1776–1808," an essay by Robert E. Cray, Jr., in the July 1999 *William and Mary Quarterly*.

Information on the Gowanus Canal, which I tend to visit several times a week, comes from many sources, including a survey in the *Brooklyn Daily Eagle* on May 9, 1885, entitled "The Condition of Brooklyn's Streets and Houses; Picturing the Pest Holes of Brooklyn"; a May 30, 1885, *Eagle* article entitled "Shanty Kings"; and a June 17, 1888, *Eagle* article entitled "The Oldest Settler." I watched a documentary on the canal, *Lavender Lake*, and referred to a Gersh Kuntzman report, "Superfunded!" from the *Brooklyn Paper* of March 5–11, 2010. A painting of Gowanus Bay, circa 1851—*Sunset at Gowanus Bay*, by Henry Gritten—can be viewed at the website of the state library of Tasmania.

In researching the Hard Winter, I utilized John Cunningham's *An Uncertain Revolution* (West Creek, N.J.: Down the Shore Publishers, 2007), and I looked back through many of Cunningham's other books on New Jersey. Cunningham is New Jersey's Herodotus. Charles Cummings, assistant director of the Newark Library and a historian himself, once told a reporter: "If you were to go into any library in New Jersey, any small library or any major library in the United States or into a great library in Europe or anywhere else and looked in a card catalog under the heading 'New Jersey,' John Cunningham would be the one author you would always find." I have taken some of Cunningham's comments from a speech he gave on the 225th anniversary of the Morristown encampment, entitled "Morristown: Where America Survived." A speech he delivered in 1979 on the two hundredth anniversary of the Hard Winter (in which he described the Continental Army as "exactly like the [American] soldiers of Viet Nam in the 1970's—out of sight, out of mind, out of sympathy") is posted by the Washington Association of New Jersey and can be accessed on their website: www.wanj.org/worserthanvalleyforge.html.

In addition to referring to Stokes and DeVoe, I referred to *A Hessian Diary of the American Revolution* by Johann Conrad Döhla (Norman: University of Oklahoma Press, 1990), as well as *Biographical Sketches of Loyalists of the American Revolution*, by Lorenzo Sabine (Port Washington, N.Y.: Kennikat Press, 1966), and *New Jersey During the Revolution as Related in the News Items of the Day*, by Richard B. Marrin (Westminster, Md.: Heritage Books, 2009). Despite being partisan, newspaper accounts describe horrible acts on both sides, particularly in New Jersey, the state most in a state of war. There was what David Hackett Fischer has called "an epidemic of rape" in New Jersey. From the January 1777 *Pennsylvania Evening Post* in a report from New Jersey: "One of the most respectable men in that part of the country was alarmed by the cries and shrieks of a most lovely daughter. He found an officer, a British officer, in the act of ravishing her. He instantly put him to death. Two other officers rushed in with fusees and fired two balls into the father, who is now languishing under his wounds."

In the first volume of his book *Early American Winters* (Boston: American Meteorological Society, 1966), covering 1604 to 1820, David Ludlum notes that spring came early after the Hard Winter, in 1780. Ezra Stiles, the noted Connecticut-based weather watcher, records sixty-two degrees at the end of February, buds arriving early in New Haven. The *New Jersey Gazette*'s farmers report remarked on human births ("On the 4th instant, Susannah Sands, wife of Christopher Sands, of Evesham, Burlington county, New-Jersey, was delivered of three male children," a report said. "The mother is likely to do well, but the children are since dead."); on the detention of rebel gentlemen ("the above-mentioned Gentlemen are still detained by the enemy in New-York"); and on the early warm weather ("The weather having been remarkably warm and pleasant for about a month past, has occasioned the buds of some early fruit trees to vegetate to a greater degree than has been remembered at this season by the oldest men in the neighbourhood"). In February, Eliza Drinker, a diarist in Philadelphia, wrote: "Ye apricot trees are in blossom." Notes on endangered plants in New Jersey came from the U.S. Fish and Wildlife Service's Conservation Library.

I referred to a 1941 *New York Times* review of Lewis Gaston Leary's *That Rascal Freneau: A Study in Literary Failure* (New York: Octagon Books, 1964) that was written by Herbert Gorman, the historical novelist and James Joyce scholar. The headline on Gorman's review: "Philip Freneau, Our Earliest Poet; His Life, as Mr. Leary's Biography Shows, Is More Interesting Than His Verse." I also referred to *Scandal and Civility: Journalism and the Birth of American Democracy*, by Marcus Leonard Daniel (New York: Oxford University Press, 2009). Richard Ellmann's notes on Washington Irving were brought to my attention by Sam Amidon. Here is Freneau on the Passaic Falls, in Paterson, New Jersey: "My morning of life is beclouded with care! / I will go to Passaick, I say and I swear— / To the falls of Passaick, that elegant scene, / Where all is so pretty and all is so green." In an essay entitled "What Made Freneau the

Father of American Poetry?" published in *Studies in Philology* in 1929, Harry Hayden Clark wrote:

> In connection with Freneau, however, we must remember that his work marks the starting-point in America of this all-important trend toward the concrete in poetry. And it is naturalism which explains why, concurrent with our political independence, he heralded our literary independence, so far as themes are concerned, by bringing into poetry for the first time truly indigenous American nature. In his work even a casual reader will find roses, daisies, daffodils, the honey-suckle, pumpkins, cedars, "the apple, apricot, and plum," "the tall chestnut," corn, "wheaten sheeves," the oak, "shrubby hazels," "dry alders," the aspin, the "sad pine," buckwheat, oats, the "weeping willow," ivy, mint, the beech and the cypress-tree, as well as the lynx, the panther, "howling wolves," the "fearless doe," the pheasant, the blackbird, the lark, the "loquacious whip-poor-will," the "timorous deer," the buffalo, the beaver, the hare, leverets, dogs, the caty-did, the honey-bee, the "angry tiger," the "staring owl," the squirrel, the parrot, and the goldfinch.

Recently, a New Jersey conservation group argued that Henry David Thoreau may have gotten the idea for *Walden* from Freneau. Personally, I doubt it.

PART FOUR: A SIGNAL

The history of various signals transmitted between New York and its environs is mentioned briefly in *The Story of Telecommunications*, by George P. Oslin (Macon, Ga.: Mercer University Press, 1992), who interviewed the last surviving Pony Express rider for the book and mentions the work of Christopher Colles, the inventor and mapmaker. (Colles's road maps can be seen at the New York Public Library, and they resemble the old American Automobile Association's TripTiks.) The history of geodetic surveys is covered on the website of the National Oceanic and Atmospheric Administration (NOAA). I read "NGS Celebrates 200th Anniversary" in the January/February 2007 issue of *American Surveyor*. I also read Margaret Long's short but beautiful pamphlet *The Revolutionary War Beacon at Signal Station No. 10* (New Orleans: Polyanthos, 1975).

The quote from Virgil's *Georgics* is taken from Janet Lembke's translation (New Haven: Yale University Press, 2005).

In addition to relying on several scholarly articles, I relied on the work of Donald Bender, a historian who created an online repository for photos and information regarding the Nike missiles that encircled New York City in the 1950s: http://alpha.fdu.edu/~bender/nike.html. The Nike missiles in the region were, according to a March 10, 2002, *Newsday* article by Bill Bleyer, topped with nuclear warheads, each bearing three times the power of the weapon dropped on Nagasaki in 1945.

The sites of Revolutionary War signals today align with parks in the region, and in 2006 large electric lights were beamed into the air from Sandy Hook north to the Hudson Highlands, as a signal reenactment. I somehow missed that, to my cost.

"Report of an Air Pollution Incident in New York City, November 1953," published in *Public Health Reports* in January 1962, details the day that an air pollution event increased mortality during the month—the smog reportedly blocked out the sun at some point, possibly because of industrial pollution mixed with forest fires.

Information on Liberty Trees and poles comes from Arthur M. Schlesinger's "Liberty Tree: A Genealogy," an essay that appeared in the *New England Quarterly* in December 1952, and from David Hackett Fischer's book *Liberty and Freedom* (New York: Oxford University Press, 2004), in which he cites what is referred to as a negative definition of liberty (no one interferes with my action) and a positive one (I am my own master). "Eric Foner," Fischer writes, "observes from long study that most ideas of liberty and freedom in America have tended to be positive and negative at the same time." The note on the dead debtor comes from a review in the December 2004 *New England Quarterly* of *Republic of Debtors* (Cambridge: Harvard University Press, 2003), by Bruce H. Mann.

My signaling was aided by Mark Satlof, a Revolutionary War history buff who has lent me numerous books and maps and kept me abreast of important Revolutionary War–related events in New York. On the day I met him, in his Brooklyn office overlooking the harbor, he turned to me, unaware of my interest in the Revolution, and said, "Can you imagine what it was like when the entire British fleet sailed in here in 1776?" I also successfully signaled with him, using a mirror from the same place in the Watchung Mountains from which I signaled to my daughter. On the phone in his office and looking toward the Watchungs, he told me he could see me without the aid of binoculars, and I heard an officemate of his corroborating, shouting, "Naked eye! Naked eye!"

I am grateful to numerous other supporters of this book-making campaign, including Miranda Popkey, Stephen Weil, John McGill, Eric Etheridge, Kate Browne, Katie Holten, Anna Wintour, Laurie Jones, Chris Knutsen, Abigail Walsh, Mark Holgate, Louise McCready, David Haskell, Adam Moss, Sally Singer, Chris Norman, Jefferson Hamer, Cleek Schrey, Ryan McGiver, Omar Alsahybi, Susan McKeown, Dana Lyn, Bill Orme, Gabe Howard, Marty Skoble, Daphne Klein, Craig Townsend, Cathy Fuerst, Mockler Marshall, Ed Cohen, Christopher Mellon, Saint Ann's School, Skip McPherson, Charlie Butler, the Brooklyn Public Library (Carroll Gardens Branch), BookCourt, Brenda Marsh, Jonathan Weiss, Paula Greif, Anna Zanes, the Oratory at St. Boniface, Clayworks on Columbia, Molly Creeden, Esther Adams, Antonina Jedrzejczak, Brigid Hughes, Elizabeth Gaffney, Eric MacSweeney, the Village Community Boathouse, Susan Morrison, D'Amico, Mark Svenvold, Kate Hutchison, John Waldman, Daniel Bauer, Mike Feller, Colonel Emmanuel Tran, Helvi Gallo, Daniele Franqui, Noel Collado, Valerie Steiker, Paul Miklusky, Riza Cruz, Geoff Brewer, Belinda McKeon, Bill Sullivan, the Muldoons, Lloyd Miller, Colm Tóibín, the Quinns, Kassie Schwann, Brian Rose, Jim Leinfelder, Linda and Donald Desimini, and my parents, Mary Elizabeth and Robert Sullivan. I am grateful, as well, to Eric Simonoff, to whom I first proposed this book on a trip to Brooklyn's Grand Canyon, and to the

Hudson River Almanac, a source of inspiration to me that has been published weekly since 1994 by the New York State Department of Environmental Conservation. Often when I read the *Almanac*, I think of a line of poetry by Thoreau: "The wind that blows is all that anybody knows." In April 2004, this *Hudson River Almanac* entry appeared:

> New York Harbor, Upper Bay: In early afternoon, with a strong onshore wind blowing, a large fish washed up against the foot of the Statue of Liberty. Alerted by 80–90 visitors, Park Ranger Ken Bausch waded out into the harbor to retrieve a four-foot-long Atlantic sturgeon. Its gill covers were moving; it was still alive. Ken worked the fish back and forth in the current, forcing water across its gills, and in short order it revived. Up above, Park Ranger Kenya Finley interpreted for the crowd what this interesting fish was and what we were doing to try and save it. Once he resuscitated it, Ken released the sturgeon which swam away to the applause of onlookers. We had to repeat this effort two hours later when the fish drifted back inshore. This time Ken gave it a good push out in the current as he released it. The fish moved away and disappeared. While Ken was working on the sturgeon the second time, he noticed several horseshoe crabs mating in the shallows. This was a good sign since their presence in this area has diminished in recent years.